To My dear friend
I hope that you will
My life.

God Bless you.

Always -

Jackie xxxxxx

Original Copy
Mistakes and all.

J.P. Lamoche

Published 4 June
2010

This is a token of my love for you.
as a friend and Sister xxx

Crossing Rivers

Climbing Mountains

Building Bridges

Crossing Rivers

Climbing Mountains

Building Bridges

Jacqueline La-Touche

To order additional copies of this book, contact:
Xlibris Corporation
0-800-644-6988
www.xlibrispublishing.co.uk
Orders@xlibrispublishing.co.uk
300188

Contents

Entry written September 12, 2008

I would like to dedicate this book in memory of my father, Robert Sydney La-Touché. My father was one of the kindest, honest, loving, and empathetic, God-fearing men that I had ever known. I thank him for the time and love that he has invested in me and for the qualities that I have inherited from him; he taught me right from wrong, and most of all he taught me to love God.

Today is September 13, my father's birthday; he would have been ninety-one years old today. It has been over six years since he passed away, but sometimes it still feels like yesterday. I know that he is always with me. I decided to dedicate this book to my father when I woke up this morning, without even realizing that it was my father's birthday today. I would also like to dedicate this poem to him.

Four Seasons

You will remember me in the wintertime when the snow is falling,
because I will always be there to warm your heart.

You will remember me in the springtime when the rain is falling,
because I will always dry your tears away.

You will remember me in the summertime when the sun is shining,
because I will shine my light for all to see.

You will remember me in the autumn time in the sound of the breeze,
as I soar through the trees, as a bird I will whisper your name.

Even though you can't see me don't worry I am always a step behind,
giving you the strength to go on, and be strong.

I cried tears of joy when you came into this world;
you cried tears of sorrow when I left.

Distant memories will become instant memories as you reminisce,
please don't mourn for me because I haven't left your hearts. I am in the four
seasons throughout the years, and throughout time. Just say, winter, spring,
summer, or fall. Just put all four seasons together, and then you
will know that love lasts forever.

By Jacqueline la-Touché

Acknowledgements

August 2008

Being asked my permission to be nominated for the Parents Peace Award is something for me to be really proud of. For someone to consider me deserving of this award has really made me look at my life for what it is today and to be proud of my achievements as a parent, but also as Jacqueline La-Touché. The fighter, the survivor.

The fighter the survivor, that's how I have always seen myself. My life has been an uphill struggle from the age of fifteen years old, one big long battle right up until now.

I have stopped asking myself why my life has taken me through all the trials and tribulations that it has done for the past years.

I have now managed to embrace what I have been through in my life and turned it into a positive outcome.

My life experiences have given me the wisdom, knowledge, and understanding to share my life with others and to be able to understand and to be empathetic, nonjudgmental, and supportive to others that have been or now going through similar situations in their lives.

I hope that someone out there will be able to draw strength from my life, and always remember where there is life there has to be hope.

We read famous people's autobiographies all the time, but sometimes they have no relevance in our lives because of their social background and lifestyles.

I am not famous. I am just a mother who has managed to overcome some of life's downfalls, and pitfalls, and managed to pick myself up, brush myself down, and start all over again.

First and foremost, I thank God, my creator, my mentor, my guiding light, my strength, and my provider. I thank him for taking negativity out of my life and bringing positivism into the midst. I thank him for giving me the knowledge, wisdom, and understanding to go forward with my life; he knows my strengths and my weaknesses, and he never gave me more than what I could handle. He stood back, only intervening when he felt that I could bear no more, the Saviour, saving me and now rewarding me for my life.

I will forever keep praying through good times, as well as bad. I will forever be thankful for the life that he has given to me.

I would like to acknowledge everyone and everything that has inspired me to start writing this book, my friends, my family, my music, and even the families that I give support too, in my role as a support coordinator; they have all played a huge part in helping me to sustain my drive and determination to reach the end of my book. Sitting down and listening to them tell me about their lives has given me the courage not to feel guilty and ashamed of presenting my life to the public, and I would like to thank them all, even if they don't know, but they have taught me a thing or two.

My husband, Benji, you have played a huge part in all of this; you have helped me to write this book. I thank you for being in one of the chapters of my life. You have been on a rough ride with me, through some of the toughest times.

You have been there for me, and I know that you will always be, no matter what. You gave me the time that I needed to write this book, you helped me with everything, and I acknowledge you for everything.

My dear friend Carol, I thank God for the day you came into my life; it's like he sent you to help sort me out. I wonder if you have any idea of how much you have inspired me. Your life has mirrored mine. I have never met anyone in my whole life that had struggles like mine, well, that's until I met you.

You're in a positive place in your life at this time. I thank you for sharing your experiences with me, making me now know that when I felt alone and hurting someone else out there was hurting too, and that's you, my friend.

Damian Cousins, one of my biggest inspirations, whilst writing the other half of this book; I got my strength through knowing that you cared. You never cease to amaze me with your patience, love, and understanding.

You have helped me to become focused, dedicated, and disciplined with my writing. Every word and every chapter that I wrote, I would say to you, "Damian, do you want me to read what I wrote tonight?" You would reply, "Sure."

Even when I was going through tough times and could not right a single word, you understood; and when you felt that I had overcome those feelings, that's when you would say, "Jackie, you haven't spoken about your book, so that means you haven't been writing." You know me so well.

You always listened attentively while I read chapters of my book to you, even correcting me on some of the things which I wrote, especially if it sounded like I was putting myself down. You even questioned my reasons for doing so. I thank you for inspiring me to move forward, sticking to the deadline, with finishing my book.

Sue, I thank you for taking up my offer. I know you thought that I was joking at the time, but I was so serious. At first you laughed, we both did, but I kept on saying it, and then it became. Your reply was "La-Touché, I would love to take this journey with you, and your book." Most of all I thank you for taking the time to proofread my book and for being serious about this.

You are the perfect person to help me, and I am happy that you are taking this journey with me.

My mother, my precious mum, the rock in our family, I look up to you for everything, your honesty, advice, and positivism; and I embrace them all. No wonder my daddy loved you so much, right up until his last breath.

You remind me of myself. Sometimes when I look in the mirror for a split second, I see you in me. You are so funny, your childlike qualities still remain, and you are still beautiful, even with your hair white as the driven snow. Writing a book like this, I had to have a sense of humor, and you gave that to me. So I thank you again for being the greatest and best role model that God could have chosen for me.

I acknowledge each of my seven children, all so different, as my father would say, seven brothers' seven different minds. My love for you all, I cannot measure. We have all been through so much, of what you won't remember, but we have managed to overcome and not be scarred by it. As a family we will always go through life's ups and downs, but my love for you all binds me unconditionally.

I would like to acknowledge my faith and love in my music, which has helped me to cross rivers, climb mountains, and now able to build bridges.

I give God thanks for great songwriters like Simon & Garfunkel; they wrote one of the greatest songs of all time, "Bridge over Troubled Water." It doesn't matter what artist sings this song, it has always been my favourite.

"Sail on, silver bird, sail on by, your time has come to pass, all your dreams are on their way." Such a very powerful and uplifting song, which now reflects my life in still a very moving and very positive way.

Little Girl

Don't be in a rush to grow up, little girl, let your youth take you
places, that amazes, little girl,

There's so much of the world to see, to be little girl, enjoy it while
It lasts, it goes so fast, little girl.

Before you know it, sow it you will reap, little girl. One day you will
Be a mother to, another,
Little girl.

So take your time and hush to a lullaby, don't cry, little girl,
'cause life won't pass you by if you just try, little girl.

By Jacqueline La-Touché

Chapter One

The Three Cs

1979

Fifteen years old and pregnant, and scared. What was I going to do? How was I going to tell my parents? What were they going to say? More to the question was, what were they going to do to me? I had to tell someone, but who? I couldn't pretend that this was not happening, this was real, and I would not be able to hide it for much longer. There was a baby coming, not going.

My little sister Mary was nine years old at the time, and she was my best friend. I used to tell her everything. I knew that she wouldn't really understand, but I needed someone to confide in, and I knew that she wouldn't say anything, so I told her that I was having a baby and made her promise not to say anything to my parents; otherwise I would not let her play with my dolls.

Eventually I had to tell my school friends because they started to suspect that something was wrong because I kept on running to the toilets at school to be sick, and I didn't want to do PE anymore. I even started to write sick notes each week, telling my PE teacher that I could not do PE that day for whatever make-believe reason which came to mind.

In one letter I even told them that I was on my period and had bad stomach pains. I became expert at forging my mother's signature.

Eventually I plucked up the courage to tell my friends at school that I was pregnant. I had missed two periods, and I needed their support to follow me to the doctor's. I could not face going there alone. I wasn't really scared about my pregnancy being confirmed, because I already knew that there was no doubt about it.

The biggest problem at the time was my doctor, because she knew my parents very well,

Dr Jessie, the family doctor and friend, a very straight forward and direct woman, who never held back a word, my father always said that her tongue was like a sword, you could say that she had a way with words. She was very cynical, with a menacing laugh, and she spoke to you like you were stupid.

My father called her Jessie, I don't think he liked her very much, and neither did I

She had this stern look on her face, which was caked with powder, at least two shades lighter than her complexion, giving her this ghostly white appearance. Considering that she was Asian, this look did not go down to well. One time for a joke, I put my mother's Yardley talc on my face and mimicked her, well my mother laughed until she almost wet herself.

Dr Jessie wore the brightest pink lipstick that I had ever seen.

When we were ill, my mother would call her to the house, the thought of Jessie coming made us feel more ill. Well before you could say, wicked witch of the west, she was here in a puff of smoke, which was blowing from her little white car, coming around the corner, like the cops were chasing her.

Without even hello, she would walk straight upstairs, with my mother walking behind

"Where are they", in the back room I would hear my mother say. Well soon as she walked into the bedroom, the first thing that she would say is "open the window", never mind if you had pneumonia, according to her, that was an excuse not to open the window. She would then reach for her instruments, out of an old crumpled brown briefcase," open up your mouth child, open it wide", I would open my mouth so wide until it felt like it was going to split, and without warning she would push the thermometer, so far under your tongue, I thought I would choke. Then out came the stethoscope, " lift up your clothe child, I said lift it up, well that happened before we knew the procedure, now we never waited, we just wanted her out, after she had scribbled down her remedy on a prescription, "give three times a day"then gone with a puff of smoke without so much as a goodbye. She didn't even tell you what the diagnosis was So you see why I was scared of going to the doctors, because I knew that there was a good chance that she would tell my parents, but I had to go, whether there was a big chance or not of her telling them.

My friends were very supportive of me and said that they would follow me to the doctor's that day after school. I remember walking into the doctor's clinic then walking back out again, before I finally plucked up the courage to walk in with my four friends in tow, slowly walking up to the receptionist with my friends on either side of me, shielding me from all ears. My friend Clare was with me, that made me feel a little brave, because she was tall, the one with the mouth, and most of all the look, she knew how to make her face look serious at 15 years old, My other friend Natalie, well she was the quiet one amongst our little gathering, well that's what I called it, not a Gang. Doreen was my other friend, she was feisty, but it was undercover because at home she was holly as the grail, so I hoped that Doreen's parents didn't show up because they had the same doctor "Jessie", and so did all of Tottenham, come to think of it, So if I didn't have the courage to tell my parents, and by a freak of nature, Jessie lost her voice at that time, then Tottenham would. I had my body guards with me that day, but only for strength and courage.

The receptionist was an elderly looking lady with spectacles sitting on the end of her nose; her white hair scraped back into a bun, which sat right on top of her head, with an expressionless face to match, to make matters worse she was deaf as a bat and always repeated every word she was told, shouting it out loud for everyone's ears to hear. By time you left the surgery you would know the reason why everybody had gone to see the doctor that day The receptionist and Dr Jessie were like two peas in a pod, one of a kind. You could say that they complimented each other, well for the wrong reasons anyway.

Well, there was no privacy with the accomplice. Even if you tried to whisper discreetly she would always say, "I beg your pardon," at least two or three times. Well, I had warned my friends that this may happen, and it did; however, they all stood close to me, to try and block out the echoes of her voice. "I would like to see Dr. Jessie."

"Why?" she asked. Feeling embarrassed I said in a quiet voice, "I think I might be pregnant." She looked at me under her spectacles and shouted, "Pregnant!" That was probably the first time she had ever heard the first time around. "Take a seat!" she shouted.

I sat down, feeling anxious and a little scared waiting for my fate, I knew that I could not turn back. I never really had a choice but to see Dr. Jessie, no matter if she told my parents or not, and believe me she wasted no time in doing so.

On the way home from the doctor's I crawled home like a snail because I knew it was only a matter of time before my parents would know my big secret; as I approached the house, to my horror parked right outside was Dr. Jessie's little white car. My worst nightmare had come true. Talk about confidentiality.

When I eventually reached the front door I stood outside frightened to go inside. I wanted to run away, but there was nowhere to run, nowhere to hide. I had to face the music. My hand began to shake as I pushed the key into the door. I told myself it was either now or never. I forced myself to be brave and strong, but my stomach was in knots. Well, I tried my best to open the door quietly and then tiptoed upstairs.

I was so scared. I opened up the wardrobe and climbed inside and sat down. The wardrobe was a place where I would always go to hide when I was in trouble. Looking back I don't know why I used to hide in there because that was the most obvious place that my parents would come and find me.

I sat down in the wardrobe for what seemed like forever with my hands covering my ears as if I could hear what Dr. Jessie was saying. I just kept on thinking, *My dad's going to kill me this time.*

My father was a very strict man; we could not get away with anything, and punishment was his middle name. We all feared him to a certain degree, however we would always try our luck, to get away with even one answer, however we knew that one answer could cost us a strapping, but it was worth it just to see the look on his face, when he was chasing us down the road, waving his belt around like a lasoo, never failing to miss, he was even good at throwing his slipper, never missing the target, which was us. Well, even though we feared him, we loved him, and we knew, and felt that he loved us too, he would always say before and after our punishment "Well you know I love you all but if you can't hear you must feel"

Well that just made it worse, talk about patronising, this made us conspire against him even more, we would sit down together planning my fathers fait," You wait until he gets old, were going to put him in a old people's home, and never go and visit him, and if we can't afford to take him there, we won't even take him to the toilet, just leave him there.

Well I was so lost in my thoughts, thinking about my father, and our plans for him, even worse what the outcome of Dr Jessie's vist would be,

I jumped when I heard my mother's voice. She was calling me to come downstairs. "Jackie, come downstairs, come downstairs now. There is nothing to hide anymore."

I sat in the wardrobe frozen with fear, my heart beating so fast that I could almost hear it, and scared to answer back, or even come out. I could now hear her coming upstairs; her footsteps even sounded different. As my mother got nearer her voice became louder. How did she know that I was here when I tiptoed upstairs? She must have heard my heart beating loud. Well, that's what I told myself.

My mother was now in my room. I could see her through the crack in the wardrobe door. There was no lock on the door, and it couldn't close, so I had to hold the door from inside with my fingers to stop it from opening.

Well, my mother walked over to the wardrobe and opened it. She looked at me, shaking her head, with tears and a look of disbelief in her eyes; and in a soft voice she told me to come out. I knew that she wasn't going to shout at me or hit me because of the soft and gentle tone in her voice and the empathetic look in her eyes, but amongst the tears I could also see disappointment written on her face. My mother was the opposite to my father, she would overlook most things, and then hold it against us, when she wanted us to do something for her "You wait till Bob get home, I am going to tell him that you, go out last night", well I would reply but mummy you said we could", well she instantly forgot about last night.

I loved my mother for so many reasons; she was funny, kind, loving, understanding and very beautiful to look at. I use to wish that I would grow up to be pretty as my mother, I would ask her "mummy why didn't you marry someone as pretty as you, then I would be pretty like you," well my mother would laugh, and say "so what are you trying to say, daddy is ugly, well you wait until he come home I am going to tell him," she would be laughing away like what she just said was a joke.

I could see why my father must have fell for my mother, because she was beautiful, her hair was a beautiful quality, very shiny and jet, as the night, and she had the prettiest pair of hazel, green eyes I had ever seen, well apart from mine,

We were spoilt children, always getting what we wanted, especially from her. My parents made sure that we had everything that we needed, and wanted as children, I guess that was because they longed for a family for so long. My mother had numerous miscarriages, and a baby that died soon after birth. She longed for a child, my mother always said that she would wish, even to have a child as small as Tom Thumb, someone to hold of her own, There were so many children in the family, but none belonged to my mother.

My mother never gave up hoping to have a family, and years later she did, Considering that she had married my father when she was a teenager, she was now raising a family, in her fourties.

Well I felt that I had let my mother down big-time; all she had ever done was love me, and now this was how I repaid her love by getting pregnant at the age of fifteen years old. How stupid was that.

I felt ashamed of myself for making my mother cry and most of all for letting her down. My mother always had high hopes for me as a child; she would always tell me how special I was and that God had a plan and a purpose for me and that one day I would find out.

My mother always said things like that to me; maybe she knew something I didn't.

I used to go to sleep at nights and have special recurring dreams. I often dreamt about God. One of my special dreams was about a stairway leading to heaven, and God was standing at the top of the stairs

With his hands outstretched to me just like he was calling me, I always ran away.

At the time I didn't realize what those dreams meant and how special they were, but my mother knew.

Well, here I was with my mother standing in front of me asking me why. I stood there with my head bowed down. "How am I going to tell Bob when he comes home from work?" Bob was my father, a very strict disciplinarian and a minister of the gospel. My mother asked me that question again, as if I had the answer.

Well, you can only imagine what happened when my father, Bob, came home and my mother hit him with the bad news. Well, he hit the roof. "You are a disgrace. Look how you have brought down shame and disgrace on this family's name."

My father was more concerned about what his friends and the congregation at church would say on Sunday rather than care about how I felt; no one cared at that time about how I felt. My mother cared more about what my father would say than how I felt, and now here was my father caring more about what people would think. "What am I going to tell the brethren, at church? I sent you to school to study your books, not man, and now you walk in my house with a big belly in front of you." I was frightened, but I wanted to laugh because my father's belly was so big. Not even when I was nine months pregnant would my belly be as huge as his, I thought to myself. My father always had a big belly,

He was a strapping man, with a gold tooth to compliment, is smile, always looking immaculately dressed in his suit, but when he took his jacket off, you were faced with his belly in front of you

Well he would sit in his chair with his arms resting on it; his plate or his mug took residence on his belly each day. My brother Robin and I would tease him about how big it was. We used to call him Big Ben, then run for dear life, shouting, "Bong bong bong." My father used to chase us round the house, along the streets, with his belt, shouting, "You wait till I catch you." Most of the time we got away; we even asked him once, "Daddy, when was the last time you saw your toes?" We never dared wait for an answer.

Well, if I was being chased for calling my father Big Ben, then what would I be expecting to happen now? My father was angry, and things did not get any better; it got worse especially when he mentioned marriage. "She can't stay in my house in this condition." I remember thinking to myself, *What condition? You're talking about me like I have the plague, and I'm having a baby.*

My father blamed my mother for me getting pregnant. He told her that she had spoilt me, and that's why this had happened. I was now charged, convicted, and condemned—the three Cs, I called it.

I would hear my mother and father having conferences in their room, even in the living room, discussing what they were going to do. I became invisible to them; they were discussing my future. "What are we going to do, Gat?" I heard my father saying. "Well, you know that we are against abortion, even though Dr. Jessie did say that was one of the options, even adoption, but no way can we ever consider doing that."

I heard my mother saying to my father that she would never forgive herself if she was to agree for me to have an abortion, and for some reason I could not have another child. "Bob," she said, "Jackie would never forgive us if that happened, just like how my sister could never forgive my mother when her baby died."

My mother once told us about her sister who had a baby when she was young; my grandmother was not supportive of her. My mother told us that every day which passed, my grandmother never stopped talking about it. Well, tragedy came when the baby got ill and died. My mother's sister never got over this and blamed my grandmother for the loss of her child. My mother did not want history to repeat itself, so from that day on there was no daily conferences and discussions about what Dr. Jessie had suggested.

After the initial shock of me being pregnant, my father soon calmed down. My parents became my rock. They supported me and tried to protect me from the wagging tongues of Tottenham. My father even stood up for me when people would pass their judgments and their remarks, but he couldn't stand up for me when I was on my own on the streets.

I knew that it was wrong for me to be pregnant at the age of fifteen years old, and that's why I probably allowed people to treat me the way they did. Maybe that was my punishment for being naïve.

I remember walking down the road in the middle of summer. I was on my way back from the antenatal clinic. The day was so hot, but that never stopped me from wearing my fur coat. I felt that I never had any choice but to wear it in that sweltering heat.

My fur coat became like a second skin to me. It was my shield from prying eyes. No one could see what was under there or even notice, because I used to hold my belly in when I walked past them. My fur coat became my protection from the gossipmongers of Tottenham.

Being pregnant in 1979 was hard; it was still not socially acceptable to be an unmarried mother, let alone a teenage one. That was a crime as far as people were concerned. My mother was told by her friend that she should let me wear her wedding ring when I went to my hospital appointments. People openly talked about me like I was invisible; they made me feel like I was a leper, not pregnant.

It was hard being fifteen years old and pregnant, because I was still at school. My mother eventually stopped me from going, even before I started showing.

At a time in my life when I was just discovering myself as a teenager, I was also discovering that I was pregnant. I thought that things would get better when I had the baby and that people would leave me alone and stop passing judgment, but that didn't happen.

At the tender age of sixteen years old, September 24, two days after my sixteenth birthday, I became a teenage mum to a beautiful baby girl. she was the most perfect, beautiful little human being I had ever seen, her hair was straight, shiny and black, laying down like a puppies coat, her little face was unlined, she didn't have the newborn look, no scrunched up, eyes and face. She was very white, I couldn't understand why she was so pale, until I realised that all black babies were born light skinned, before they acquired their true colour.

I didn't really care what colour, or look that she had, because I loved her long before now.

Well I never really got a chance to hold her, before they bundled her into a cot which resembled a goldfish bowl, and away to the nursery, where she would sleep for the first few days of her life. I was labeled a mother now, and very proud to be.

However I was a child still living at home, and my parents were responsible for my well-being, and here I was a young mother now responsible for this tiny infant which I held in my arms but still only a child myself.

A child holding another child, and she was mine. I had to take responsibility for the life I had just brought into this world. I remember the nurses speaking to me like I was a child, explaining to me that I had to feed the baby every four hours. Well, I couldn't think about anything apart from my baby.

I was alone when I gave birth to her, no family, no friends, no one to hold my hand. At that very moment I started to think that this was my punishment for being a teenager and getting pregnant. "You made your bed, so you must lie in it." So here I am lying in my bed, alone looking at all the other mothers who were probably twice my age looking over at me with their bag of thoughts.

I watched their visitors walking in and taking a seat; everyone looked happy. Mums were looking really proud of themselves for having their babies. Well, I felt proud too, proud of my perfect baby. She had five toes, five fingers, two eyes, and one mouth which looked like it needed to be fed,

I felt nervous as I looked around. I felt like the whole room was watching me. I was scared to pick my baby up. I wanted to, but I felt that all eyes were on me waiting to see how I would manage. Well, all of a sudden I looked over to the door, and in walked my family one by one. my sister Patsy with a huge smile on her face, and trying to push past everyone to reach to the baby.

My face tried not to show how happy I was, because I didn't want my father to think that I was happy for being pregnant and having a baby two days after my sixteenth birthday. Truth is she was the best birthday present I could ever have.

My sister asked me if I had picked the baby up from out of her cot yet. I told her no; she asked me why, but I couldn't tell her that I didn't know how to. I had never held a newborn in my arms before, older babies yes, because you hold them with more grip and strength, but newborns, you pick them up, like glass, gently because you don't want to break them.

My sister was the opposite to me, you would never believe that we were sisters, she was totally different, she wasn't scared of anything, or anyone, Patsy knew how to defend herself, with her mouth. She was bold, and never really feared, not even our father, she would always put herself in the firing line, she never really bothered about the consequences do now and think later , was Patsy's motto. So she wouldn't fear, taking the baby out of the cot to hold, like I did, at the time.

Well My sister leant over the cot and gently took my baby out of her glass case and handed her to me. "Oh, Jackie, she's beautiful," she gushed. "Let's name her Chantal." "Okay," I said. I'd never really thought of a name for her like mothers did, because I was too busy watching and thinking and hiding from people, wasting my time and energy living my life for people and caring about what they thought of me when I could have been choosing a name for my baby.

My family loved her the first moment they saw her. Well, my father forgot everything negative that he had said to me. All that was forgotten when he looked into her tiny face, looking at her sleeping eyes and looking every much the proud grandfather. My mother started making her plans for my baby, what cot, pram, clothes, feed, and nappies the baby should have.

I just lay there watching them and thinking about my plans for my baby. I was a mother now and had to take responsibility for this child. I could not allow my parents to raise my child in the way that they wanted. I could not let them make choices or decisions for me as much as they used to. I had to take control, not my parents. I would still ask their permission for most things, but not everything. Making decisions for my child was my responsibility, not theirs. I had just turned sixteen years old; however, my life had just changed. I had grown up overnight, from a child to an adult. Well, that's how I felt.

My hospital experience was a great one. I met other teenage mums, and we all had one thing in common, you could guess, babies, and our parents all felt the same way when they first found out that we were pregnant.

We all became good friends, and mothers, sticking together and going for lunch together. We would listen out for each other's babies. We were like one big happy family. We would all be in the television room just relaxing and some of us smoking a cigarette. We just slouched out on the couch, chatting away about our babies, then we would hear cries down the corridor. I always knew my baby's cry, and that was not her. It's funny how that's one of the first things mothers hear and recognise when you have a baby.

I was an expert to my baby's cry, and I was beginning to learn more and more and get to know my baby's needs and wants. The funniest moment was the very first time when I had to change my baby; that was scary. Well, to cut a long story short, I ended up being covered, face, hands, fingers, and my blue frilly baby doll nightdress which my mother had given to me. She told me that she had worn it when she had me. I wondered to myself, did this happen to my mother? But I guess not, because she was twice my age and not a first-time mum.

I was in a complete mess you could say, feeling and looking embarrassed. A lady walked over to me. She was twice my age and looked like she had a dozen children. Full of experience she smiled at me with an understanding, probably thinking about her first time, those dozen children ago. She took over with such ease and helped me to clean myself and my baby up.

From that day on my confidence and my love just grew to such a height. I was going to be a proper mother to my daughter. Just because I was a sixteen-year-old teenager it didn't mean that without good support I could not be a good mother to my child as a woman twice my age, or even better.

The relationship between my father and me improved. My father became a doting granddad; he was never without the baby on his belly. My father's belly became a cushion for my baby's head. She loved the soft warm feeling. As soon as her head would touch that soft cushion, she would be out like lightning. Even at nights when she wouldn't sleep my father would come into my room and take her to his room, or I would carry her to him, and he would just take her, wrap her up in his arms, then turn to lie on his back, then hey presto, one baby fast asleep before I could close the door and say sweet dreams. I was very much supported by my parents, but it started to feel like they were her parents. It felt like they wanted to take over. Her first two words were directed at them, "Mamma and Dada." However, I still held on to the fact that I was her mother, and soon they began to respect that I was a good little mother.

I did everything for her. It was hard leaving her with anyone. Wherever I went she went. She was a little doll. Well, my sister said that I treated her like one. I would comb her two, three times a day. I was so in love with her and proud of my baby.

I walked through the streets of Tottenham, pushing my baby in her buggy, the latest. I had to argue with my parents to get the latest buggy, and no, they were not having it.

"You are not bringing that wheelchair into this house. It is not good for the baby. Babies need to be flat out in prams, you know, just like the one that you all grow up in."

"Well, Mummy, that pram could fit four of us in there and still have room for shopping. No, I don't think so."

I stood my ground on everything after that. So here I am walking along Tottenham high road. Nothing has changed. I might have, but not the same gossipmongers who stood on the same road nine months ago passing their judgment. I held my head up high and stepped tall like the trees.

Being a young mother was hard, but being stigmatised by older mothers was even harder. I can remember an incident where my friend's mother looked at me in the street and said, "You should be at school reading your books instead of pushing a pram." She then told her daughter that she could not be friends with me anymore, because she would get pregnant. The older mothers would often give me scornful looks at the baby clinic, probably thinking in their minds that I was only a baby myself.

These were just a couple of many prejudices I faced as a young single mother. I remember going to the Social Security, to see if I could claim benefits. I was asked by the man who was interviewing me, "When did you have sex, and where did it take place?"

I was young and vulnerable to his questions and felt that I had to answer to this man, so I told him everything he wanted to know. In my heart I knew it was wrong to ask me those questions, but I needed money.

I loved being a mum; my baby was the most precious thing in my life, and she now came first.

However, I did pay the price of losing most of my school friends. I guess we didn't have anything in common anymore. I was a mother, and they were still schoolgirls.

I had to grow up overnight. I had to be responsible now. I was a mum. My friends wanted to go to the discos and cinemas and talk about boys and probably got fed up with me talking about how many times I had woken up during the nights, how many bottles I had to make, how many nappies I changed in one day, and how many teeth my baby had.

I had no time for hanging around with my friends, and the friends that I did have left. Well, they stayed around for a while, but I guess they got fed up too. They had their whole lives ahead of them, going to college or university and probably carving out a career for themselves, not becoming a mother at the age of sixteen years old like me.

Even though I had lost my friends, I couldn't blame them because we had nothing in common anymore; let's just say I had outgrown them like an old pair of shoes. Well, that's what I had told myself.

I was happy staying at home looking after my baby and trying to prove everyone wrong. I was young, but I could be as good as any mother, even as good as my mother. I quickly found new friends, and we all had the same things in common, babies and dirty nappies.

I settled into my new role as a mother like fish to water. I was a natural, even though I was still a child. It was not that long ago that I was sitting down on the floor playing with my dolls, playing out with my friends, and running around having fun; and here I was making bottles, changing nappies, and washing my baby's clothes. I had grown up overnight into a responsible parent.

Chapter Two

Right or Wrong

1980

Well, six months into motherhood, back on track with my parents, baby crawling around, my life took another turn, when I realised that I was pregnant again. There was no doubt about it. Each day I would wake up and think that today was the day that I would discover that I was wrong, and everything would be back to normal, and my periods would appear, and no more feelings of constant tiredness would plague me. I was struggling to get up each morning. I was sleeping more than the baby was during the day. As the days passed there was still no sign that I was not pregnant, and for some reason I managed to put my pregnancy to the back of my mind and just carried on like everything was fine.

Things became more apparent to my mother. My mother was a very clever woman; you couldn't hide a thing from her. She knew everything. She could even predict things that would happen before they did, especially with her dreams. Well, here was my mother walking around hinting that something was wrong in the house. "Jackie, how come all of a sudden you're getting lazy," she would say. "I had a dream last night that I was frying some fish." Well, according to my mother that meant that someone in the family was pregnant. "What's coming is not going," she would say. Every day she just kept on hinting. However, this was never in front of my father; it was always when we were alone.

I couldn't tell my mother that she was right, because there was no way that I could get away with it this time. They would definitely turn their backs on me; that's after they murdered me. Well, that's what I thought. As the reality of being pregnant started to settle in my mind, I began to feel frightened, scared, and alone with my daily thoughts of what my life would be like if my parents knew my secret. What was I going to do? I even fooled myself that this would go away, when deep down I knew that it wouldn't. My mother was right, this was not going, it was coming.

One day as I sat down in my brother's room reading through his comics, I noticed a few of my magazines sitting between the comics. My brother Robin was the only boy in our family. I was very close to my brother, we were a year apart in age, I guess that when my mother found out that she was able to have children, after being told that there was a possibility that she would never, well eleven years later after losing her first child she gave birth to my sister prematurely, she never gave up hope of ever becoming a mother, well it was all system's go from there on, and she managed to fit us all in, a year apart from each other, except from my little sister Mary, who came along five years after my brother, I was the second in line, and then came Robin, so you see, we were all close, especially Robin and me.

Robin was the only boy, so he felt like the odd one out, We were very competitive with each other, everything, he could do, I could do better, that's what I always told him, I was his older sister, and I never made him forget it. We never left each other's side, in good and bad times, especially when father Bob was out to get us. Robin was my accomplice in everything.

Well Living with three sisters, he got to like the same girlie things as we did. I remember him feeling left out, he once asked my mother why he was different from us. He wanted to be a little girl, playing with our dolls, even wearing our clothes. It was funny, because I wanted to be a boy, especially when it came to sports. The fighting gloves would be on and me and Robin, would compete, then fight, I would always win, and he would always end up crying, "Mummy Jackie beat me up, and I never done anything to her"

Well, even though it was quite a few years ago when Robin would wish that he was like us, things had changed as he got older, he was now playing football and getting dirty like most boys his age, however, Robin still enjoyed reading our comics, *Bounty, Jackie, Tammy,* and *My Guy,* as we got older and started to buy magazines; he still continued to read them.

Well, here I was, sitting in his room. As I looked through the magazine, reading some of the stories, and skipping from page to page, I came to the last page. As I looked at it, I noticed that there were little columns of adverts, for abortion. One read, "If you think that you might be pregnant, please call this number for advice," while another read, "Abortion advice." There were even addresses for abortion clinics.

Well, there was one advert which caught my eye; it was about a private abortion clinic. For the first time since this happened I was able to admit that I needed help.

I couldn't go through this alone anymore. So many weeks had now passed, and I had lost count of them. Well, to be honest, I was never really counting. It was just one long blur of a situation that I had blocked from my mind.

As I continued to read the adverts, I noticed that they all had a price tag written on them. This was not like the National Health Service (NHS), free for all at the point of use. This was not what Dr. Jessie provided at her surgery. This was a private clinic in Harley Street with consultant fees. Just to listen and give advice; even that had price tag written on it too.

As I sat staring at the page, thinking that this was out of the question, and so was Dr. Jessie, I shuddered when I remembered sitting in the wardrobe hiding from my parents. The feelings of fear came back to me. There was no way I was I going to go through that again. I picked up a pen and took down the numbers and addresses. I had to do something. I knew that I could not have this baby; even the thought of proving my mother wrong, facing the shame, and people talking about me again, made me more determined to try to get some help to deal with this.

I found myself a quiet place, a pen, and a piece of paper and sat down to write a letter and pray that I would get a reply and some help. That was the first time in my life that I had ever written since I left school. This was not an essay; this was me pouring my heart out to a complete stranger for help.

Well, within a week I received a letter asking me to come for a consultation at a private clinic in Harley Street, London. Well, that freaked me out because I had no idea where Harley Street was. I knew it was in London, but London was a big place. I had never travelled such distance on my own. Come to think of it, the only places I really knew were in Tottenham, and I had only ever been on buses and in cars, never on a train. I felt a little nervous about the distance; however, getting there was the least of my worries.

Well, the day arrived for my appointment. God knows how I managed to get there without getting lost; even I surprised myself. I remember walking into a really nice building. It didn't look at all like Dr. Jessie's surgery. It was welcoming with lovely décor; it looked more like a nice home than a surgery.

A very nice receptionist with ears as clear as a bell greeted me. As I sat nervously waiting for someone to call me, I thought to myself, *Here I am again in the same situation only a few months on. How did I allow this to happen? Why did no one advise me after I had my baby six months ago that this might happen again if I did not have any protection against getting pregnant? They just let me leave from the hospital to get on with it, and why didn't my mother tell me that this could happen again? They just left me to my own devices.*

Reflection 1976

I guess that sex might have been an embarrassing topic to talk about, back then. Even periods were taboo; that was not a thing that was openly spoken about. It was all hush-hush. Even going to the shop to buy a packet of sanitary towels was like a military operation. My mother would give me a special bag that was not transparent to put it in. She would even give me a scrap of paper with the name written on it to give to the shopkeeper.

I remember feeling embarrassed, standing outside the shop waiting for the person in the shop to leave before I went in; and as soon as I would pluck up the courage to go in, someone would appear from behind me opening the door and walking into the shop. I couldn't go in now. Well, sometimes I would be outside the shop for ages, before I finally got the chance to go in and hand the shopkeeper the piece of paper that my mother had given me. The shopkeeper would look at the paper and discreetly reach for a packet of Dr. White's sanitary towels which he kept under the counter, out of the reach and eyes of the customer, like it was a shame to have them on the shelf. I sometimes felt that it was a shameful and embarrassing thing to have a period. So you see, my mother would be the last person to tell me anything about sex.

Well, as I sat deep in thought, my name was called; and I went in to see the consultant. She was a very nice and kind-looking lady, not like Dr. Jessie, with that serious look and that laugh that made you feel stupid. I remember my mother fussing around before Dr. Jessie visited our home. When we were ill, my mother would clean the house from top to bottom. She even said, "Do you think I want Dr. Jessie to go and tell Mrs. Copings that my house is dirty?" Mrs. Copings lived two doors down. Well, Dr. Jessie always had something to say about all her patients, especially the ones which lived on our road. This included Mrs. Copings. Well, this was a far cry from Dr. Jessie and her surgery.

Well, this nice lady sat and told me that she had read my letter and was very moved by it. As she sat down attentively listening to every word she had a very empathetic and nonjudgmental look in her eyes. Well, after I finished talking to her, she explained the procedure to me. She even told me the cost. I couldn't believe my ears when I heard the price. There was no way on earth I could afford to pay that price; this was out of my league, £200. It seemed like the price tag got higher according to how far pregnant you were.

After being examined, I was told that I was almost fifteen weeks pregnant, which didn't really mean anything to me at the time. I was more concerned about causing more shame to my parents. I was more concerned about proving my mother wrong than thinking about how I really felt about all of this.

I didn't even know what £200 looked like or even felt like. I had never held that amount of money in my hands ever. The most I had ever held was £80 and only ever managed to save as much as £40, and even that took ages to do.

This was out of the question. No way could I afford this price tag. The total was £240, including consultant fees. Well, after she quoted me the price she turned to me and asked me how much money did I have. I told her that I had only had £40 saved at home. The lady looked at me and said, "Okay, Jackie, if you could afford to have this operation, would you be able to come in on Monday morning?" Well, it was now Friday. "Sure," I replied.

"Well, come in on Monday and bring the £40 with you."

I got back to Tottenham in no time. As I walked along my road I thought about how I was going to leave home on Monday morning to go and have an abortion, and not telling my parents the truth, and also leaving my daughter for the whole day and possibly night. How could I get away with this? Where would I tell them that I was going? All these questions raced through my mind.

As I approached my gate, I suddenly came up with the answer: a job. Yes, I would tell them that I had found myself a job in a shoe shop in the West End, and that's where I had gone today, for the interview, and I wanted to surprise them that's why I didn't say anything this morning. Yes, I had my answer. Soon as I walked through the door, without saying hello first as I always did, I shouted to them that I had got a job in a shoe shop and pretended to be really happy and proud of myself. My mother asked me who was going to look after the baby while I was working. Well, that's the only thing that I never thought about. "Well, I don't know. Maybe Patsy, she's not working or anything like that," I replied.

Well, my sister agreed to look after the baby while I went to my new job, in a shoe shop in Oxford Street, West End. I even promised her that I would give her some money when I got paid next week.

Over the weekend I did a lot of thinking. Was I doing the right thing? Well, a voice in my head said yes, while the other said no. I wished that I had the courage to talk to my mother about it. I know that she would be shocked and upset, like she was before. They both would be, but they would eventually get over it like they did before and support me, but I couldn't do this to them again. Just the thought of another showdown confirmed that I was doing the right thing.

I lay in my bed deep in thought feeling alone, and no matter how much I tried to justify what I was doing, it now started to feel wrong, but I still felt that there was no way out of this situation that I had created for myself. There were times when I felt so desperate, I even contemplated throwing myself down the stairs. One time I even tried to punch myself in the stomach. I couldn't even manage to do that properly. Every time I went to punch myself, I would close my eyes. As soon as my fist got near to my stomach I would flinch and draw it away, ready to try again.

Over the weekend I even told myself that maybe if I tried to pluck up the courage to tell my mother, then she would understand; but the more I told myself this, the more reluctant I became of telling her, especially when she hinted again that I was always sleeping like a pregnant woman. Well, that was it; there was no turning back. This was the only way forward, and proving my mother wrong, and anyway how would I cope with two babies at the age of sixteen years old?

Sunday night, and alone in my room staring in the mirror for the first time since I realised that I was pregnant, I noticed that I had developed a little bump in front of me which for the first time I was acknowledging. As I stood there looking at myself for the first and the last time pregnant in the mirror, I felt sad. As I reached down to touch my bump, I felt like a little butterfly was fluttering its way around inside me. I now realised that it was not a butterfly but my baby. I stood there for what seemed like forever with tears streaming down my face and asking God to forgive me.

Early Monday morning I kissed my daughter goodbye and held on to her tiny hand; she cried as I turned my back and walked through the door, holding a picture of her in my hand. The nice lady at the clinic had given me a list of things to bring with me; the list included a nightdress. Well, I couldn't think about anything on the list, just what was in store for me that day.

My parents waved as I left the house telling me to mind how I go. Come to think of it, they even looked and sounded very much the proud parents again, just like they used to when I was knee high, and I would win a drawing or fancy dress competition, or even better, when I sang at Sunday school.

Reflection 1972

My parents were always proud of my little talents, especially when their friends came round. I was their little entertainment. "Come and sing for us, Jack," or play the piano or the guitar or the mouth organ or the accordion. They would even ask me to dance, their faces beaming with pride.

As I walked down the street, I started to feel sorry that I had lied to them. I felt ashamed of myself for deceiving my parents; however, the farther I walked away to face my fate, the more I knew there was no turning back. I began to think about what was in store for me at the clinic. For the second time in my life I was very much alone and scared, sixteen years old, and making the second biggest decision in my life.

In no time I reached my destination. It's funny how we lose all sense of time when were wrapped deep in thought. Time just slips through our fingers like sand.

As I sat down waiting, I noticed that mothers were there with their daughters, women with their partners, single women with their friends, and here I was alone with my fears. As they called me into the room, I saw a young girl being wheeled out on a trolley with her mother in tow holding on to her hand. Well, that shocked me because the girl looked like she was dying. Her eyes were closed, and she was mumbling and groaning like she was in pain. Well, that freaked me out. I wanted to get up and leave straightaway. Who would be there to hold my hand when I was mumbling and groaning? No one, but I couldn't let that put me off, and if I got scared and walked out, that would be it for me, no more chances.

I had to fill in a consent form, and I was even told that I would have to spend the night here. That shocked me. No way, that was out of the question. My parents would call the police if I never arrived home, and if they didn't and I returned home the next day, there would be hell to pay, and there was no way that I could spend the night without my daughter. I had never done that before, and even though she couldn't talk she would be wondering in her tiny mind, *Where is my mummy?*

As I sat there with the consent form in one hand and the pen in the other and all those thoughts racing through my head, I knew that I had to sign it. So I did; however, I knew that somehow I had to get home that evening. I could not stay here for the night, and not signing meant that they could not go ahead, so I signed with the intention of breaking the agreement.

As I took my clothes off and slipped into a white gown, tears rolled down my face, because it suddenly dawned on me what I was doing here. I had never once looked at this baby the way that I had looked at my daughter. I loved her from the very first moment I realised that I was pregnant; with this baby I had distanced myself from the possibility of becoming attached. I made myself think of all the reasons why I couldn't and stuck by them.

I climbed onto the bed, which was shrouded with crisp white sheets, tears falling onto the pillow as I laid my head down, and all I can remember is someone saying to me, "Jackie, count to three, one, two, three," and then someone calling my name, "Jackie, Jackie, it's all over now. Wake up, love."

As I slowly opened my eyes, they told me, "Jackie, it's all over now." The tears were still in my eyes; it felt like I was sleeping for ages, but I wasn't. It took me a little while to come round, but then it dawned on me what had just happened, what I had just done. As they wheeled the trolley upstairs, all I could think about was how I had proven my mother wrong, but the truth was that I had proven her right.

Well, they put me in a lovely room, with beautiful pictures on the wall. There was even a large vase with freshly scented flowers sitting on the table, like they had just been picked for me. There was even a television. Everything about the room was luxurious, just like a five-star hotel room, but it never meant a thing to me. All I could do was cry until I fell asleep.

I was in pain, and there was no one there for me. I wanted to get up and ask for help, and when I did, I was horrified with what I saw; the crisp white sheets were now stained red. I screamed out for help, and the nurse came running in only to assure me that this was normal. Normal, I thought, nothing about this was normal for me. I wanted to go home now.

Well, I managed to calm down as she changed the sheets. She gave me some painkillers and tried to make me feel comfortable like I was at home by turning the television on. She even asked me what channel I wanted to watch. I thought to myself how insensitive could she be. *Here I am in pain and you're asking me what I wanted to watch on TV.*

I reached for my bag and took the photograph of my daughter out, and I put in on the bedside table next to me, hoping that this would make me feel better, but every time I looked at her little round chubby face with those bright brown eyes and that huge smile I wanted to go home even more.

Evening came and the staff ended their shift as a new lot took over. By this time I was getting anxious. It was getting late, and it was time for me to finish work at the shoe shop. I had to go, and no one was going to stop me, agreement or not. I was packing my photograph and leaving.

When the evening doctor came I was adamant that I was leaving, even though she warned me of the implications and the seriousness of the operation which I had just had not that long ago. She told me that I could hemorrhage and end up dead. Well, I was willing to take that chance, I told her as I packed my bag. When she saw how determined I was to leave, she made me promise her that I would call my family or my boyfriend to come and get me; and if I did that she would discharge me, however, only if they came to get me with a car, no public transport.

I remember her giving me a list of the complications regarding the operation and telling me that if I should experience severe pain and hemorrhaging I must go straight to my local hospital, but I must not tell them that she consented to me leaving. I should tell them that I discharged myself against their will. Well, the way that I was feeling, which was pretty much desperate to get home, I would have agreed to anything.

I promised and even made her believe that they were on their way to collect me; the truth was that I was heading home alone just like I had come here alone that morning.

Later on that evening, I left the clinic heading slowly towards the station. I walked at a snail's pace, trying to take it easy, keeping in mind what she had told me. I sat on the train deep in thought, thinking that this morning I wasn't alone when I came here even though I had thought that. Well, I was now alone with no baby. I wasn't pregnant anymore. I felt relieved but empty and sad inside.

When I got home the first thing that my father said to me was that I looked like I worked really hard that day and that I looked tired. I replied yes before slowly walking upstairs and crawling into my bed.

I couldn't even hold my daughter, because I didn't want to put too much strain on myself. That night I just lay there feeling numb, restless, and in pain as feelings of guilt plagued my mind. As I lay there gently sobbing I held my empty tummy until I fell asleep. My life was never the same again because even though I still had my daughter I always imagined whether the other baby was a girl or boy. I couldn't really dwell on the past forever, so I had to let it go and concentrate on my daughter.

Chapter Three

Big Changes for Everyone

1982

My life changed again when my parents decided to immigrate back to Jamaica; my whole world felt like it was falling apart. My parents had been my rock; even though they were disappointed and ashamed when I got pregnant, being devoted Christians they still stood by me and helped me in every way they could, so now they were leaving. How was I going to manage by myself?

My parents begged me to come to Jamaica with them, along with the rest of my siblings, but I couldn't go to somewhere I had never been before and to live, so I stayed.

There was not a day that went by without me crying for them. I missed my little sister Mary and my brother Robin. I missed Mary the most because, I had no one else to confide in, I missed seeing her walking up the road, on her way home from school with her friends, There were so many things which I missed about my sister. I reminisced about taking her to school, combing her hair in three bunches, dressing them with ribbons, and getting her dressed.

Mary was the baby of the family, and very spoilt she was, she got away with everything, even lies. My parents believed everything she said, even if she pointed, Mary was an angel, she babbled, then spoke gospel, the golden child of the family, she could do no wrong as far as my mother and father were concerned, even if she did do wrong, we would get the blame for it, even if we told them what she had done, they would say that we were telling tales on Mary.

Sweet Mary with her cute little face, she had the rosiest flushed cheeks, that you ever saw on a kid, she was forever running away from everyone in line ready to squeeze pinch or bite them, she used to walk around with her rag doll in her hand, full of dirt, my mother had to wash it every week, she would not put it down, to compliment the rag doll, she would walk around with a discoloured cloth nappy in her hand, sucking the end of it, until it turned to a piece of rag, everywhere Mary went, so did the rag doll and nappy. Now I would give anything to see Mary, and the rag doll, and the raggy nappy.

Alone with my little Chantal, and my memories sitting down in a flat with nothing but my thoughts about my family.

I felt sorry for my daughter Chantal because she had lost her family too; however, she was too young to realise what was going on at the time.

My daughter's father was still around; he was three years older than me. I had known him most of my life. We had grown up together in the church, and his parents and mine were friends; they all went to church together.

I had grown up with a very religious background; my father was very dedicated to his ministry. Going to church was our whole lives; everyone in the church was one big happy family, and I certainly did not know it any other way.

My father's dream was always to go back home to Jamaica and build a church as well as a home for the family, and now his dream was about to come true; they were going and leaving me behind, but that was my choice to stay.

No matter how much they begged me to come I could not leave; it wasn't fair to take my daughter away from her father and me away from everything I had known all my life.

The day came for them to depart. Looking back that was one of the saddest days of my life. I was now alone without my parents for the first time ever in my life, and I felt like a motherless child.

With my parents gone I suddenly realised that I didn't have anyone around to rely on. There was no support from anyone and anywhere. I was alone for the first time in my life, alone with a child, and pregnant again as I soon found out.

My children's father did try his best to support us. He had a job as apprentice mechanic, but he only earned £50 per week which could not support a family.

When I found out that I was pregnant, it was different from my previous pregnancies. Even though I missed my parents I felt more positive about being pregnant this time around. There was no shame involved, and no one to answer to. For the first time in my life I had embraced everything about being pregnant and was looking forward to being a mum again. Maybe this time I would have a son.

I had never gotten over having that abortion. I knew that this child could not replace the other one, but maybe becoming a mum again would take away that missing feeling that I had carried around in me for the past two years.

Well, just as I was beginning to come to terms with my parents not being around, even feeling more comfortable with myself and so much looking forward to this baby, everything changed for the worse when Tony became ill; and the doctors could not find anything wrong with him, even though it was clear to see that something was wrong.

I was eighteen years old at the time, and I could not cope with what was happening to him. His hair began to fall out, leaving him bald, apart from a tuft of hair left in the centre of his head. His skin started to look infected and raw. He looked like he had just been in a fire. The palms of his hands looked like they were being eaten away red raw and ready to bleed.

I remember him taking off his shirt and his skin being stuck to it, with water oozing from the sores that had engulfed his whole body. I remember waking up in the morning with bits of his skin stuck to the sheets. God, what was happening; no one could give us an explanation as to why we were going through this living nightmare.

There were times when he couldn't help himself. I had to bathe him and sometimes help him to put his clothes on; he could no longer drive because of his hands. I felt like I had two children and one in my belly, which made three.

Life became more difficult as time went on. There seemed to be no change with his illness. It was getting worse, and there seemed to be no end. Come to think of it, looking back to when my parents were here, that's when my mother noticed that there was something wrong with Tony; she even commented on his face looking swollen.

I can remember her saying to him, "Tony, you need to go and see a doctor. You're not looking well." She even noticed that he seemed to always be wearing a hat. One day when he came round she asked him to take it off, and that's when the first signs of his hair loss became apparent. Tony had been hiding the fact that his hair was falling out, clumps at a time.

Reflections

I had known Tony you might as well say all of my life; we had both grown up together. We both grew up in the church, and his parents were devoted Christians just like mine were, church in the morning and church in the evening, during the weekdays and even on a Saturday night, then bright and early first thing Sunday morning, and back again in the evening until late.

Sometimes we would get home after eleven o'clock in the night, because we had to give the church brethren a lift home in the van. The ones who lived

the farthest got home first. We were young at the time. I can remember falling
asleep in church and my mother waking me up when it was over, then no
sooner had I woken up than the journey would start in the van. After a while I
would fall asleep again. Come to think of it, we were probably second-to-last
drop-off of the night.

This was all we knew as a child; however, I must say that even though my
father was a very strict man he did allow us to have fun, within reason. We
were allowed to do most of the things that other children did. He never stopped
us from being kids. Our childhood was a wonderful and magical experience;
however, it was disciplined.

I grew up with manners and respect for everyone and everything; right
from wrong, we knew from a very early age. However, we were just as naughty
as other non-Christian kids.

We were supposed to be different. Sometimes it felt like I had a label
on me. "That's Pastor La Touche's daughter," they would say. "That's the La
Touché family." So you see, our labels made it impossible for us to get away
with anything; however, it didn't stop us from trying. We wanted to rebel.

I didn't want to go to church anymore as I grew older. I wanted to go out to
discos and to the cinemas with my friends, and I wanted to play and hang out
longer with my friends.

Well, both our parents were pretty much on the same level, so I thought,
but I later realized that their childhood was not as rosy as everyone thought. We
used to call them the Jacksons, because that's how they came across.

At that time we were in the early 1970s, the Jackson mania. I idolized the
Jackson 5, we all did, and now here were the Smith Brothers with their big
afros, I use to wonder, how many pats, did it take to get it in shape, how long
did they stand in front of the mirror raking up their hair to perfection. They
would stand in front of the congregation every week with a different song
belting their little hearts out. with their little bell bottom trousers, and platform
shoes, with their shirt collars pointing to the north and south. *Poor little souls,*
the brethren must have thought, *they must have been up all night practicing
with a belting in mind.* If they went out of tune, especially at the high notes, it
must have been such a relief for them when they heard us all clapping, which
meant that we loved it, and most of all they had made it to the end of the song
with every note intact.

We had to do as we were told even when we didn't want to. Children in
those times did not have much say especially if you came from a West Indian
background, and discipline was always on the menu.

I wanted to be like other teenagers my age, free to talk about boys, go to
parties, and have fun. Standing up for my right as a teenager and letting my
parents know that I had ideas, opinions, and choices too, they only saw that as

me being rebellious. Well, I thought to myself, if that's the way they think of me, I might as well not disappoint them and live up to my new title as a rebel.

Don't get me wrong now because even though my parents thought that I was out of control, I never came home and cursed them. I still retained my manners towards them and did what they asked of me. *No* was not a word that we used towards our parents; willing to please we were.

Well, here I was fourteen years old and the party scene was my dream. Sneaking out in the late evenings and sneaking back in became a regular thing, going to parties and staying out until the early hours of the morning became regular, drinking and smoking became regular, arguments in the family home became regular too. My father said I was out of control. However, the more he tried to put me back in control, I became more out of control.

I once ran away for one week, Christmas Day. That's when I made my exit, round the dining table with my family, eating the wonderful Christmas meal that my mother had spent all Christmas Eve and Christmas morning preparing, all chatting away happily, until I told my father that my friend was having a Christmas party that night and that I wanted to go. "No, you're not going anywhere tonight. This is Christmas Day, and people must stay in their house."

Well, I wanted to go to this party; everyone was going except me, and there was no way that I was missing out on a Christmas party. I had never been to a party on Christmas Day. This would be my first, and anyway I couldn't tell my friends that I wasn't allowed. I would be the laughingstock of Tottenham County School when I returned in the new school year. It was bad enough being the laughingstock all year round when our friends would pass our house on a Saturday night and hear "Praise the Lord," "Amen," and "Hallelujah" coming from our living room, when my parents were having their weekly sessions of prayer meeting.

Well, for the first time ever in my life I stood up to my father and told him that I was going and that he could not stop me. "If you leave this house don't come back!" he shouted. "I won't!" I shouted back as I stormed out of the room and upstairs, to pack my bags. This was the first time that I had said no, and I meant it. I ran upstairs and grabbed a few clothes, not forgetting my party outfit; well, this was the reason why I was running away, so best not forget it.

I ran away for a week to stay with some friends. I stayed with Tony and his sister Althea. They had rebelled and left home too and had come back to London to live.

Christmas was fun, and I did go to the party, and I was having the time of my life. There was no one to tell me what to do. This was the life. I was living the teenage dream of independence, drinks flowing, music playing, but no money to buy food; between us we had nothing.

I spent most of the Christmas holiday hungry. Well, New Year's Day came. I had a great time. We all did, but my belly was crying for food, and there was only one place to go, and that was back home, and I was missing all the comforts of being at home, my nice clean warm bed, clean clothes, breakfasts, and my mother's cooking, so as much as I was enjoying my new life of independence, I was suffering.

I was so hungry and didn't think twice about going home. I wasn't even scared of the consequences. All that I could think about was the last time that I had a good meal. I kept on thinking about the turkey, the potatoes, even the brussels sprouts, which I never really liked. I appreciated them now. I hallucinated about everything. I just wanted to go home, and most of all I missed my family, even my father too.

I packed the few pieces of clothes which I had brought with me, not forgetting my Christmas party outfit, which had led me to this adventure; and I left for home.

"The prodigal daughter has returned!" my father shouted when he saw me walk through the door. "Look, Gat," he shouted to my mother, "if we did know she was coming home we would have cooked Christmas dinner all over again." Well, I learnt my lesson from that day on that there was no place like home.

Chapter Four

Fending for Myself in This Unholy War

1983

So now here I am eighteen years old and caught up in something that I didn't understand. I was a mother and a nurse and very scared; there was no one to turn to. We were both young with one child and another on the way. I needed my mother, but she wasn't there. There was no one to help me, no one to understand and explain what was happening. None of us understood, that is, until we sat down and started to try to make sense of what was happening to Tony.

It was a Sunday evening, and Tony's sister Althea and Desmond and some of our friends sat down in the living room. We felt helpless to the situation. We could all see what was happening; however, we had no solution to this. Times were hard, and money was scarce, but that didn't matter because whatever we had we would all put together.

There was no diagnosis, and we could clearly see that there was something happening to Tony. However, the doctors said that they could not find anything wrong with him. We even went private, but they still did not have an answer as to what was wrong.

As we all congregated in the living room discussing what we should do next, the room went silent as we thought, then we all came to the same conclusion. Well, if the doctors cannot find anything wrong and they've done all these tests for everything, then there is only one answer: "obeah." Someone must have done this to him.

I could not believe what we were saying; it was hard to listen to what everyone now agreed with. Why were we now thinking like this? Surely this was not what had happened to Tony, but what else was there to think?

As a child I had heard stories about people who had done this kind of thing, inflicted this torture upon their friends, families, partners, neighbours, and enemies or had it done to them. However, it always sounded farfetched to me.

Well, I found it difficult to digest that it was witchcraft, "obeah," as it is called in Jamaica. Here in England surely those things did not exist, or did they? Why had we come to this conclusion? I guess we had to explore all the avenues; we couldn't rule that one out. The funny thing is that until that day none of us believed in witchcraft. However, that was all about to change forever.

As we sat dumbfounded one of Tony's friends said, "We have to try and get some help. We can't just ignore this, because if the doctors can't find anything wrong, then we've got to take this seriously."

Well, he told us that his father could help us and that he knew someone that we could go and see. We needed to know what was happening. I had to know what was happening because I was suffering. I was the one who was living with Tony and watching him deteriorating each day, watching his features change in front of my eyes.

I was pregnant, and fighting this unholy war I couldn't allow myself to be scared. I had my daughter to think about, also this baby that I was expecting very soon, so I had to try my best to be brave for all our sakes, so that meant confronting whatever we had to, even witchcraft.

So we all agreed that we would go and see this person who could help us to understand what was really happening. When I look back, it was really spooky how we all were on the same page and singing out of the same hymnbook, but not songs of praises and joy.

The day came when we got our answers. Eight of us, including Tony's friend's father, set off into the van ready to confront our fears. While everyone chatted away I just sat there waiting for answers. We finally reached our destination. If anyone was to ask me now if it was north, south, east, or west, I could not tell them. All I can do right now is to describe the house.

The house was huge from outside. It looked like a hotel, not a home. Inside it looked like a doctor's surgery waiting room. Chairs made a circle around the walls, but they were empty seats, not like in a real surgery where people with all different ailments sat waiting for an answer.

The walls were empty and cold, not like in a real surgery where posters with diagrams and information hung on its walls. I could hear music playing, but the melody was not sweet. I could hear bongo drum beats faintly coming from below the floorboards.

As we sat down and waited a man came into the room and sat down with us for a while. He never spoke to us. He just sat there in silence, waiting just like we were.

We sat there for what seemed like ages, then the man got up and left the room, leaving us behind feeling impatient. I now know what seemed like ages was not, but when you are racked with anxiety a moment can feel like forever.

Well, the door opened, and in walked another man cloaked from head to toe with a white gown and his head bandaged with a turban; every finger on his hands was surrounded by gold and silver rings.

I can still remember the huge snake rings which wrapped itself around his thumbs. I felt a little nervous because I had never met anyone in my life who dressed like that.

He introduced himself as Dr. King, and that's when I realised that he was the same man who had sat in the room with us, just waiting. Well, he was not just waiting; he was watching and observing. He then asked us to follow him. We all got up, but only a few of us could go. We stood in our tracks for a moment as we thought who should go. Well, his brother and his sister and I knew that it was definitely me; the others sat down as we left the room.

We followed behind Dr. King, the man who would help and give us the answers that we needed, and definitely a solution to what was happening. The farther down the stairs we walked, the music and the bongo drum beats became louder and clearer in my head. I felt nervous, but I could not turn back. I suppose we all must have felt that way, but we were here for an answer this evening.

Dr. King invited us into his room to take a seat; I looked around nervously with my heart beating a little louder than normal.

The room was dimly lit with candles; and dolls decorated the room, Barbie, Sindy, and wooden dolls, with needles stuck in them. I was scared as I looked at the circle with a triangle and numbers inside it, brightly painted on the floor.

"Someone has done this to you, someone close to you, a family member, has done this, a man and a woman." *What man and woman?* we thought. Then it hit us, what man and woman he was talking about.

Well, Dr. King went back into time, talking about Tony's childhood. Some things that he said were exactly true. We were astonished by this man, the man who sat observing us; he knew so much it was amazing. I had never met someone like that before. He spoke of such certainty. "Thank god you came on time. By the end of the week you would have died. The person who has done this to you is no longer in this country. She has packed her bags and gone back to Barbados. However, the other person is still here."

This person who had gone back to Barbados was a lady that Tony had met at church who had developed a crush on him without him even realising it; everyone else knew that this lady had a liking for Tony.

I remember his friends teasing him about it. No matter what they said, he refused to believe that this lady fancied him.

Reflection 1974

Before we started to live together, Tony went back home to live with his mother. We were both young even though he was three years older.

I remember being a ten-year-old girl, who had a crush on Tony Smith. Well, I was not the only girl; my sister Patsy and my friends and even some of the adult church sisters took a shine to him. They used to drool over him, especially when he used to hit those high notes just like the young Michael Jackson and he was cute just like Michael.

I remember wishing that I stood a chance with winning his attention like the older girls, but I was just a kid with a crush. Well, maybe one day when I got older he would notice me; that's what I told myself.

Well, all those wishes ago, and here I was with my wish, Tony Smith, but this was not what I had wished for.

As Dr. King took us through a summary of this horror story, I tried to block out the last letter of each word, but I could still hear every word that he said. "This woman has a wooden doll, and she puts the doll in the fire. She's trying to change your features. She has your hair. She took it out of a comb. She wanted you, but she couldn't get you, so she has hurt you instead."

Tony had got this woman a room in his mother's house, another devoted Christian sister, and it was a very charitable offer of a room at the inn. It used to strike me how everyone used to go on about this woman, like she was some great prophet, Sister Lesley this, Sister Lesley that. Well, this woman had wormed away into Tony's mother's affections and house; and now here was the great Dr. King telling us that this woman had set out to harm Tony because if she could not have him, then she would make sure that no one else would want him again.

Tony had told us that a few months ago he felt that he was coming down with a cold, and Sister Lesley had made him a drink which she said would help him to get over his cold. He told us that he only managed to take a few sips because it tasted awful. He told us that it tasted so bad he could not drink anymore after that. Did that drink have something in it to harm Tony? He told us everything, and we believed him. Well, we had to because we hadn't found an answer yet, so this had to be it.

Well, Dr. King spoke about being surrounded by good and bad spirits in the room, doing good and bad for a price. I sat there trying to be brave, my legs getting ready to stand up and leave, but I was just glued to the seat listening to this man giving us instructions what to do to rid this. I looked to the left and then to the right, relieved that I was sitting between two people. Even though I was in the middle I felt that I was on the outside.

The unexplainable happened when he asked us to throw some coins preferably coppers into the circle. As we obeyed him throwing the copper coins into the circle, we waited for them to hit the floor, but they didn't; they dropped nowhere and fell into obscurity. Well, that was it for me. I just freaked out and left the room. Talk about fright, and flight.

We left with our diagnosis and a list of instructions to follow. Tony was also given a silver guard ring to wear and a white envelope with instructions never to open, but carry with him in his pocket wherever he went. He was told to have a bath in a cocktail of ingredients which you could not imagine; it was crazy. Everything became crazy after that night, the bath rituals, the ointments, and the smells, it was madness. I felt I was in one of those horror movies, but this was not on screen, this was my life.

I had become another Florence Nightingale or some would say Mary Seacole leaning over the bath, filled with water and a variety of ingredients, wiping down this man. I tried tenderly not to rub the sores on his skin with the sponge too hard, just in case the skin rubbed off. Every night and day I would do the same helping him to prepare for this cleansing ritual.

For the next few months we lived our lives with instructions, given to us by Dr. King. I couldn't take this anymore. It was hard doing some of the things which we were told to do. I was scared and felt alone, and I couldn't tell my parents what was happening or what I was going through. They couldn't help me anyway, because they were thousands of miles away in Jamaica.

I couldn't even tell my friends because I felt that they would not understand. No one would, but God.

I needed looking after myself, and here I was with a few weeks left to have my baby, and it felt like Tony was my child too.

The morning of July 7, the exact day that my baby was due, he came. It happened so fast there was no time to call an ambulance. It was just like you see on television, the woman is walking along, then suddenly she's screaming in agony and on the floor. Well, that was me. I woke up at four o'clock that morning and ready to push this baby out. I thought I had died and gone to hell. My legs were paralyzed, and I could not walk. I couldn't even put my clothes on. There was no time for an ambulance, so Tony had to drive. God knows how we got there.

I could see the pain and tears in his eyes as he drove. The palms of his hands were sore. He told me that he felt as if his hands were on fire, but he had to forget his pain and concentrate on getting us to the hospital.

I kneeled down on the floor in the back of the car trying not to push and just praying that we would get there on time.

When we got to the hospital I tried to walk, but I had no feelings in my legs, then suddenly I heard a loud pop, and there was water everywhere. The nurses came rushing out to help us and carried me into the labour ward. They managed to get me onto the bed just in time for the baby to make his entrance. Michael, that's what I named him. I had chosen his name way before his birth. I thought to myself that he did look like a Michael and then realised looking down that I still had my shoes on my feet.

The joys of motherhood were marred with Tony's illness. My life became a nightmare as time went on. I had two children now, and I was supposed to be happy, just like every other mother who had just had a new baby, but I wasn't.

I felt very emotional all the time, but I put it done to having the so-called baby blues, and in a few weeks I would feel normal again. Well, that's what I told myself.

Well, things never got any better. I felt depressed, and I cried all day. I never came out of the flat, unless I really had to. I used to sit down on the couch wearing my pyjamas and dressing gown all day, with the curtains drawn shut. My life felt dark and gloomy. I felt that there was no reason to have them open, because at this time I could see no light in my life, just pure darkness, day in day out.

I never even smiled anymore, and my baby was so sad he cried all day long. I had always been the best mum that I could be, but I felt like I was losing my mind.

Trapped in a council flat on a notorious estate with two young children feeling like you don't want to live anymore and no one to turn to because you don't want anyone to think you are mad thinking crazy thoughts, doing crazy things, I needed someone to help me, but who.

I became violent towards Tony. No one knew what I was going through. If my friends only knew how much I was suffering, but I couldn't tell anyone. Why would they believe me anyway? My children and I never looked like we were suffering, and everyone always commented on what a fantastic mum I was. They always told me that my children were always nicely dressed. Well, nicely dressed on the outside, but we were all naked on the inside and suffering.

Not once did I write to my parents and tell them what I was going through. I kept silent. Not knowing or understanding my feelings, my agony went on for one year. That was until I self-diagnosed my illness.

One morning I was sitting down listening to the television. I couldn't watch it because the picture had gone. I was lucky that we still had the sound. We could no way afford to buy a new one. Someone had given it to us, because they had bought themselves a new one, and you don't get people giving you televisions every day. Anyway GMTV breakfast show was on, and they were talking about postnatal depression, and that is when I suddenly understood what I had been going through for the past year. I didn't know whether I should laugh or cry. It suddenly dawned on me, *Jackie, you're not mad, you're not crazy, you're not mental.* I wanted to shout out the windows. *I'm not mad, I have postnatal depression, and I am going to get better,* and I did.

That day I went straight to see my health visitor at the baby clinic. As soon as I got there I burst into tears and told her that I had postnatal depression. I told her what I had been through for the past year and how I thought I was losing my mind. I had suffered in silence and in fear of being judged, and I was scared that Social Services would take my children away, if they found out. Well, if I had known then what I know now, I would never have gone through that alone in silence.

I felt like a burden had just flown away. For the first time in a year I felt like my old self. I felt strong again. I felt free from my torment; and my kids were happy again even though we didn't have carpets, a sofa, or any luxuries in the flat.

Things did not get much better on the financial front. Tony could no longer work because of his health, so things got so bad, but nothing could have been worse than the year that I had just left behind me.

After buying food and providing for the children we hardly had any money left to pay the bills. Some weeks I had to rotate it where I would buy a little food and pay towards the bills. I would always pray that the shopping would at least last until Friday, but that was wishful thinking because it never did. I would struggle all through the weekend praying that a saviour would come and save us, and they always did.

I thought that things could not get any worse, but they did. We couldn't afford to pay the electricity bill, so we ended up living without electricity for one year. Choosing between paying the gas bill or the electricity bill was not a hard choice to make. I would rather have gas to keep warm and to cook rather than have electricity to have light to see. What a decision to make

Living without light and sound in that flat was like living in a graveyard. You could hear the cockroaches singing, yes, cockroaches everywhere crawling around in the dark on my food, in the oven, in my children's clothes. Even the wallpaper was peeling and falling off the walls because of cockroach infestation.

I went through summer without electricity. Thank god for summer, because it was bright outside until ten o'clock in the evening, but then summer turned into autumn, and the clocks went back, and it slowly but surely got darker. Then autumn turned into winter. By three thirty in the afternoon, darkness was on its way. I used to try to rush and cook the dinner before it got too dark.

Bath times became a nightmare for my children, because we could not see in the bathroom. There were no windows. The bathroom was just a box with a bath, sink, and toilet. It made no difference whether I bathed the children day or night because it was completely dark.

Candles were the only means of light; that's only when I could afford to buy them. The bathroom soon became caked in candle wax, which had turned into some decorative piece of artwork. Around the corners of the bath, drippings of colour stuck to the sides.

I used to sit down on the floor in the dark, with just a candle writing letters to my family in Jamaica, telling them how everything was fine, when it was far from that.

One Sunday evening as I gently rocked the baby to sleep, I rocked myself to sleep as well and almost burnt the flat down. Tony had gone to his mother's house and had taken Chantal with him. This became a regular thing because some Sundays we couldn't find the money to buy even a chicken. On a Friday that's when I would be thinking about Sunday dinner. Well, I had to think two days in advance. I couldn't wait until Saturday. I had to give myself forty-eight hours and hope that something would turn up, maybe money, maybe someone coming round with some money that they had borrowed whether it was last week or last year; however, that was wishful thinking.

Tony would always say if worse came to worst, then we would go to his mother's house for dinner; that was the only solution at the time. Well, Sunday would come, and he would get his bowl, and Chantal, and get in the car, and off they would go to get their Sunday offering. I used to thank God that at least I didn't have to worry about not having food for two children. It was just one, because the baby had his milk, tins of it, which I would get from the clinic each week with my milk tokens. I had tins upon tins stacked high. All you could see was SMA, milk powder, more than anything else, no beans, no spaghetti, just milk.

Well, that evening I woke up to find a film of fog like smoke hovering in my room. I felt like someone or something had just woken me up. It didn't sink in what was happening until I saw a trail of smoke seeping in through the bottom of the door. That's when it hit me that the flat was on fire, and I knew exactly why.

I had left the baby's bottles to boil in a pot. Well, that was my way of sterilizing the bottles. I couldn't afford to buy the sterilizing tablets. Anyway I had heard that this method was good just as the tablets, and it was, until that became the reason why we could have lost our lives. The water had evaporated, leaving the plastic bottles to melt and blaze to such an extent. Well, realising what was happening, I jumped up and without thinking opened the door to greetings of thick white smoke. I never thought twice as I fought my way to the top of the stairs, flashing my arms in front of me, like a blind man feeling for security. As I reached the top of the stairs all I could think about was putting this fire out, but I had to see how bad it was first, and there was no electricity. I couldn't let anyone in to help me because they would know how we were living. Well, as I jumped down the stairs missing steps in between, I wasn't thinking about breaking my bones; all I could think about was finding out how bad the fire was.

As I opened the kitchen door all I could see were orange and yellow flames dancing around the cooker. I couldn't fight that fire. I had to get help fast, and I had to get the baby out. I shut the kitchen door behind me as I ran out the front door shouting that the house was on fire. I didn't care about people knowing that we had no lights. All I could think about was getting help to stop the flat from burning down.

Thank god my friends lived a couple of doors away because they were able to help me that night, by putting the fire out and taking the baby next door. Both of us were lucky that night. Maybe if I hadn't woken up my story could have been different.

For one year living without light and taking the children to school, no one knew until that night.

Well, even though this had happened, I still never went to Tony's mother's house on a Sunday for dinner, not once. Tony would always bring dinner back in a bowl. I guess I felt too embarrassed and ashamed to have to rely on going to his mother's house on a Sunday for dinner because I felt that I should have been in my kitchen preparing a roast dinner or rice and peas with chicken for us all.

A few months later and all this behind us, I thought my troubles were over when I was offered temporary accommodation. At least I would have electricity, and things would get better, but I was far from being right.

Temporary accommodation has become somewhat a luxury for people, compared to what it was like twenty years ago. Today we have decent temporary housing, which comes fully equipped with beds, cookers, fridges, all the necessary things that we need. Some even come with microwaves, beddings, curtains, washing machines, and cutlery. Today these things are not deemed as luxury, but in my times they were.

Well, I was given this temporary flat to live in. There was nothing in there, only the walls and floorboards, not even a heater, no central heating, nothing, only damp, condensation, mould, and mice. The only positive thing that it did have which was now a luxury to me was electricity.

The flat was so cold. I should say freezing to the point where not having a fridge did not matter. I was told by the Department of Health and Social Security that a fridge was not a necessity, only if I had a child who was ill and needed to have medication which should be kept in a refrigerator. I did not qualify for that. Thank god my children were in perfect health.

I couldn't afford to buy a bed, so I slept on the floor with my two children, wrapped in blankets donated by my next-door neighbour.

I tried to make the flat homely as possible. It was hard to do this especially when there was mould, mildew, and ice dripping from the walls. I used to leave my frozen food on the shelves, and when I woke up in the morning they would still be frozen. I couldn't live there anymore; I was living in an igloo, in London in 1984.

In that time I commuted between two flats. I would stay there in the daytime, and as soon as it got dark I would make my way back to the other flat which belonged to my sister. I would rather live in darkness than to be cold. I had to do what was best for my children, so I went back.

Every Saturday evening, we would visit Tony's sister Althea; we spent a lot of time visiting his family. I got on very well with Althea, she was funny, because she laughed about, everything, I use to make her laugh, then she would make me laugh too. I loved being around Althea, she felt like my sister, more than my own sister, Patsy, was hardly around, I guess she was getting on with her own life, and was too busy to consider mine Patsy was the only one that I had left here, but sometimes it felt like I had no one, Althea, Derek, and Anthony, Tony's family became my family.

Well we were hardly ever at home because there was nothing to be at home for. Althea's life had taken off, and she seemed to be doing well for herself. She had managed to get herself out of her struggles and was now living comfortably in a nicely decorated, fully furnished flat with her partner and child, a nice cozy home with all the trappings, something we never had.

Sitting in Tony's sister's nicely decorated home, I wished I had a home like that to carry my children back to, a home full of pure light, upstairs and down. My children's home was dark with no light, and no money to pay the bills.

Well, it wasn't long before I was offered a permanent flat on the same notorious estate. My life was about to change again for the better, so I thought.

I moved into this flat. It wasn't my dream home, no beds, no chairs, no carpet; but it was much better than what I had been used to.

My children were happy. I felt happy, more than I had been for the past few years. The children were settled, but money was still a big issue in my life. I couldn't really afford to buy much food.

Sunday evenings I would often sit down and write my shopping list, being careful not to make it come over £35, but it always did. I would sit down for hours adding up, taking away doing the priority list, choosing what to take off the list: should it be tomato ketchup or baked beans, should it be biscuits or bread.

I adapted the skill of adding up my shopping before I got to the checkout, and I often prayed that my maths was right because I didn't want to get embarrassed at the checkout when the cashier said that my shopping was £40, and I only had £35. I needn't worry about that because I was always correct, and my shopping was always under.

Chapter Five

No White Christmas, Only Blue

1984

The relationship between me and my Tony was holding on by a thin line. The pressure of his undiagnosed illness which no doctors could fix took its toll on the relationship. Deprivation also played its part.

I was only nineteen years old but sometimes felt like I was ninety-one years old instead. I didn't go out anymore. I just stayed inside and cooked, cleaned, and looked after everybody. Surely there must be more to my life than this; and why did I feel like I was trapped at nineteen years old, in a relationship that felt like it was stuck in time, burdened down with all problems which we had faced, and no one to help me? Where was I going? Was this my life? Some people would say, "You made your bed, so you have to lie in it," but for how long could I continue to lie in the bed that I had made?

Things hadn't always been like this. There were times in between this misery and before Tony got ill that we were young, carefree, and happy. Although we had very little money we did manage to have fun, with Tony's family and friends. Well, we were all one big happy family who did everything together. We went everywhere together, and the fact that we had children never got in the way.

We still managed to party and go on outings. All of us would just pile ourselves into a car day or night and just drive to wherever we wanted to go. There were no set times to have fun. We would just be sitting down just like we had done when we had all come to our conclusion about Tony's illness.

Money was never an issue. Even though we didn't have any between us we all managed to support each other like families do. We had known each other most of our lives.

Tony was ambitious. He had plans and dreams for our lives; but all those had to go on hold because of his illness, deprived of his health and me with two young children, no qualifications, a young girl who looked destined for a life filled with deprivation, failed relationships, and still searching for happiness and peace.

I had never understood what the word *peace* meant. Was it a feeling of sure utter bliss, because I had never felt it before. Would I ever know that feeling? But you know what, I never gave up hope of finding it somewhere in my life. I knew I would, but I had a long road ahead of me, to fight for peace.

Times became harder. Sometimes no money and no food, I would often sit down and watch my children eat. That made me feel so good to hear them say, "Mum, I'm full, I don't want anymore," but sometimes I would wish that there was just a little left over for me. Sometimes there was, and sometimes there wasn't. That's the way the cookie crumbled for me. My children only said those words up until Friday, then it was "Mum, I'm hungry."

I would turn the house upside down looking for money to buy potatoes. You know, there is always change somewhere. The places that we look for money are the sofas and under the carpet, but I never had any of those things to look for money.

December 25, 1984, Christmas Day, no Christmas tree and no presents for my daughter to open. I felt so sad. She was four years old at the time, and she knew that it was Christmas and very excited like every child is on Christmas Day, but there was not one present, because I had to choose between Christmas dinner and presents. I couldn't even afford to buy a proper Christmas dinner with all the trimmings, just chicken potatoes and stuffing, the basics. No Christmas crackers, no stockings, no decorations, and no tree with flickering fairy lights and shiny baubles hanging from it. There was no evidence of Christmas in our house.

Reflection 1970

When I was a little child, Christmas was the most magical recurring event in our lives. Each year my parents would pull out all the stops to make it memorable in their own way. I remember Christmas Eve with great fondness and a smile on my face. Christmas Eve, Christmas Day, and Boxing Day were just awesome in our household.

Christmas Eve was a day when my parents would be so busy preparing for that special day. My mother would be running around fussing about what curtains she should hang and looking for new sheets to decorate our beds, while my father would be finishing off the last bits of decorating that he had started to do earlier on that year. Freshly scented paint gave our home a new feel, look, and smell each year.

I would be in the kitchen sitting down on my little stool watching mother steadily icing the Christmas cake. She used to have this serious look on her face while she was icing the cake. I dared not say anything just in case she lost concentration.

My father was busy putting up decorations all over the house. It was amazing how the house was transformed by a few pieces of paper, tinsel, and balloons. Christmas cards strung throughout the rooms, brightly coloured lanterns decorated the ceilings, and flashing fairy lights surrounded the windows and the tree. The Christmas tree stood tall and gracefully decorated in our living room and now became the focal point of the room.

My father never really played music, only at Christmas, whilst he was concentrating to make the house look pretty for us. As we ran around, laughing and playing, the sweet voice of Jim Reeves echoed so sweetly from the record player around the house, "Silver bells, soon it will be Christmas Day." I could see my father was enjoying the music and the atmosphere, because he would be tapping his foot. You could say that we all had the Christmas spirit in us.

After everything was done, tree beautifully decorated and all, my father would tell us to put on our coats; and we would all take the long-awaited trip to our local off licence to get our Christmas drinks and goodies with our trolley in tow. I can still remember standing in the shop all excited, while my father made us choose which Christmas drink we wanted. The shopkeeper would always give my father a bottle of sherry as a present. I suppose it was for his loyalty and custom each year.

After our trip to the off licences we would return home to greetings of wonderful smells coming from my mother's kitchen. I couldn't wait for Christmas Day.

As we all sat looking at the beautifully decorated tree, there were no presents under or surrounding it; however, we knew that when we awoke in the morning it was guaranteed to be full with presents.

Going to bed on Christmas Eve was so hard. We couldn't sleep, anticipating, wondering, hoping, and praying that we would get the presents of our dreams. Excitement filled the house. All I wanted was the latest talking doll, not the one that you held on to a loop and pull the string attached to her back. No, this was the doll which had records, little plastic discs which you would open up a little box in her back and put the disc in. That's what I prayed for, and I knew that my parents would not let me down.

We used to lie awake imagining the day and what we would play with first, then we would hear the door gently open as my parents tiptoed into the room and laid our Christmas stockings filled with goodies at the bottom of our bed.

We would close one eye and leave the other open, sleeping and spying at the same time. We even made little snoring sounds; the whisper of my parents' voices seemed so loud. I was happy because they even sounded happy and excited like children, just as if they were getting presents too, excited about giving and watching us opening our presents and seeing the smiles on our faces and feeling they have managed to fulfill this year's Christmas dream.

We finally fell asleep, waking up in the morning running downstairs into the living room, standing in front of the Christmas tree that had no presents under and now miraculously packed with presents of all shapes and sizes, with our names on. I believed in Santa Claus.

Now all those years later, here I am, just like my parents were those many Christmases ago. The only difference was that my circumstances were the total opposite, no job, no money, no food, no presents, and certainly no tree. There were no nice smells coming from the kitchen, no decorations hanging from the ceiling, no nicely coloured lanterns and tinsels, no flashing fairy lights around the windows. Come to think of it, no proper curtains too, and no Jim Reeves. This was a far cry away from the Christmas that I used to know and loved as a child; there was nothing magical about this at all.

Well, I never mentioned the word *Christmas* all day. I just treated it like any other day. I never even looked out the window that day, to be reminded of what day it was, especially with the flashing Christmas lights that decorated the neighbour's windows. No one came round that day. I prayed for the day to end. I looked at my daughter who was blissfully unaware of how I felt. I had never shown her how sad I really was. I felt like a bad mother. I felt that I had let her down on the one day that meant so much to every child, the day which had meant so much to me when I was a little girl.

Well, the day came and went, and the Christmas weekend was over. Well, the first thing I did was to go to the post office and cash my benefit book and straight to the toy shop. I bought my daughter a Sindy doll, and I bought a rattle for the baby; that's all I could afford because I had to pay my bills and buy shopping. I also bought some wrapping paper, and I couldn't wait to go home and wrap the present up and give it to her.

Well, I got home and excitedly wrapped the present up. I even put a big bow on it. I couldn't wait to see the look on her little face when I gave it to her. "Happy Christmas, baby." You should have seen her little face. Her mouth dropped open, and her eyes lit up, and she gave me a great big hug, and in her sweet little voice she said, "Thanks, Mum, this is the best Christmas I ever had."

I felt happy because she was happy. I even bought some sweets and chocolates and cooked a nice meal. Today was our Christmas Day.

There was no way that I was going to put myself or my children through another Christmas like that ever again. I loved my children, and I would die for them and steal for them if I had to, and that's what I did.

With no one to turn to, with my pride desperately trying to hang on, there was no one that I felt that I could turn to.

I felt like I was in this world by myself, and there was no one whom I could turn to, so I had to fend for myself and my children. I turned to shoplifting. Shoplifting gave me a buzz. I felt that I was now able to contribute to my family, and my children would no longer be without. I started hanging around with people who were established in this occupation, who would teach me the skills of shoplifting.

I didn't feel proud about what I did, but it was a means to an end, so I thought. Well, my newfound occupation came to an abrupt end when I got caught stealing jumpers and coats for my children. I felt so ashamed about what I had done. I remember the judge asking me why I had done this. I told him that it was winter and that my children needed jumpers and a coat to keep them warm and that I couldn't afford to buy them a coat or jumpers.

Well, that was a long time ago. I told myself that there had to be a better way. Thieving was not the answer to my problems, it only added to them.

I found it difficult to cope with everyday life. Financially it was even harder because I only had my benefits to live on, but I managed somehow and with the help of my friends. Most of us were in the same situation, single mothers, on benefits; only difference was that they had their parents around, but I never.

We became a family, and we were always there for each other, financially and spiritually. We gave each other strength. We shared a lot with each other; we shared clothes, food, chores. You could say we were like a mother's support group and a children's play group, because all our children were happy together.

The relationship between me and Tony ended. I just could not go on living this way anymore. I didn't love him anymore. Come to think of it, I don't know if I had ever loved him in the first place. Bogged down by family life at an early age took away whatever it was that I had felt for him in the beginning, his illness, having no support, lack of money, they all played their part in the breakup of this relationship.

When Tony left he never looked back. He saw the children a few times after that; but then his visits became less, and lesser, until they faded out and stopped completely, when he started a new relationship. He got on with his life, got married, and started another family and just forgot about the family that we had together; no contact was ever made again. I never saw his sister or brothers. No one came around to visit the children. Christmases and birthdays were forgotten by all.

Chapter Six

From the Frying Pan into the Fire

1985

I was also in a new relationship. He was an old friend that I had grown up with. I was happy because I had someone in my life who was there for me, someone to talk to and someone to share my life with. Chantal and Michael loved Patrick, and he loved them too. He treated them like they were his own and made sure that they never went without anything. Financially things were better. I was able to buy nice clothes for the children. I was able to afford to buy more food, the bills got paid, but my life he controlled.

Things were great at the start until I had his child. On November 6, 1985, I gave birth to a beautiful baby girl. I named her Sacha, she was Patrick's first baby, and I must say she looked just like him, she had no resemblance to me. Sacha had milky white skin, I was overly shocked when I saw her for the first time, well I never expected to have a white baby for sure Patrick was mixed race, but he was darker than me. I had built up a mental picture in my head of what my baby would look like, and she did, but hence the colour.

I remembered saying to everyone "if I hadn't seen her being born and they I brought her to me after, I would have sworn she wasn't my baby. Well I must say she was absolutely a little beauty, she had ivory skin and lovely golden brown hair, her little face was perfect, with a little mash mouth, well that's what we called it, referring to the look of someone when they had no teeth, well that's how Sacha looked, and that made her look more cute, she was defiantly a doll. Everyone always commented on Sacha, Sacha was the bomb, and her mouth was like fire, she was a little chatterbox, at the age of one year old, you could have a fluent conversation with her, and she would still be questioning you longer after, Sacha was amazing.

Three years later, I had another child for him, a son named Raymond.

Now I had four children, and that's when things changed for the worse. We were so different. He always wanted to be in control of everything and made all the decisions. At first it didn't bother me, because that's how I thought it was meant to be; a man was supposed to be in control of everything. I didn't know any better. When I was with Tony I was more in charge of things than he was, and that's because he was not able to do much because of his illness, so you could say that it now felt good that someone had come into my life masterfully and was taking care of everything. Patrick described himself as a soldier, very regimental, I often felt that he was coming from the old school, where discipline was at the top of the agenda.

He loved to be, and feel in control, of all the big, or small decisions, He wasn't bad looking, I wouldn't say that he was a charmer, or even had charisma. He was loud, and always wanted his presence to be felt, everyone knew when Patrick had landed. I must say that he had a funny side to him, especially when he would walk around the house singing Bob Marley songs, well that's when things were ok, and we all loved when he was in that mood, because we were all happy and relaxed. and I didn't feel like I was tip toeing around.

Patrick wanted to take care of everything, he was good at that, and I allowed him, too.

There were times when I felt like I was living in the background of my family, I felt like I was not noticed anymore, just the mother of Patrick's children, and nothing more, I never felt that I had ever meant anything to him, well if I did, would he have treated me this way. Well that's how he made me feel, like I did not have a say any more about the direction that my life was heading in, well that's how it seemed, and that's how I felt.

I soon realised that I was losing my independence, and my voice, and I didn't know how to get it back. I felt anonymous. The way that he spoke to me began to sound condescending. I felt belittled, stupid, and I soon started to feel powerless.

I became dependent on him while he controlled my life and everything in it. Sometimes I used to feel like I didn't have a mind of my own anymore. He even made sure that I wore sensible clothes, no flesh on show.

I remember my sister buying me a dress, which he did not approve of because he said that the back was too low and you could see my bottom, which was not true. I loved that dress so much. It was bright orange, and I felt good each time I put it on. Well, I did defy him by wearing it, and he soon made sure that I never wore it again because he ripped it in half, as I stood watching.

I stood up to him by running upstairs to get one of his shirts to rip; fighting fire with fire didn't work. My home became a battlefield as I tried to defend myself.

All my life I had always been able to stand up to anyone, small and feisty. I had an answer for everything. Well, that's what my father would say. I would not let a soul take liberties with me; but here I was allowing a man to do this to me, disrespecting me in front of my friends, my family, and my children.

He would insult me in front of his friends and his family too, and I allowed him to do that, not because I wanted him to but because I felt helpless. The name-calling and insults just came one after the other. "Look at you," he would say, "you are worthless, you're nasty. Don't let me do you something." There were times when I did manage to stand up for myself; however, I would always come out worse off.

I was not allowed to have a telephone in the house because he said that I didn't need one, and if I did have one then I would be giving out my number to men and that they would be ringing the house when he wasn't there.

I had to ask his permission to go out with my friends. Sometimes I would get my friends to come round and ask him, "Is it all right if Jackie comes out with us tonight?" His answer would be "No, it's not."

Sometimes I would be there all day trying to muster up the courage to ask him if it was okay with him if I went out with my friends. Well, I would be there all day taking two steps forward and three steps backwards; and every time he looked at me, I would lose the little courage that had taken me all day to get. Come to think of it, I don't know why I bothered because most of the time it was no.

On a few occasions when he did say yes, I would always pay the price for going out and enjoying myself because two days later when I was blissfully unaware, I would get a great big punch in my face and get pushed to the floor; and he would lift his foot up and step on my head. Someone had told him that they saw me at a party dancing with another man. Lies, lies, lies, that was his way of not making me want to go out with my friends anymore because I would be too scared to, just in case he did have his spies out there.

After that incident happened, I remember my friends coming round to visit. No one really knew that this was going on in the relationship. I don't even think my family knew that much. I can remember my friends knocking the door. I wanted to go and open the door to let them in, but I couldn't. I even told the children to keep quiet just in case they heard us. My friends knew we were there and shouted through the letter box, "Jackie, open the door. We know you're in there." I put my hand over the baby's mouth just in case he decided to cry at that time. I remember once he told me that someone had told him that I was sleeping with some Jamaican guy that hung around on the estate where we lived. Up until this day I still don't know who I was supposed to have slept with. The fights between us grew more frequent, even spilling out onto the street.

I was even told that I could not go to my nephew's first birthday party because I was not to be trusted. Did he think that I would run off with the clown? Believe me, I wish that I could run, but where to, and with whom, because he would not let me take the children. He lived his own life because sometimes I would not see him for days, and when he did come home it was always with some lame excuse.

He always gave me the one where he was locked up for two to three days in a police cell; he would even pretend to smell himself and make his face up just like he smelt something bad. After a while I got used to him staying out. I didn't mind anymore when he never came home. I was happy when he was not there anyway, and besides, he treated my home like a hotel, bed, and board, so at least I wouldn't have to feel on edge, just in case he decided to kick off, over nothing, so the less the better.

Kicking off happened a lot, especially on a Saturday morning, when he would eventually come home from the night before, or the night before that, sometimes looking for an excuse to argue or fight.

I remember my first coffee table. I had saved a little of my benefits each week to buy it, the latest nest of glass tables from Argos. However, I used to tell myself that they were only there until I could find a table that I really liked. I told myself that they were only there to fill up the space in the middle of the floor.

The flat was starting to look like a home just like Tony's sister's flat. It had taken me years to get it up to this standard. Anyway I had my eye on another centre table, but there was nothing wrong with this one apart from it rocking from side to side when you touched it. Well, I prayed for it to break. That would be easier to justify why I needed a new table.

Well, every Saturday morning when Patrick would come home, the first thing that he would do is get angry and kick the nest of table for whatever reason he had in his mind. One minute we would be sitting down watching the television, the next we would be watching where the table was going. The amazing thing was that it never broke, when I wanted it to, so I could buy the table that I really wanted.

Living on edge was really hard. I never knew what mood he would be in when he came home. Even worse was when he woke up; he would spend all day sleeping and then get up wanting to cause an argument over anything.

He always made sure that he bought himself and the children nice clothes. I always came second to none. I was happy that the children were well taken care of.

If I needed anything I would have to wait until Monday morning when I got my benefits, and whatever was left over I would try to buy myself something out of it.

I couldn't really afford to buy nice clothes out of what I was getting, but you know when you don't have much money you stick to what you can afford, by going to the cheap shops which cater for people like me.

Sometimes even going to the cheap shops I still could not afford to buy things that I wanted. Sometimes I used to hide a blouse or skirt that I liked right at the back of the rail and hope that it would be there when I came back next week, when I got paid. Anyway I would return to the shop on Monday hoping that it would be there, but it never was. I guess other people had the same idea too.

The worse thing for me was to sit down and try to rack my brains about what to sell to get money to buy myself something to wear. It was even worse when I would realise that I had nothing to sell. Sometimes I would think to myself that I dare not ask him for money for anything, because the few times that I did, I was told to try and budget better with my benefits so it could last.

I would always try to pluck up the courage to ask for money, then he would surprise me by saying yes, and then he would try to give me half of what I had asked for. It wasn't long before I caught on and started to ask for more than the cost of what I wanted to buy. That way I knew that I would get the full amount of money to buy the item I needed. It took me a while to catch on because I was scared to challenge him. I guess that I just felt grateful that he gave me. I would just have to save the other £20. I soon got over my reservations and learnt to play his game very well.

I once wrote a letter and left it around the house for him to find. It was about having very little clothes or proper shoes to wear on my feet. Well, that day I did realise that there was a heart in there somewhere, because that day he gave me enough to buy myself some much-needed clothes.

I cannot remember a time when we ever went out together as a couple. By now I had started to resent him for everything, most of all the way that he treated me, just like a housemaid. A woman's place was in the home, that's how he saw it. Women had no voice, only men. He definitely believed that this was a man's world, where women should not be spoken to, but at. He spent all his time with his friends. There was no time for me. Even when he invited his friends round, every Sunday to gamble and drink, I would always end up in my room or in the kitchen, cooking and serving them.

My home sometimes never felt like mine. It felt like I was just passing through; that's how he made me feel. He was king of the castle, sleep by day and roam the streets at nights, and ordered me around to make him breakfast, lunch, and dinner. I was tired, fed up, sick, and scared of this man.

Tony stopped coming around to see his children. He didn't really like Patrick. He felt that Patrick disrespected me each time he came round to the flat. It was true what he was saying; however, that should not have stopped him from seeing his children. That was just an excuse.

Reflection 1886

I remember one time when I was struggling on the street, coming home with my shopping bags. I couldn't afford to take a taxi, so I walked as usual. Well, as I was struggling down the road, Tony was driving past and saw me, and he offered me a lift home.

Well, the first thing I thought about was what Patrick would say if he saw me in Tony's car, but then I thought that it was okay; after all, I was buying shopping to cook his dinner.

Well, as we drove up to the flat, Patrick was there. He waited until Tony left, and then the argument started. As I ran out of the flat, he ran behind me, whacking me so hard in my head in front of whoever was passing. I was in total shock and disbelief, because that was the first time he had ever laid into me, and it wasn't going to be the last. For one week, it felt like I had water in my eardrum. It sounded like an ocean in my head. I had put up with his moods and his temper, and I didn't want to put up with it anymore. I had truly jumped from the frying pan into the fire. I had gone from one bad relationship to worse. Tony must have been laughing behind my back, saying and saying "Serve her right". Tony loathed Patrick", and it was made worse by the way that Patrick would exalt himself in front of him, like to say "she is mine now this is my family, and I run it in the way that I see fit" Tony didn't approve of the way he saw Patrick talking to me, and especially in front of him, causing Tony to pull him up over it.

Well, I managed to get away from him with the help of a friend. My friend Jackie Pinnock had moved off the estate where I lived. She had managed to flee from a very violent relationship and sort her life out. I hadn't seen her for months, and here she was, looking like her life had completely changed.

I couldn't believe how great she looked. Her hair was immaculate; she was nicely dressed in a bright red mohair jumper and a pair of dark blue jeans, with the nicest pair of black boots I had ever seen. She looked like she stepped off the cover of a vogue magazine and had just stepped off an aeroplane freshly back from holiday.

She was glowing, and her face was lightly covered with makeup. I was amazed at how good she looked. She had even gotten back her confidence and self esteem, everything that had been stolen from her, in that abusive relationship, she now got it back. Wacky Jackie she had become again.

Jackie was the funniest person I had ever met, she was a funny character, and she made you laugh so effortlessly, and unintentional, she always reminded me of an old west Indian woman, true to her roots, she used her Jamaican accents, when she needed it, we were like to pair of kids, when we would get together, we would even pretend to be two elderly Jamaican women, sitting down talking about life, and our aches and pains, it would be so funny, she would take on the character, we both would, and this could go on for ages. Jacqueline La-Touche and Jacqueline Pinnock, two of a kind, but different in mind.

We had always looked out for each other, Once, we were both pregnant at the time, the best thing about being pregnant together, was the sharing. We supported each other in many ways, we counted the weeks together, we spoke about the sickness, and aches and pains, the weight gain, and we would even stand in front of the mirror measuring our bellies, and looking at the two different shapes, pointed and round, we would even try to predict what type of baby we were having, well I wanted girl, and Jackie wanted a boy. The most memorable moments that we had together was sitting in my bare living room, on the floor together, admiring the new stripy grey carpet, that had just been laid, after living there for at least three years, there was no furniture in the living room, but we didn't care, we just laid on the floor, with each other, connecting with our babies, "quick quick Jack, come feel, the baby just moved" sometimes we both would have either hand on either tummy at the same time feeling each other's baby move in sync at the same time, it was a wonderful experience, away from the experience that we were having at the time, away from the control, and abuse, and violence, even if it were just for a while Jackie and I, in my living room.

We both gave birth to two little girls, Sacha and Safron, Jackie's daughter was Safron, but sometimes, I would think that Jackie thought Safron was more a Simon. Sacha was all pink, and Safron was always blue.

Well my friend had long since moved on, she had managed to get away, from the monster that she once lived with, I remembered the day when Jackie's mum rescued her, she came to get her, everything packed, and she was gone, leaving me behind. Jackie's mum didn't stand for rubbish, as soon as she found out that this man was abusing her child, she came down there in a flash, in her green sports like car. She was a strapping woman, with very dark skin, and her mouth was something else, you always heard her, before you would see her. The first time that I had met Jackie's mother, I was a bit nervous, because, I had heard her so many times before, and to tell you the truth, she frightened the hell out of me, she was one of those people, if she liked you, she would give you anything, if she didn't like you, she would let you know straight away, not only with actions but with words. Well I and Jackie mum, got on like a house on fire, we clicked instantly, "Jackie with the green eyes", she would refer to me" yes I like Jackie, well right now Jackie Pinnock was in a much better place, and away from everything that she had encountered, New beginnings for my friend, but here I was stuck right in the middle of my situation,

The last time I had seen my friend Jackie, she looked a right mess: her hair looked like an old shag pile rug, her clothes looked tatty and stained, her shoes were leaning to the left, and her face was covered with different shades of bruises. Well, now she had come back to visit me, looking like Vidal Sassoon had given her the latest hairstyle, her face enhanced with different shades of lightly covered makeup this time, and not heavily covered with bruises.

We had a lot of catching up to do. I wanted to know everything, how she managed to get away from that monster and get a new flat in a nice area, and most of all how she managed to look so good.

My friend spent the night with me. I remember putting my arm around her. We huddled together just like two little girls, and we talked all night. She even managed to make me laugh, which was something that I rarely did anymore.

Daylight welcomed us in, and that's when we fell asleep. Jackie promised me that she would help me to get away from my life and the notorious estate which she had left behind, and she did.

It was easy to get away because my children's father had moved out. We were always having arguments, and he was always moving out, but then I would always take him back. This was a regular pattern for us. He would leave but then try taking furniture with him. Once he tried to take the sofa. Well, I tried to stop him, so he tried to set it on fire, but it was flame resistant; however, he still managed to break into the flat and take the sofa when I was out shopping.

I had saved up for so long and sacrificed really hard to buy this sofa. For a long time my children and I would sit on the floor watching television and eating our meals. Even my friends were used to sitting on the floor when they came round to visit. Well, I managed to save up £300 towards the sofa but still needed £100, so he contributed £100 toward it and now felt that he had ownership for one of the armchairs.

I had seen the way my friend was treated by her ex-partners whom she once lived with. They always took the furniture out of the flat when the relationship was over, leaving her with nothing but the kids. I could never understand how a man could walk out on their family, taking the beds, chairs, and television, leaving their children with nothing. Today, I wouldn't really call someone like that a man; I would say more a boy, a child.

My friend Jackie said to me, "Jackie, you got to get out this place. You don't want to end up living on here forever."

The estate was known as the Notorious Broadwater Farm Estate since the fateful night in October 1985 when a policeman was murdered. The Broadwater Farm riot is what happened to give this once-happy family estate its bad name. Well, to tell you the truth, I had always loved this estate since I was a child. I didn't live on the Broadwater Farm Estate, but I had friends who did, and I found it an amazing place to have fun as a child. It was like an adventure playground and a maze.

However, the police saw it as an adventure playground for crime, and that's how it became.

So now I've ended up on the estate, and it's not such fun and adventure after all, especially as an adult. Well, even though Patrick had moved out, he wasn't that far away because he lived in the next block to me. He had lived on the estate since he was a child, up until now. I even noticed that everyone who had grown up on the estate as a child now had their own flats with their own family. Everyone lived close to each other; everyone looked set to stay on the estate for the rest of their lives. I told myself that I was not one of them.

Well, I was able to get away from the estate with the help of my friend Jackie Pinnock. It was difficult, because I had to stay in one room in a bed-and-breakfast with my children, not what I was used to. I found it very difficult sharing a small kitchen with people from all different cultures, different foods, different smells. It was even worse sharing the bathroom. We were all strangers, there for whatever reason.

I was in this strange place signing a register to come and go. I felt like I was being monitored. I had left my home with all my belongings in it, just as if I were still there; and here I was living in this one room huddled up at nights, like a dog with her puppies. I didn't have a home anymore. I had fled from my flat, never to return to live on the Broadwater Farm Estate. Even though it was not the ideal situation, it was far better than the situation which I was in before. My mind felt free, and I was in control of my life again. No Patrick to try to take control.

Well, that was only for a short while because he eventually found me. I went back to the flat to pick up a few things, and he was there. Even though he had gone back to his flat, he still had keys for mine. Well, we hadn't seen each other for a couple of weeks, so it was a bit awkward when I walked into the flat and saw him there. He came across like a different person. He told me how he had missed me and the children. Well, I tried to be strong. I listened while I packed the things that I had gone there for. "So where are you staying now?" he asked me, and without thinking I told him that I was staying at a bed-and-breakfast in Seven Sisters Road. Well, that was a big mistake because that night he didn't stop until he found the place where we were staying. He told me that things would change for the better between us, now that I had moved off the estate. Little did he know that the estate was not my problem, it was him.

Anyway I fell for it. I believed everything; he told me that we could make a new life, get a new house, and be happy. My big mistake was believing him and letting him back into our lives. Eventually I got somewhere to live. It was temporary but beautiful, and guess where it was? Right across the road from my friend Jackie's flat. I couldn't believe it; that must have been fate, not luck. So you could say that I chose to stay in this progressively emotional and violent relationship, having my clothes ripped up, punched, degraded in front of my friends and family. I even had hot porridge thrown in my face, even my children's food thrown into the sink, and the taps turned on to the food, because he didn't like what I was cooking. I remember my head being stamped on until I almost blacked out. These were just a few of the things that I endured. Some of the others are still too painful to talk about or to remember.

Most of the things that Patrick did or said to me, he always tried to justify why he had to do or say them and why I deserved it. He even told me that this was the only way to keep me on track, because sometimes I had a tendency to come off it. So putting the fair of God in me would help us both, me not to come off the track and him not having a reason to hit me.

The mental pain was far worse than the physical pain. I could cope with the physical pain because the bruises would always heal; but the mental pain just got worse, with the name-calling, worthless, stupid, ugly, and nasty.

I chose to stay because I didn't want to go back to what I had come from a few years ago. Looking back, that was a better place to be at than the one where I was right now. Any woman who has been in a violent relationship will know and understand how these men's minds work, ever so full of remorse.

Some people would say, "Why didn't you leave? It's your fault. I would never let a man do that to me. How can you be so weak?" Well, for all those people who have said those words, I consider myself a strong woman because of what I had been through in the past; but there are men out there who will eat away at a woman's confidence and self-esteem, until he's got her where he wants her, under his control.

I felt like I had no control over my life anymore. I wasn't the same person anymore. I didn't feel like I knew who I was anymore. I became a robot, mechanical. I wanted to try and regain some of the control that I had lost, but how.

Chapter Seven

Love-Hate Relationship with Food

1989

It was a Friday afternoon, and I had just returned home from the dentist. I just had three of my teeth taken out, so I was in a lot of pain and could not eat. All through the weekend I hardly ate a thing because my gums were aching and sore.

After having a very painful weekend, I felt much better on the Monday, but I didn't really have much of an appetite for food, so I never forced myself to eat. Over the next few days I began to notice that I was losing weight rapidly. I even realised that I could go the whole day without eating, and whatever I did manage to eat I had to force myself to eat it.

My friends noticed my weight loss as soon as they saw me. "Jackie, you've lost weight. You look good. You look slim." Everywhere I went I got the same reaction from everyone. They all noticed me, and that made me feel really good. I felt like I was in control again.

I could control how much I ate, how little, when, and not at all if I chose not to. The weight just continued to fall off; within two weeks I had lost a stone, wow!

My skirts were swinging around my waist, my trousers were falling off me, and I was feeling great. I felt like this was an achievement.

Some days I would just eat a packet of crisps or an apple; some days I could go through the whole day with just a glass of water. As the days went by I was getting smaller and smaller and weaker and weaker, so I made the decision to start eating properly again, but I couldn't. Two spoonfuls of anything and I felt as if I had just eaten breakfast, dinner, lunch, and dessert all in one go. I knew that I had a problem; however, where I thought I was in control my problem was now controlling me. I had totally lost control of my mind and my health. I had to eat whether I felt hungry or not. I was slowly losing control of something that I thought I had under control.

I had to learn to eat again. I used to love eating. Food and I were like best friends; and after it being so scarce in my life, for a long time, I developed a love affair with food and appreciated it. Now food was no longer my best friend, but my enemy. I hated food.

I knew that I had to eat to get strength because I was so weak. However, I wanted to stay small. I didn't want to be the way that I used to be. It's not like I was overweight in the first place.

I wanted to be noticed, but I began to get noticed for the wrong reasons. Everyone thought that I was taking drugs, because I had lost a lot of weight. My weight loss was very drastic.

My cheekbones stuck out, my eyes became sunken and dark, my collarbones looked like bowls you could drink water from, my ribs you could actually start to see, and I had an arch between my legs; but I felt great even though everyone started telling me that I looked sick, including Patrick. He would say to me, "Look at you, you look disgusting, like one of those skinny girls, with the big arch between their legs. You're putting me off." I used to think in my mind that he had put me off long time ago.

I told myself that everyone who was now commenting on how bad I looked was jealous because they wanted to look like me. I kept telling myself that I looked fantastic; I couldn't see anything wrong with the new me. I started to gain back a little of my confidence, which Patrick had stolen from me. I became a little more outgoing, and the more I looked at myself in the mirror, the more I saw nothing wrong. However, I was on the boundaries of anorexia. Well, I started to find new ways of keeping in control, binging, eating vast amount of foods, then making myself ill. I even went as far as using laxatives which made me feel so sick, even though the results were quick.

I chose to binge, because that way I could eat whatever I wanted and then get rid of it after.

I became a slave to bulimia.

Bulimia controlled my life. I started to walk with carrier bags in my handbag, just in case I had to use them. I stopped eating out. I refused invitations where I knew there would be food. I rarely sat down with my family to eat, and when I did, I would leave the table straightaway to reject my unwanted food. It served no purpose in my body; that's how I felt.

I used to be a slave to the scales. First thing in the morning, last thing at night, and right through the day, I stepped on and off the scales. I lost count of how many times during the day that I did this. Even if I ate a biscuit I would weigh myself. I counted every calorie I ate or drank. I survived on little or next to nothing. God knows how I survived.

Mealtimes became a huge problem for me. I hated it. I would prepare and cook food fit for a banquet, sharing it out and laying it on the table for everyone to eat but myself, and I always made excuses why I wasn't hungry yet. Two of my biggest excuses were I was picking at the food, nibbling away when I was cooking, or I'll eat later. Truth was, I wouldn't. There were occasional times when I was told to sit and eat up, just like a child.

It wasn't long before Patrick clucked on that I was making myself physically sick. I was always so careful to cover my tracks, making sure that I left the bathroom clean, especially the toilet, and not leaving any plastic carrier bags with unwanted food still in my handbag, which was a place he would sometimes look in.

He became worried about me; however, he didn't understand what was happening. He would shout at me, saying, "Look at you, you look disgusting. Look how skinny you are." He would sometimes call me names. I think that he was trying to get through to me, and that was his way, or trying to shame me into eating my meals.

Well, something had to give, and it did. I got so ill. I was so weak I could not make it up the stairs. I had to sleep downstairs because my legs would not carry me upstairs. I fell asleep with my bracelets on and woke up to find that they had melted off my wrists. I had so much acid and very little water in my body.

I had fluid coming out of my belly button; the stench was awful. I realised that I could die, and I wanted to stop, but how. Who could I tell? No one. This was my secret. I had become ashamed of what I was doing, but there was no way I could tell my secret to anyone. No one would understand; everyone would think that I was crazy.

I started to hate myself for hurting myself. I was this disgusting person that ate all this food and made myself ill, carrying plastic bags around, throwing up in McDonald's after eating six french fries, turning the taps on so that no one would hear me, making myself ill. I had become an expert at deceiving my family and became so clever at lying to myself.

My bulimia gave me the strength to stand up for myself. It made me feel smug inside, to say, "I have a secret that you don't know about. You can hit me, you can verbally abuse me, you can mentally abuse me and try to control some of me, but bulimia is controlling the rest of me." My life was like a bridge over troubled water.

Years had passed, and I can't say it got any better. I lived with the man and the monster, as I now began to see him, and bulimia the monster in my mind. God knows which one was worse.

Chapter Eight

Jamaica, Here I Come

1990

I finally got the opportunity to go and visit my parents in Jamaica. He told me that he was sending me on holiday, and I deserved it. I was happy to go because I had not seen my parents since I was eighteen years old. I was now twenty-six years old. Seven years ago was the last time that I had seen my parents, so going to Jamaica would be my dream come true. I had only ever imagined, fantasized, or dreamt of seeing my parents again; and now my wish had come true.

My four children, my sister Mary and her son, and I all went to Jamaica together. I never realised that the journey to Jamaica was so long and tiring. Well, we all landed in Jamaica, with jet lag, which lasted for exactly one week. Can you imagine going to bed at six o'clock in the evening? Well, I couldn't until then.

It was a strange experience, but a wonderful strange experience being in Jamaica for the very first time, driving along the Jamaican roads and seeing children walking around selling snacks, music attacking you from all different angles, and people standing on the street corners dancing. In England, you would be arrested for all three. In Jamaica, everyone was a free spirit.

Arriving at my parents' house in the night was beautiful, even though it was dark, and waking up in the morning in a strange place was the best thing I'd ever experienced. I remember waking up and going outside even more beautiful. I thought to myself, *Amazing grace, how sweet the sound,* when I heard the birds twittering and singing away.

I remember my first waking morning in Jamaica. I felt strange, happy but strange. I couldn't believe that I was in Jamaica and that I was with my parents, seeing all of us, seven years older. Chantal was almost ten years old. She had only just turned three years old, when they last saw her.

I was proud of all my children, and loved them all, but Chantal was my first, and she was the only grandchild, from me that my parents had known, a toddler when they left, and now ten years old, so I had always imagined this time, all my family under one roof, for the first time in years.

Walking out onto the veranda for the first time and feeling the warm sunshine melt on my skin, it was awesome. Everything was picturesque. I had never seen such beauty. Acres of greenery stood around me. In the far distance I could see the different shades of blue sea. Looking through the binoculars I could see a ship sailing on the ocean. I loved Jamaica. It felt like I had come home, and what a homecoming it was.

Well, we spent three months in Jamaica and the happiest I have ever been since I was a child. I felt just like a child again, being with my parents. I was free and happy and felt at peace. I didn't want to go back home, if that's what you could call it.

My mother and father were very happy to see us, and all the grandchildren. When my parents left to go back home to Jamaica, I only had one child, and now I had four. This was what you would call a family reunion.

This was Mary's first time back since she had left Jamaica, to come back to live in England she was an adult now, with a child of her own, Mary was only a child when she went to live in Jamaican. She never really had a choice but to go. She was only twelve years old at the time. My brother Robin also returned back to England. I guess it was their home, so Mary was no stranger to Jamaica. She had lived and gone to school there, and she must have a few friends, so we should have a great time.

So here I am in Jamaica, with my family. I felt like I had won the lottery; this was a miracle. I never imagined this day would come, even though I had always imagined a reunion. This was more than I had prayed for. The children were happy. None of us had ever experienced anything like this before. Come to think of it, we had never been away together as a family, not even to the zoo.

Well, I couldn't tell my parents about the hardship that I had suffered when they left me, the violence that had been inflicted on me by Patrick. I knew that it would break their hearts, so I pretended that my life in England was a bed of roses. Meanwhile, in my head I was working out how was I going to leave this man. My parents had only ever heard about Patrick in a good light. You could say that I made him sound like every parent's dream for their daughter, not their nightmare.

I went to Jamaica to visit my parents. I wasn't there looking for love, but I found it. Jamaica is an island with beautiful eye candy. As a woman coming from England, well, in Jamaica, you suddenly become priority for whatever reason. I had never seen so many good-looking men in one place. Everywhere we walked, my sister and I would be commenting on their good looks. My sister would say to me, "Jackie, did you see that one?" or "Look, Jackie, there's another one." We even counted how many good-looking men we would see as we walked along the streets. One thing that I can say about Jamaican men is that they really know how to woo a woman. With their sweet lyrics, I used to think that they were all reading out the same book. I actually believed that this book existed because surely they all couldn't be like that, but they were.

Well, time slips away when you're having fun, and boy, did we have fun for the three months that we were there. It was like being a child again living at home with our parents; they fussed over us like we were children again.

Three days before I returned back to England, I met someone. I had seen him around for the past three months; however, I never really spoke to him. Eventually I got the chance to speak to him, and he told me that his name was Benji.

Well, that day I had gone to the hairdresser's to get my hair done. I wanted to look better than when I had first arrived in Jamaica. I wanted to go back home looking like a new woman, new clothes, new hairstyle, and a new attitude to life. I came out the hairdresser's feeling on top of the world. You know what it's like when you get a new hairdo. You have so much confidence, not to mention the spring in your step when you know that your hair looks and feels good.

From the moment that I met him I knew that he was the man for me, but I only had three days to return back to England.

There was something about Benji that I fell in love with instantly, he had a calm nature about him, very peaceful, charming and handsome, too. He even had a way with words, and he acted so cool, He even had cheekiness about him, I liked this man, I fell completely for him, because of the way that he stared at me, as if he were looking inside of me. I thought to myself that I could easily fall, head over hills, for this man, in a very short space of time, like right now.

I remember telling him that I wished that I had met him when I came here three months ago and that it was too late to get to know him. Well, he quickly replied, "It's never too late for a shower of rain." He was telling me that it was not too late for us to get to know each other.

Well, he was right because for the last three days we hung around together, it felt like three months, not three days. We talked and we laughed like a couple of school kids. We walked on the beach together holding hands. We sat down on the veranda watching the sun go down and watching the moon shine as we looked at the stars. It was so romantic. Here I was with this man whom I had only known for three days but felt like I had known him all my life.

I had never done anything romantic in my life before. This was the very first time, and it felt so good; we became inseparable in those three days, but I had to go. My holiday had come to an end. It was time to go back to my miserable life, which I had left behind. I couldn't bear to go back and leave my parents. God knows when I would see them again, and here I was with this man, feeling that I had known him all my life.

The airport journey was really hard. We were all on edge. My parents were the worse, especially my mother. She snapped every time one of the children would laugh, or we would be chatting away just like we were going out for the day. She had gotten used to us being around, and now we were leaving, and she was taking it really bad. "Shut up, you wouldn't understand how we feel," she said. I felt sad for my mother, and most of all I felt sad for myself.

Time to say goodbye to this stranger I had grown to know over the past three days. As I stood in the airport telling him my goodbyes, I knew that it would not be long before I would see him again. I felt like he would be around in my life for some time.

I felt sad leaving him behind. This was the first time in my life I had felt this way about someone.

When I got on the aeroplane I could have kicked myself. I couldn't stop thinking about him; he was stuck in my head. I thought to myself, *Oh boy, if three days with him feels like this, then a lifetime must be magic.* At the airport he gave me a piece of paper with his name and address written on it. I felt that this could not be one-sided, so without thinking I gave him my address. What had I done? I didn't live alone. I lived with a man who would frequently ask me, "Do you want me to do you something?"

When I came back to England I started to write to Benji. As the weeks went by I noticed that I was writing him more and more. There was not a day which passed that I didn't write a letter. I would receive replies from Benji, sometimes two letters at a time. I lived for the postman; he became my best friend. I would wait at the window for him, knowing that he had something in his sack for me.

I couldn't forget Benji. The more we both wrote, the more we grew closer.

I thought to myself, what was the point of this, because I wouldn't be going back to Jamaica for a long time.

Over the next few months things were fine between me and Patrick. Spending some time away helped. Things were a lot better between us. For some strange reason I did miss him. Well, he even told me how much he missed me and that things were going to change, more fool me for believing him, but I did.

A few months later I was pregnant with my fifth child, oh no. I was beside myself. I had planned to get away from this man, and here I was pregnant again, with his child. Well, I decided to have the baby, but things just got even worse. When I was five months pregnant he kicked me in my back. I was sitting on the stairs at the time. I remember gasping. He had found a letter from Benji. He had gone through my handbag looking for God knows what. I wasn't aware that he had found the letter. He kicked me then recited some of the things he had read.

By now I had stopped writing to Benji. There was no hope for me and him anyway. Here I was five months pregnant for someone I never loved anymore, someone who treated me like a doormat, and here was this man in Jamaica sending me such positive letters.

I couldn't really tell him that I was pregnant because I had told him what my relationship was really like.

I thought that he wouldn't really understand, and he would probably think how I could have another child with someone who treated me so bad.

There was nothing in that letter which could incriminate me that I was having an affair, because I wasn't. I had only met Benji three days before my return to England, so at this point there was nothing about declarations of undying love between us, or anything sexual in this letter. It was just about two people corresponding with each other, from two different parts of the world, and also about friendship, but I think Patrick knew that this friendship would blossom into something more, and he now felt threatened by this letter and by this man who was thousands of miles away. Well, to add insult to injury he even said to me, "How do I know that this baby that you're having is mine?" I thought to myself, *Do your maths because I got pregnant almost four months after I came back from Jamaica.*

Chapter Nine

Realisation

1992

My son Steven was born on the twenty-eighth of April. It was not that long after I had him that my mother returned to England for a holiday and to attend her brother's wedding. This was the first time she had returned since leaving England all those years ago.

I was happy that my mother was here; she had come just at the right time to help me with the baby. I felt proud to know that my children had a grandmother that was here in this country and I could turn to her for support. It felt good to know this. I used to look at my friends' mothers and wish that my mother was here to help me too.

I never really got any help from Patrick because he spent most days sleeping until the late evenings; then he would get up and eat, shower, and leave until whenever he decided to come home. He never really told me when he was coming back. Whenever I would ask him he would say to me, "Why are you asking big man question?"

When he was at home he was no use anyway. I remember after Steven was born, it was April, and there was snow outside. Would you believe that there was snow on the ground in April?

Well, one morning I had to take the children to school. Patrick told me to take the baby with me, because he was going out. The baby was five days old.

Well, I had to wake him up and get him dressed to go out into the snow. When I came back Patrick was fast asleep.

It was always like that. He was one of those men that made excuses about the reasons why they don't like holding newborn babies or changing them. Even if he did hold the baby it would be not for more than five minutes, and then he would pass him back, like it was enough bonding time for him.

My mother spent six months in England, and it didn't take her much time to work out that I was really on my own and had no help from Patrick. My mother soon realised that he had no respect for me.

I could tell that she didn't really approve of him and his lifestyle.

He never respected, loved, or cared for me; he never once took me anywhere nice. He always went out with his friends. He slept all day and would get dressed to stay out all night. He even had the cheek to ask my opinion on what to wear that night, if he couldn't make up his mind.

His side of the wardrobe was full with clothes, while my side was full with empty hangers. He also had boxes on top of boxes of shoes, whilst I only had one red shoe. It didn't match any of the few pieces of clothes that I had. He walked around with designer shoes, and I walked around with my red shoes, with the insoles made out of a cornflakes box to stop my feet from getting wet.

Eight years of abuse and five children later I grew stronger, and I was no longer afraid of him. I found that I could stand up to him, and I felt strong enough to get out of this abusive relationship. I felt like I was fighting for my sanity. I had now started to sleep with a knife under my pillow just in case he came home and started on me.

I was no longer frightened of him, and he knew this. I had started to retaliate against him. I stood up to him. I stopped getting out of my bed to warm his dinner up on the cooker. I even told him that I would rather fight him than to get out of my bed to warm his dinner. Well, he knew that I was serious.

For years I had let this weak excuse of a man control my life, but now it had to end, and it was time for me to change my life. I couldn't put my children through this anymore because it was affecting them, especially my son Raymond who was six years old at that time. I remember him pointing and laughing after his father had hit me. "Ha ha ha, Daddy hit you." It had now become a joke. Well, I didn't want my sons growing up and thinking that this behaviour was normal and that it was fine for a man to treat a woman like this, so I had to forget about him paying the bills and providing for the children. I couldn't worry about who was going to pay the electricity bill. He had to go. I would rather live in darkness for another year if it meant getting him out of my life.

My mother was due to return back to Jamaica; she had spent six months in England, and I couldn't imagine what it would be like when she left. I had gotten so used to her being around.

Well, things remained calm between me and Patrick. I think he knew that my mother was watching him, and he was on his best behaviour when she was around. My mother made sure he knew when she was around and even warned him a couple of times jokingly. She saw how difficult things were for me; and she saw how hard I worked in the home, making sure that there was always a meal waiting to be served, clothes washed and ironed, house spotless.

People used to say to me that they would never have guessed that I had children, because there was no evidence of toys or children's clothes around the house. Everything was always neatly packed away, in order to prevent the abuse.

My mother thought I needed a break from all this. She asked me to come back to Jamaica so that she could take care of me. She said that I needed a rest. Well, I couldn't even find any space in my head to analyse what my mother had just asked me. "No way, Mummy," I said, "there's no way on earth he would allow me to go."

"Well, let me see if he can tell me no," my mother replied.

The next day all forgotten when my mother unexpectedly came out with it. "Jackie, come back home with me. You need a break." Well, I told her that I didn't think that he would allow me to go with the children, and I had just not that long ago had a baby. I was playing the game, pretending that this was the first time I was hearing my mother's proposal. You should have seen his face that hit him out of the blue, just like one of his punches, he wasn't sure about what to say.

"No no, she can't go anywhere." Well, my mother just looked at him and then said, "I am taking my daughter to Jamaica with me. She needs a break." Well, what could he say? Nothing. I couldn't believe it. He was speechless for once. He was a big coward who could not stand up to my mother the way that I had allowed him to stand up to me, for almost nine years. My mother was a feisty little woman, full of vitality and strength, she was strong in mind and character, and she wasn't afraid to speak her mind. My mother had no fear of anyone, except creatures yes, she would shout the house down, but man, no way was she scared of Patrick," I have been married to Mr Bob, for over fifty years, and Mr Bob never once put his hand on me, or treat me any less than he should", well that's what my mother said, I don't think that my mother understood how much Patrick had affected my life, emotionally, and mentally.

Within two months I had saved up all our fares to go on holiday. I even managed to buy clothes for our holiday. I bought everything.

God knows how I did it because he had refused to contribute towards us going, and he even had the cheek to tell my mother that "yes, she can go, but she has to pay for everything," and he meant it. I didn't really care if he helped me to go or not. I was going to Jamaica, with or without his help, and blessing.

Well, that was the first time in my life that I really truly believed in miracles. In two months I had managed to raise the money for all our fares.

It was a huge sacrifice. I sold some of my belongings to the secondhand shop, anything that I could find. I taught myself to knit babies' hats, in all different designs. I was getting orders from all over the place, especially from the baby clinic.

I put my budgeting skills into good use. I cut down on all the luxuries. My mother had said to me that I was buying too many biscuits and fizzy drinks, and she was right. I stopped immediately. We even became vegetarians for a while. That saved me a lot of money too. We even ate tuna and pasta, until we got fed up, but it all paid off because we were on our way to the sunny island of Jamaica.

That's when I really started to believe in the power of thought, and how to make things happen; and that's when I realized that I had the power to get what I wanted, and to change my life.

Thinking about Benji and seeing him again also gave me the incentive to save more. I guess it was just me imagining what it would be like to feel truly happy, because I had never felt that way in any of my relationships.

I had never received another letter from Benji, after I had stopped writing to him. I had to take him out of my mind. For the next six months I managed to do that by focusing on preparing for my baby, but as soon as the baby was born, I soon realised that I had not taken Benji out of my mind. I had just put him to the back of my mind, and now he had worked his way to the front again.

I had all these thoughts going through my mind. One of my thoughts was what if he's forgotten about me? Well, I knew that he knew about the baby, because my mother had told him that I had another baby. When my mother told him, she said that he was very surprised, because he never really knew the reason why I had stopped writing. I never gave him any reasons. I didn't reply to his letters anymore. After a while they stopped.

Well, the second time in Jamaica was just as good as the first, maybe even better, because I was familiar with the place. I had friends there, and I was looking forward to seeing Benji again.

I will never forget the time I spent in Jamaica. I had never known such happiness. I thought I had died and gone to heaven. I was free again.

Meeting Benji again was good; however, I did feel a bit awkward, when it came to telling him the reason why I had stopped writing and why I felt that I could not tell him that I was pregnant at that time. Well, I needn't have worried about what he thought. I think that he was more pleased to see me than to hear about the reason why I hadn't written. The reason was here with me anyway.

My son Steven was nine months old, and this was his first visit to Jamaica. He loved being in Jamaica, and Benji loved him being there too. I used to watch them together, and if no one knew any better they would think that Steven was his son just by the way he attended to him. I had never seen that before. I never had any help from Patrick, especially with Steven. It felt like he had lost or never had interest in him from the start.

I remember when I was in labour with Steven and I was getting ready to leave for the hospital. My friend Heather was there with me throughout the night and day. Well, when it was time to leave she said to him, "Patrick, are you coming to the hospital to see your child being born?" Well, his reply was "You see one birth you see them all." I remember my friend saying to him that all babies were different and births too. "Nah, you go with her. You're her friend." Well, he just continued to watch the football match. I guess that was one of the reasons why he couldn't be bothered to go.

Well, I should be grateful that he did go to one birth; that was our first child, the second child. My next-door neighbour Dorothy heard from my friends that I had made my way to the hospital to have the baby, so without thinking, she turned up at the hospital asking for me.

When the nurses told me that there was a lady outside, I couldn't imagine that it would be Dorothy, because we had never spoken about her coming to the birth. Well, she was here now, at least someone was. Dorothy was like a mother to me, she helped me in so many ways, giving me food, baby sitting, and she gave me my first refrigerator, Dorothy was the Florence Nightingale of Broadwater Farm, she was the mother Teresa, everyone loved her, she was always giving, Well she was here tonight giving me her support

I asked her where Patrick was, and she told me that he had gone to a party. My neighbour had seen him, and he had also told her that I was in hospital having the baby. He even had the cheek to tell her to go up there. Dorothy was there when I gave birth. At first I felt a little embarrassed with her being there because she was like a mother to me. She even had a daughter who was much older than I was. I thought that having her there would feel like my mother being there, and the thought of my mother being there and seeing me all over the place made me cringe. Well, all that cringing went out the window when the pain set in. I never really cared if the whole world was there that night. Every piece of my dignity and pride went out the window that night, and I was just glad to know that Dorothy cared enough about me to leave her little daughter at home and to be there for me. I wished my mother could have been a part of that too.

The next day Patrick came to visit me and the baby, acting like the proud father, saying that he had a son now, his firstborn son. He even told me that he had heard the news at a party that he now had a son; he told me that he celebrated the birth of his son that night. While I was alone lying in my hospital bed, celebrating my son's life, by thanking God for giving me this perfect baby boy, he was out celebrating with his friends.

He spoilt Raymond; he doted on him so much. Raymond was the spitting image of him, another version of Patrick, how fortunate, and that's what he loved He used to walk round saying, "No one can't say this is not my son." Raymond was the little star in Patrick's eye, especially when it came to playing football. Football became the highlight in Patrick's life, and was now Raymond's too, but was it? Every week, once twice, or more, Raymond would be off behind Patrick, who would be anxiously waiting for him to score a goal, Patrick was living his dream, inside Raymond, well that's how it felt, "where going to make money from this boy", Patrick would say, he's going to be a footballer raking in the change, So you see, he was to busy with foot ball, to even witness the birth of his other son.

Well, Steven looked more like my side of the family. Patrick couldn't resist commenting on this, saying, "Jack, he's not as good looking as the others, is he." He even joked about me giving him an ugly baby; he always said out loud that Raymond looked better. Well that was not necessarily true, because to me they were both handsome little boys, but with different looks, Steven was light brown with, light brown eyes, that stood out, his hair was a little different to Raymond's. Patrick said that Steven was a La-Touché, not a Marshal, like Raymond. Marshal was Patrick's surname, Well to me Steven did look like a La-Touche and a Marshal too.

When Raymond was born, he looked more Asian, his hair was so beautiful, as he grew his plaits grew longer and longer, and hung from his little head, everyone always commented on how much he looked like a little girl, or mistook him for a on, he had very delicate features, a cute little button nose, and a tiny little mouth, you could just about hear is cry, he sounded like a kitten, I must admit that he was a beautiful baby and he did resemble Patrick, so much, everything about Raymond was Patrick, the walk, talk, actions, facial expressions, and the attitude.

Patrick had always paid more attention to Raymond than he had ever done to Steven.

Well, here was Steven in Jamaica getting all the attention from someone that wasn't his father.

From the first time that I met Benji I knew that we would get married. I was still in my nightmare relationship, but I never stopped dreaming about how my life would be with him; this kept me going.

When I realised that I would see Benji again I started to read his letters. He told me that he had never stopped reading mine. I was in this nightmare relationship, and I was pregnant at the time. I had no choice but to forget about ever being with him. Benji accepted my five children.

I was always told by Patrick that no man would ever want me with five children and that I was lucky that he was with me and that he took me on with two children; for years I believed him until now. No man had ever made me feel like I belonged on a throne.

This new man in my life loved and respected me, and it never made a difference to him whether I had children or not.

I became alive again. My eyes lit up every time I mentioned his name. I was in love for the very first time in my life, and the feeling was mutual; however, the big problem was how to tell Patrick.

Ten weeks of happiness and talking about my life and what I had been through, opening up to my parents about what my life was like after they left me, the pain I had suffered at the hands of this man, the deprivation that I had suffered when they had left me, I had to disclose all of my past to them, to be able to move on with my future and to make a new start.

Doing that gave me the strength that I needed to make the decision to end the relationship with Patrick as soon as I returned back to England.

I was not going to back down. This was the only happiness I had ever known in my adult life, and I was not going to make this opportunity of happiness pass me by. I had made up my mind that it was over, dead.

Leaving Jamaica was the hardest thing in my life that I had ever done. I was leaving heaven to go back to hell. I was leaving my parents. I was leaving the man that I loved. I couldn't bear being apart from all this.

It was so heartbreaking saying goodbye. I had found happiness, but I was leaving it behind. I never wanted to let him go; we held on to each other like it was the last time we would ever be together again. As I said my last goodbyes and walked away, I looked back and saw him pressed against the window with tears falling down his face, watching me as I checked my baggage in. I wanted to go back, but I couldn't. The glass window at the airport divided us, as we walked along running our fingers along the glass in sync until we could see each other no more.

I cried all the way back to England, but I had made up my mind that as soon as I reached home, my nightmare would be over.

Well, when I got home there was no one there, so I had time to relax and prepare for when he came back; he never came home until the following day. I remember him coming up the stairs, but he only came as far as the bedroom door and stood there looking at me. I looked back at him, and I just heard myself saying it's over. I expected there to be a huge fight between us. I didn't have a knife to defend me this time. I had no one to call. I was alone, me and Patrick. Well, he looked at me and said, "I know." I couldn't even look him in the face. I just hung my head down, and I said, "It's over." I repeated myself because I thought maybe he never heard me first time, but he did. I couldn't believe that he was accepting this, as if he was accepting an award for coward of the county.

The room went quiet for what seemed like forever. Well, he had to give one last cowardly speech. "That is why I let you go to Jamaica, because I knew that it would be over when you got back. I was only testing you, that's why I let you go, and I was right because you passed the test. You went to Jamaica to find a man."

Yes, you are right. I did find a man, a real man that loved and respected me which is more than you ever did. How kind of you for setting me free. After all those years when you kept me as your prisoner, humiliating me in front of my friends, my family, your family, your children, and strangers too, and now you are setting me free. Don't you know what you did to me? Do you know that you robbed me of my self-esteem, you robbed me of my confidence, you robbed me of my tears, you made me sink so low? Sometimes I didn't even know myself. You silenced me. I could not whisper what you did to me, the way you treated me at times. You owe me a lot.

Even though I had made up my mind that I was walking out of this abusive relationship, I still hadn't gained the voice and courage to stand up and say all these thoughts that I was now thinking whilst I was telling him that our relationship was over.

I thought really hard to myself, wishfully thinking that he was telepathic and that he could read my mind and every last thought. I continued with my thoughts, thinking and saying in my mind, *I had managed to get eight years of heartache out of you, but three beautiful children.*

Patrick the Monster was how I now saw him in my mind. *I thank you for every time you raised your hand to me, for every little tear that you made me cry, because those tears have turned into a river of strength, and that's why I am standing here today saying goodbye.* I stood there listening to him waffling on about how he allowed me to go and even admitting that things were getting bad between us, so maybe it was for the best.

Well, he had to top it off with the we-can-still-be-friends speech.

He was setting me free to go, to be happy; it was easier than I had imagined. Well, that's what I told myself; but knowing him I found it hard to believe that he would just let me walk away without a punch, kick, or slap, or a whole load of verbal abuse. He'd called me most names under the sun, so why not call me the rest now.

Well, not long after the speech he left. I never saw him again for a while. He had left me and the children, but he had not taken his clothes. I saw that as a statement: "Don't think that you're getting rid of me so easy."

In a weird unexplainable way I missed him. I felt that I couldn't breathe without him. I felt lost, alone, and confused. I couldn't sleep without him. I used to open the wardrobe and stand there smelling his clothes and feeling like he was still here.

I was grieving for this man, and I couldn't understand why; I welcomed confusion into my head, with love and old habits die hard. I knew that he would never change; my life would always be miserable if I stayed with someone like that, so why was I feeling these feelings? I needed him, and I had depended on him for so long while he controlled my life.

I told myself that I must still love him if I felt this way. I tried to compare the love that I felt for Benji, the new man in my life, and the love that I felt for him; they were worlds apart. It wasn't love that I felt for Patrick. I had become an addict to the treatment that I had received from him, without even knowing it.

I was like a drug addict who couldn't live without their next fix. For me, my fix was abuse, and I had grown accustomed to it, and now I wasn't used to not having that part of my life gone.

I walked the streets day and night looking for him, asking his friends, anyone who knew him, if they had seen him.

Well, I had heard that he was living in West Green Road. Well, I walked from the top to the bottom of that road, knocking on doors and asking people if they knew him, if he lived there. I walked any hour of the early morning in the dark, going to places that I wouldn't normally go, areas were drug pushers operated, just looking for him; it's like I was obsessed with him. It's like half of my heart still belonged to him while the other half belonged to this new man in my life.

I did eventually find him, and I did the unthinkable. I begged him to come back home, I cried, and I almost got down on my knees; but something inside me stopped me from doing that. I came to my senses. No way was I going to bow down to him and degrade myself anymore. No matter how much my heart was breaking I had to let go, but how.

It was time to let go of this unhealthy feeling. That day I packed every piece of clothes that was in the wardrobe into black bags, all the designer suits, shoes, everything; and I put them in my son's buggy. I had to get them out of the house. It was hard to do that. All the years I wished that I had the strength to do this, and now it seemed like everything had backfired on me. I was now the one who was hurting. I was the one who dumped him, and I was the one who was feeling like I had been dumped.

I didn't have any money, but I walked miles with his clothes in the buggy, then I dumped them on the floor in the community centre where I knew he always went. I told his friends to give them to him. Well, doing that almost cost me my life, because he beat me up so bad that I almost lost consciousness. I couldn't defend myself, as he laid into me with his fists. He beat me up in the corner at my sister's house. I couldn't even run. I just took every last punch and listened as he hurled abusive words at me, one after the other. The names that he called me were so low, but I knew that it was the last time that he was ever going to do that to me again, and it was. I stumbled back home, battered but free.

I had to get away. I wanted to be happy just like I had been while I was in Jamaica. It took me almost a year, but I managed to save up my fare to go back to Jamaica, and I wasn't coming back.

I tried to be happy in Jamaica, but I wasn't. I thought running away from my problems would be the end of my misery, but it wasn't. I soon realized that my problems were very much still with me. I tried my best to be happy, but something was missing. My parents helped me a lot with the children. I didn't have to worry about them at all. I spent a lot of time with Benji. We were inseparable; we did everything together. My children accepted him, and so did my parents. His parents also accepted me.

I loved him very much, but my old life still overshadowed my happiness.

I had now been in Jamaica for five months when I was hit with a bombshell; my whole world fell apart.

I couldn't cope with what I had heard. I just wanted to go back home to England. I couldn't cope with my new relationship either. I felt that it was unfair to inflict my troubled life upon Benji, who loved me. I loved him too, but I was so confused I just had to go. I had told him about the life that I had in England, but it never made no difference to the way he felt about me and my children. I guess it was just too hard for him to imagine, because I was always this happy-go-lucky, fun-loving person around him, not like the unhappy, tortured soul that I was in England.

I ended the relationship between us, even though he cried and begged me not to. I was confused about everything and needed time to clear my head and sort my life out, then maybe one day I would be well enough to come back to Jamaica, and if it was meant to be for us, we would end up getting back together again. I couldn't give him more than that. It broke my heart to walk away, but when I did I felt some of the confusion leave me. I needed to do this alone. I needed to find myself again. I had to discover who Jacqueline La-Touché was.

Chapter Ten

The Meltdown Near Breakdown

1994

When I arrived back in England, I started to hear things about Patrick and things that he had done to me behind my back when we were still together, some of them going back years.

The full extent of everything, the affairs he had and with whom, was worse than being slapped in my face a thousand times. I was the last one to know as always. I didn't think that something that happened years ago could come back to tear me apart the way that it did.

I was in a worse place than I had ever been before. I almost lost my mind because of this. What happened to me next is not something that you would imagine, but it did. This almost tore me apart. I was so alone, you could say in a wilderness by myself. I had to hold on to my faith, and I did a lot of soul searching. I even reached out to God for help. I felt like my life was falling apart.

God knows how many times I contemplated taking my life over this. Suicide plagued my mind. I agonized over a bottle of pills. I wrote letters to my children and put them in envelopes with their names written on it. I kept them in a box under my bed so they would be easy to find.

I couldn't function in the outside world. I tried to, but it was really hard. I even tried to go out with my friends; but all I wanted to do was go back home to my room and draw my curtains, turn the lights off, and go to sleep.

The only escape that had from my tormented soul was sleep. My bed became a safe haven. It was the only place that I felt safe in. I was a nervous wreck.

I couldn't listen to songs about love because I would cry. I couldn't even watch television just in case there was a programme on about happy families. I couldn't sleep at nights. I used to lie awake all night just thinking.

My health deteriorated, and I started to suffer panic attacks, to the point where I would lose the feelings in my hands. I would start to panic, because my arms became lifeless. I couldn't even raise my hand. I would try to lift my arm up and let it go, but it would just flop down, then I would start to have a panic attack. My heart would be beating so fast, and I would lose control of my breathing. Sometimes I couldn't even breathe. I gasped for air. This always happened at the same time during the night when I was alone. I was afraid to tell anyone. I felt so alone. I became depressed to the point where having a bath and getting dressed seemed so hard to do. I suffered in silence.

When was this going to end? When was I ever going to be myself again? Every day was a bad day. I just wanted this pain that I was suffering to subside.

I fought between a rock and a hard place. I loved my children very much; they were my life. I couldn't leave them. What kind of mother would I be? Who would protect them? Who would love them like I did if I was not here anymore? No one, no one could or would love them like I did.

I prayed to God to take those selfish thoughts out of my head. I didn't want to commit the ultimate sin by taking my life. I wanted to live to see my children grow up. I wanted to be there for my sons and my daughters, to see them have children of their own. I wanted to be proud of them and see what they had achieved in their lives. I didn't want them thinking that "my mum was a coward, that's why she is not here today." I wanted to see all that, and that is why I am here today, thank God.

God said, "Forgive them that trespass against you." Whilst on the cross, he also looked up to his father and said, "Father, forgive them for they know not what they have done."

I have my hopes, I have my beliefs, and most of all I have my faith; and no one can take that away from me.

I learnt to pray. I had to. Prayer was my only means of getting through those terrible times. There was no one I could turn to. I felt alone and helpless. The only one that I could turn to was God. At first I thought, *How is God going to help me? No one can.* I thought that I had lost everything, and there was nothing more to lose, so this was my last resort. I needed someone to talk to, so I called on him, and he did answer me because from that day on, my life changed; the darkness that had overshadowed my life for so long had disappeared. I couldn't believe the power of prayer.

I would be on my knees praying for hours in my room. I always felt strong after praying.

The first lesson I learnt was to love myself again. Being constantly put down all that time took away my self-esteem and my confidence. I had to try to rebuild my life; however, I still had a long way to go, but I knew that I would get by with time. As they say, time is a healer.

Chapter Eleven

My Awakening

1995

As time went on, I started to feel much better. I told myself that I had to take each day at a time. I knew that it wouldn't be easy, but I was in a much better place than I'd ever been. One day I found myself walking into a clothes shop. For so long I had lost interest in looking good. I didn't feel good inside, so I never really bothered about the outside, so here I was standing in between the rails, without a clue. Well, the clothes looked really pretty the way they were displayed in the window and on the manikin. I didn't really want to buy anything, but the window dressing enticed me to go in and have a look.

I walked around the shop admiring the beautiful clothes, then I found myself touching them as I walked along, feeling the quality of the clothes. I hadn't bought myself clothes in ages. To tell you the truth I felt like I had lost my identity. Well, as I walked along the rails of clothes I started to pick them up, imagining myself in them. This shop was expensive and out of my reach, so God knows what I was doing in here, but I did feel as if something had drawn me here, not just the beautiful clothes.

I knew that I could not afford to buy anything in this shop, but for the first time in what seemed like forever I started to fall in love with clothes again.

I picked up a black dress. It was so elegant. I wanted to be elegant too. Well, the shop assistant came to my aid. "Would you like to try this dress on?" she said. I told her that I was in a hurry, and I didn't have the time to try the dress on. Truth was that I could not afford that dress. "Oh, it won't take that long to change. Rooms are empty. Just quickly try it on. I can see that you want to. You don't have to buy it. Just try it on."

Well, as soon as I tried the dress on I fell in love with it instantly. It had been years since I had looked this good. I stood there looking at myself in the mirror wondering how I could afford this dress. Well, that day, I came home with the dress, and accessories to match. I had just bought myself an expensive dress that I couldn't really afford, but it didn't matter, and that's when I realised that I had just done some retail therapy.

I was so excited but thinking at the same time, *Jackie, what have you done? You've just spent nearly all of your benefits on a dress. You have nowhere to go, and now you can't afford to go shopping.*

When I got home I rushed upstairs with my bags and tried my new dress on, and the accessories to match. I couldn't really see the full beauty of the dress because my hair was not done. Anyway I got the comb and some hair clips and pinned my hair up into an elegant style to match my elegant black dress. I stood looking at myself in the mirror for what seemed like hours. I couldn't get over how beautiful I looked and felt, then I heard myself saying, "You are pretty, you are beautiful." I take my mind back to when I was a child, standing in the mirror dressed in my mother's prom dress.

Reflection 1974

This dress was the most gorgeous dress I had ever seen in my life. The brightest yellow there ever was, with sequins and diamantes sparkling in their full glory. I twirled and swirled in my mother's yellow prom dress, imagining my mother wearing it. I was ten years old and felt so grown up standing looking at myself in the mirror.

As I held on to my father's arm, walking down the avenue, dressed as Cinderella for a competition at school, I felt like a little princess as I stepped proudly with my father with that proud look on his face, down the avenue, onto the stage to win the competition.

Standing here twenty years later, I told myself, "You are gorgeous. Wow, look at you." For the first time in my life I told myself that I was worthy and deserving of this dress, and so much more. Well, you know I never wore that dress again, but that was spiritual healing for me.

Financially things were much better. Patrick was still providing for the children; so I never had to really worry about expensive items like trainers, shoes, and coats. I never worried about buying clothes for the children, because he would always make sure that they were catered for. I started to concentrate more on myself. I went out and treated myself to a new outfit whenever I wanted. I even started to go to the hairdresser's each week to pamper myself.

I never knew about pampering until then. I even changed the colour of my hair. You know what they say, a woman's hair is her beauty. Wow! I looked different. When I looked in the mirror, the person that I saw looking back at me was beautiful; she looked like someone that I used to know. Well, I wanted to be that person in the mirror again, looking and most of all feeling beautiful inside.

I had to make a change, and the first biggest change that I made was to cut my hair off and dye it even more blond. This was the new me. I was surprised at how much confidence it gave me back. I had never wanted or planned to cut my hair, but it just happened without me really thinking about it. One day I just took up a pair of scissors then started cutting away. My hair was quite long at the time, but now it was short. I think that was a real turning point in my life at that time. It was a statement. I felt great. The awakening of a brand new me.

The awakening of my new life saw parties after parties; a new party dress was at the top of my shopping list each week.

I acquired a taste for beautiful dresses, which drew attention to me for the right reasons. My haircut drew attention too. I became confident in myself and outgoing again. I began to attract men like bees to honey, especially on the dance floor. I knew that I was good at dancing, and it showed. I had always loved dancing as a child. Well, I stopped dancing when I lived with Patrick. There was nothing to sing and dance about anymore. I was suppressed. I had lost my rhythm.

Well, I got it back, and here I was with men queuing up waiting to ask me for a dance. I remember one man thanking me for dancing with him; it was all fun.

I was out to have a good time and make up for the years of dancing that I had lost. I remember another man shaking my hand at the end of the night and saying to me that I had done well, dancing all night, considering the heels that I had on. That was a laugh.

Men were giving me their phone numbers, already written down on pieces of anything, cigarette packets, bus tickets, and my hand. They used to wait for me outside the club, until I was leaving, then thrust their numbers in my hand. This became a joke for me and my friends. We would be counting numbers at the end of the night. I had never experienced anything like this before.

I had lived a very sheltered life, as a young mother missing out on teenage years, when girls would laugh about things like what we were laughing about right now.

I used to end up with loads of numbers in my bag; I threw most of them away when I got home. The attention which I received from the men that I spoke to me made me feel special, and they respected me too. I felt like a celebrity with the compliments I received. Funny thing is, when I told them that I was single, they never believed me. They used to say, "What is a beautiful woman like you doing by yourself?" I used to laugh about it. The biggest compliment that I still remember was someone saying, "Tell your boyfriend or your husband that I said that he is a lucky man to have you, if he doesn't realise that." I remember asking him why did he think that, because he didn't know me. His reply was "Because I can see that you are a good woman and that any man that has you if he doesn't see that then he doesn't deserve you at all." Biggest compliment ever, definitely a confidence booster.

Now that my head was in a better place, and I had begun to feel alive again, I found myself thinking about the man that I had left behind in Jamaica. I had never forgotten him. I always thought about him, where was he, what was he doing, who was he with, did he still love me, would I ever see him again. I felt guilty because of the way I treated him, but I couldn't do any better at the time. I felt suffocated by everything and everyone around me. I hadn't written him in three years, and I hadn't received a letter from him, so I guess he must have moved on and forgotten about me a long time ago.

I still loved him, but at this time, I had grown to love my newfound life. I started to enjoy myself and felt relaxed in myself as a person. I became independent and funny again. I was always the clown in my family. I used to make everyone laugh, until they cried. Well, I started to make people laugh again, and I was having fun again. I was having a ball, and life became one big party.

Meeting men, fancying them, all those chat-up lines, getting to know them and going out on your first date, all those things I never did, when I was supposed to; so I found that I was doing them now.

I was enjoying myself, and I wasn't afraid to show it, especially on the dance floor. I had always loved dancing, even as a child.

Reflection 1977

My parents used to call me to dance for their friends, and I always did. I can remember when I was eleven years old, I went to my friend's birthday party, dressed in my pink frilly bell bottom suit, looking like Tina No one was dancing; they were just standing there looking at each other. Well, my favourite record came on, "Ring My Bell." You could say I forgot myself, and I ran into the middle of the dance floor and started to do my thing, Tina Turner had nothing on me, Next minute I had everyone in the middle with me following my dance steps.

Music had always been like food to me. I had come from a musical background. Most of my family sang and played instruments. Some even had recording contracts. I believe that is why I had became so passionate about music. Music became my rock, and I worshiped it. I found that I couldn't get through the day without listening to music. I was so inspired by it, because it had brought joy into my life. Learning to express myself through music was awesome. However, I still felt that there was something still missing in my life, and I was not going to find it out there on the dance floor.

Late-night parties and clubs started to subside. I was burning myself out, and even though I was out there enjoying myself, I knew that my lifestyle would soon have to come to an end.

I knew that I was not a child. I was a woman, and most of all, I was a mother to five children at that time.

I soon realised that those nights that I was out boogying on the dance floor and getting my groove on, I should have been at home curled up on the sofa with a cup of cocoa, and my children. Instead I was out there raving until the early hours of the morning. I also knew that this was something that was supposed to have been done at some point in my life when I was younger but never did, so now it had to come out of my system.

Chapter Twelve

A Whole New World

1995

Well, it was the days of the ecstasy. Everyone was going around hugging each other, peace and love on the dance floor in the form of a tablet. I soon realised that this lifestyle was not what I wanted anymore. After three years of partying hard, Thursday, Friday, Saturday, and Sunday nights, I decided to bow out from the party scene, still having respect for myself and from people whom I had met. I didn't want to get caught up in drugs, even though I knew that I was a very strong-minded person. Maybe a year or two ago, I probably wouldn't have been able to say that, but now everything had changed, and anyway there was no way I could be easily led. I always thought about my children first.

Things had to change from now on in my life. I had experienced another life over the past few years, partying and going out having fun, but I couldn't live that life forever. My children were my priority, so I decided to hang up my party dresses and dancing shoes for a while.

Not only did my life change, but my children's fathers' life changed too. Patrick started to live the dream. Well, his dream of a champagne Charlie, lifestyle, pure designer labels, fancy car, and girls young enough to be his daughters.

Well, I thought at least when I was out there reliving my teenage years, he's now out there reliving his nursery days, dating six former girls. He needed money to impress them, so in order to do that, he stopped giving his children money. We never really saw him that much again; I guess he never had the time or energy to see his children anymore, because he was too busy running after young girls and feeding his big ego.

He used to take the children shopping and buy them whatever they wanted. Christmastime he would shower them with presents. I knew he loved his children; he used to take them on outings. He always took the boys to play football, religiously, and he still managed to be a part of their lives, but then the day trips and the time he spent with them and the money started to slow down. Soon his visits stopped completely.

He would ring the children and make empty promises to them. "I'm coming to take you all out, and make sure that you're ready for me when I come." Well, you can guess the rest, letdown after letdown until they didn't care anymore whether he came or not. They didn't really mention his name anymore. I had always felt that the only child that missed out on having any time with his father was Steven, because he was the youngest.

Well, it was approaching Steven's tenth birthday. He never really had a strong bond with Patrick, like the other children did. He was only a baby when we broke up. He had no memories of living with him, where the others did. But he still loved him. Well, Patrick promised to come and take him out to get whatever he wanted. That day Steven waited with great patience, until he started to feel anxious. Well, Patrick never came for him.

That evening as I lay in my bed Steven came into my room and lay across my bed. He started to tell me how he felt about being let down by his dad. "Dad promised to take me out and buy me a present for my birthday, and he never came, why? Doesn't he love me anymore? He didn't ring me to say happy birthday. Even if we don't see him all the time he never forgets our birthday." He looked at me for confirmation on that. Well, I said, "Yes, that's true." Patrick had never let them down at birthdays, Easter, and Christmas. He would always buy them the best. To be honest he did have a good side to him, and a funny side, which to be honest was something I had forgotten because of the way that he treated me. It was hard to remember the good side and the good times because he was Mr. Jekyll and Mr. Hyde. I felt like I was living with two different people rolled into one, because when he was good, he was great, but when he was bad he was horrible. Patrick had some good qualities about him; however, they were marred by the other side of him.

Well, here I was, lying on the bed with my son, and the next thing that he said made me realise how children feel rejected when they are let down by their parents. "I would never treat my child like this, when I grow up and I'm a dad and I split up with my girlfriend. I'm not going to forget about my children." *Such grown-up words from a little boy,* I thought to myself.

I could not believe that he was saying these powerful words at such a young age. Children at that age shouldn't be questioning whether they are loved or not, because you know when you are loved, because you feel it just by the little things that your parents do for you. Actions speak louder than words. Words can be empty without meanings; but our actions say a lot, even though children will always need that confirmation, of those three little words that are so big, *I love you.*

Well, we spoke for a long time. I tried my best to comfort him by answering his questions, and whilst we talked I recorded every last word he said before I hugged him and we exchanged good nights, before going to his room.

Listening to him really broke my heart. Here was my ten-year-old son thinking that his father didn't love him anymore all because he broke his promise to him. Well, I had learnt a lesson from that, and it was never to make a promise about anything to anyone.

You could now say that I was a full-fledged member of the single mums group. I never received anything more from my Patrick. Both fathers had disappeared into thin air, or just walking around with no conscience. I just had to get on with my life. There was no way I was going to go looking or begging either of them for a penny.

I hadn't seen Tony for about a good eight years, and neither had his two children, and here was this other one following in his footsteps. By now we hadn't seen Patrick for almost two years.

Life was a little hard, but I managed to get by. I was a lot happier in myself and never let anything get me down. Things were looking much brighter than they ever did. I even thought more about what I wanted to do with my life. I felt like I had crossed a river.

My life had changed for the better. The children were getting older. To make ends meet I found myself little dead-end jobs here and there. I didn't stay in these jobs that long. As soon as I worked there for a couple of months I would leave. I only did it to get extra cash to buy things that I needed for the house or to go on holiday. Yes, I wanted to go back to Jamaica, to see my lost love.

Three years of discovering myself again and taking back control of my life, there was still something missing, and it was love. In the past three years that I was out there enjoying myself rediscovering my lost youth, I never once met anyone out there that I would say that I wanted to share my life with. I met some nice men along the way, but I kept them as friends and nothing more. My lost love was still very much in my head whether I believed it or not. Come to think of it, maybe that's one of the reasons why I never gave any of the men that I had met a chance because I was already in love with someone.

I felt the time was right for me to bring love into my life again. I had never given up on Benji. Somewhere in my heart the candle still burnt for him. The flame had never gone out. It still glowed brightly for him. I thought to myself that if we were meant to be together then nothing or no one could come between us. I knew that I still loved him, and this was a true and sincere love. Well, even though I felt like that I couldn't help but still have doubts in my mind. Did he still feel the same way? Did he still have that candle burning, or had the flame gone out a long time ago, when I walked out on him?

My life had now become more settled. I was more positive about life in general. The children were getting older, and I was able to do a little more for myself. I had become independent. I loved it. I had never been independent. All my life I had always depended on someone, my parents, and both my children's fathers. I never believed in myself and the abilities that I had to function as an independent woman.

I started to discover my qualities. I would never have had the opportunity to find out about them if I had not been on my own at that time in my life, to discover my hidden talents, my strengths, my weaknesses, my capabilities, and even my intelligence. I even discovered that I was multitalented and gifted. Surely things could only get better from now on. Or was I jinxing my thoughts?

Chapter Thirteen

Wearing the Same Shoes

1996

My father arrived back in England. He had come because he needed medical treatment. He had become unwell, and coming back to England was his last chance to find out what had happened to his arms. My father had lost the use of them, and no one could tell him why or what was wrong with his arms. My father ended up staying with me. It was my sister Patsy he had come to stay with; however, that didn't work out. I was pleased that he chose to stay with me. It was nice having him around, but he wasn't the same anymore. Time had mellowed him.

Well, everything seemed to be going all right, but that was until I received the bombshell that my eldest daughter was pregnant. Chantal was sixteen years old and pregnant. Now I know how my mother must have felt sixteen years ago when she found out that I was pregnant, "disappointed."

I had high hopes for my daughter. She had always been academically a very bright child. She was a beautiful girl who always had her head on her shoulders. She was smart, intelligent, and so loving. Everybody spoke so highly of her. We all had great, big expectations that she would make something of her life, which was more than I ever managed to do. I was thirty-two years old and still trying to make something of my life.

I wanted a better life for all my children because they never really had a good start in life like I had when I was a child, and I never gave up hope of them ever having a good life. I always told myself that where there was life, there was hope and that one day I would be able to provide more for them.

Well, Chantal was now pregnant, and it was so despairing to me. It felt like it was only yesterday that I gave birth to her, and I became a mum, and here was my baby about to do the same. I found it hard to accept because I didn't want her life to be a mirrored image of mine. I wanted the best for her. I wanted her to get an education and become someone. I wanted her to have the chances and opportunities that I never had. I never wanted my daughter to walk in the same shoes that I once wore.

I had to quickly overcome these thoughts and feelings and try to focus and concentrate on how she felt. I didn't want to treat her like how my parents treated me when they first found out from Dr. Jessie that I was pregnant. I knew how Chantal felt, because I had felt that way almost sixteen years ago. Well, I didn't want her to feel ashamed like I had, or you could say, how I was made to feel. I had to protect her because she was still very young, too young to take on the responsibility as a mother. She was only a baby herself, as once was said to me.

I had to try and turn it around. I told myself that she really needed me to show her my love and support. I had to be there to see her through this, just like my mother had done for me; I could not condemn her for getting pregnant or judge her, because I had done the same. If my mother had turned her back on me at that time how would I have felt?

I remembered what I had been through at that age when I was pregnant. All the stigmas I faced and all the judgments that was cast upon me by people. This was a different time now, and there was no way that I was going to make my daughter face all those things alone, or at all. I was going to protect her, to stand up for her, and to support her in any decisions that she would now make; and I was sure that she would not go through her life, struggling, knowing deprivation, and most of all without support.

The first thing that I did was to go out and find myself a job working in a factory sorting out junk mail. It was a boring brain-dead job, but at least it paid me enough to help my daughter out.

It was difficult working and looking after my father, but I had no choice. I had to support her financially and make sure that the baby was provided for.

Each week when I got paid, I would go baby shopping for my daughter. I made sure that she had everything that she needed; I made sure that the baby had everything too. I worked to buy them both the best. This was my first grandchild, and I was going to make sure that he came into this world feeling loved. I was going to be a grandmother, and I was only thirty-two years old, talk about young grandmothers. Well, I was now about to become one of them.

My daughter had to grow up overnight just like I had once done. I still had to get on with my life. After all I was only thirty-two years old.

I worked for the next six months until I had bought everything for my daughter and baby. I made sure her hospital bags were packed, for when the time came, even the baby's clothes were packed. We had since found out that the baby was a boy, so we were prepared.

My father was totally dependent on me for everything. The doctors had since told him that the muscles in his arms were completely wasted. They also told him that if he had seen a doctor three years ago, maybe it would not have reached to this stage. Well, my father had to accept that the doctors could not do anything for him, or his arms anymore. It was too late; however, he never gave up hoping. This once strapping belt wielding man, had become dependent on me, I never held anything against him, I loved him, he was my father, I didn't approve of his techniques of keeping us on track, however I did think that it wasn't his fault, he had come from a different time, where discipline came in the form of using impliments.

My father had grown up with the rod, he even told us that the last time that his father hit him, was when he was a man. Well all that was behind us now, and here we were father and daughter,

I became my dad's carer, his nurse, his full support system. I even felt sometimes like I had become his mother too.

I did everything for him. I fed him, nursed him, bathed him, brushed his teeth, took him to the toilet, cleaned him, wiped his nose, and combed his hair, all with the help of my children. It was sad to see my father in this way. Simple little things that we all take for granted and never really think about were now the hardest things for him to do.

The first time that I had to bathe my father was a difficult thing for me to do. I remember lying in my bed that Sunday morning and asking God to give me some strength to do this. I wasn't asking for physical strength, just to be mentally prepared to do this. I had never seen my father without any clothes on in my life, so I knew that he was probably lying down and thinking and praying for the same thing too.

Eventually I got up and thanked God for listening to me. As I walked into the room the first thing I said was "Daddy, I know that this is hard for both of us, but there is no one else here to help you, only me, but I prayed and asked God to give me strength." All I heard was my father saying, "Okay, daughter, do what you have to." After that things just got better.

My father climbed into the bath and held on to my arms for support. I climbed in after him and stood in the bath with my trousers rolled up to my knees, bathing my father and thinking to myself, *Oh, how the tables had turned, role reversal.* Here I was, bathing my father, something I would never have imagined ever doing.

When we were finished I would call the children to help us. We would all count to three, as we eased him out. Sometimes we would all end up wet and laughing as we counted over and over again. This became easier as time went on. Eventually I never needed any help from the children, just my father and me. Only God knows where my inner strength came from. After his bath, I would stand there with the towel drying him all over then kneel down to make sure his feet were dried as they were swollen, then I would cover him with moisturiser and his favourite talcum powder, before putting his nightclothes on. We would chat away like old friends, then I used to put him to bed and tuck him in just like a baby and make sure that that the last thing I did was read to him. The bond between my father and me grew, and I looked forward each evening for our little bath time chats, before we would tell each other good night and God bless.

I knew that my father felt that he was a burden to me, but he wasn't. I felt that it was my duty to serve him at this time. My father had always done the best for me, so I was just giving back what he gave to me. I loved him, and even though it was hard going to work it was even harder coming home and doing my duties as a mother, and a daughter. So many nights I would fall asleep reading the Bible to my father; that was something that he couldn't do anymore without help. He could no longer pick his Bible up and turn the pages like he used to do on a Sunday morning standing in front of his congregation at church. My father lost so much when he lost the use of his arms. My father was a musician. He played the mouth organ, beautifully, and strummed the guitar with such grace. My father had the sweetest singing voice I had ever heard. I used to think that a lot when I was a child.

Reflection 1969

As a child, I would sit down listening to my father sing; he had the sweetest voice. I would sit down for ages just looking at him sing. Well, he now thanked God that he could still do that. My father was so many things, a musician, a wonderful chef, a baker, a carpenter, even a gardener; and now all of that had gone.

At first it was hard for all of us, especially my mother, to accept. My father took it much better. He would say, "If it's God's will that I should be like this, a pastor who can no longer hold his Bible, well, I couldn't look at it like that."

I never once complained. Looking after him I was honoured to have had the opportunity to help my father in the way that I did. It was great having him around. I enjoyed his company, and we would give each other support.

Well, I could not believe my father's attitude to my daughter being pregnant. When I had first told him, I thought that he would hit the roof just like he did with me, but he didn't; he was so calm about it and said to me that she was put on this earth to have children even though she was still young. He even reminded me that I had done the same. Wow, what a difference a day makes.

Almost seventeen years ago when I was pregnant with my daughter it was a different story. My father was so disappointed in me that he did not speak to me for weeks. He could not even look in my face anymore. He was so ashamed of me and wanted me to get married because of the disgrace that I had brought to his door. However, he still forgave me for my mistakes and supported me.

My father helped me to take care of my baby. She was like a cat on his lap. My dad was the only one who could put her to sleep. She loved falling asleep on his big soft cushion belly. There was no room for him to rest his mug on anymore because the mug had been replaced by the baby. He loved her so much, and here was this baby having her own baby.

Well, I was upset about my daughter being pregnant, and I expected my father to be upset too, but he wasn't. He just said that's life, a far cry from sixteen years ago.

Six months was almost up, and my father was soon to return back home to Jamaica. I was going to miss him terribly. He was my company, and we would sit for hours just talking about the past. Sometimes he would get really upset at not being able to help me around the house, or with the children, because he saw how hard my life was. He couldn't believe how I managed to do everything and still stay positive. He would often get upset about his hands and cry, so I had to be strong for him, but seeing him just sitting there would upset me so much. I never cried in front of him. I never showed him how upset I really was and always tried to make him look on the bright side of life.

Reflection 1977

My father was always a strong independent man when it came to the domestic side of life. He was a fantastic cook. I remember me and my sisters and brother sitting down licking our lips when my father was cooking. My mother was a fantastic cook too; however, they both would debate on who was better. My mother would always try to find some fault and would look at us for confirmation. Well, we couldn't take sides, so I guess we had the best of both worlds.

My father loved baking. He was a fantastic baker. His specialty was baking Easter buns. I remember our house being filled with buns, waiting for collection. Yes, my father would bake buns for everyone in the church. The orders came flooding in from January. It's Easter time, and the entire congregation would be turning up on our doorstep to collect their buns. Our house had the most wonderful smell of Easter.

My father now sat staring out of the window, with the saddest look ever in his eyes, with tears rolling down his face. I asked him what was the matter. He replied, "I want to buy all the children outside an ice cream, from the van, but I can't take the money out of my pocket." I hugged him and said daddies don't cry. I went through a lot of those days with my father, constantly putting himself down, but I would always be there to encourage him and to console him. After spending almost six months with me, it was time for my father to return back to Jamaica.

During the time that my father was in England, I had managed to save up money to go to Jamaica for Christmas. My father left three weeks before. I didn't want to leave my daughter behind, but I knew that she would be fine, and she wasn't alone. I was leaving her in the hands of her father. Well, that's how she saw Patrick. She had never really grown up with her real father, Tony. She had always been dependent on Patrick, who was still in their lives, when it suited him. However, he promised me that he would take care of her. Patrick and I had started to get on a little better now that we both had separate lives.

Well, the baby was due in January. I wished that I could have cancelled my holiday, but it was already booked before I found out about the baby. Those days you were able to pay your fare in drips and drabs, which made it easier to consider a holiday. Each week I would go to the travel agent and pay down whatever I could afford at the time, so you see I couldn't cancel, or I would lose my money, and besides, the baby's due date was a week, after I returned home, so I hoped, and that he wouldn't make his appearance before my return.

Chapter Fourteen

A Never-Forgotten Love

1996

I arrived back in Jamaica in December, almost a month after my father had returned. I was just in time for Christmas. I was so happy to be back. A lot had changed in my life since the last time I was here. I had come to spend Christmas with my parents and brought the younger children with me too. The only one that was left behind was my daughter. For the first time ever, I had left her. I felt a little sad, but I couldn't make that dampen our holiday mood; we were going to have a wonderful Christmas.

I hadn't spent Christmas with my parents since the first time I had come to Jamaica. My mum wanted to make it as happy for the children as she could. She said that she wanted them to feel at home because she knew that in England, Christmas was a big thing. Huge Christmas trees decorated in their full glory, decorations draped around the house, and shops and even on the roads, Christmas fairy lights flickered on and off. Christmas carol singers and the Salvation Army brass band played "Oh Come All Ye Faithful."

In Jamaica Christmas is celebrated in a huge way, but not over the top like it is in England. It felt strange when we arrived in Jamaica because there was no fuss at the airport. You see, when the children left Heathrow airport there was a huge Christmas tree, standing tall and proud in the middle of the airport; but when they got to Kingston airport, there was no trace of Christmas anywhere. I can remember my youngest son asking me where had Christmas gone.

Well, here was my mother getting excited about this Christmas. She took out the same box of decorations that I remembered from back in England, and we all started to decorate the house, even the veranda. We put up flickering fairy light, tinsel, balloons, and the same colourful lanterns that once decorated the living room. We even had crackers and fireworks, but in Jamaica it is known as clappers. My father sat down watching with a smile on his face, but a glint of sadness in his eyes, probably thinking that it was once his job to put the decorations up at Christmastime. Well, Mummy, Daddy, you sit down. We're putting the decorations up this year. The children and I decorated the tree, blew up the balloons, hung the decorations, while they looked on and gave their instructions on where to hang what.

I almost felt like a child again. I even got the same feelings of excitement that I used to get when my father was putting up the decorations. This was deja vu, a feeling of being here before. We played music and danced around the veranda. This was the first time I had seen my mother dance in years. This was heaven.

I couldn't wait to meet Benji again. He knew that I was here, but I wanted to go and see him first. I didn't want him to come up to the house until I knew where I stood with him.

Well, I needn't have worried because he still felt the same way that he felt three years ago. He had never given up hope that I would come back, and he never resented me for ending the relationship between us. Looking back now, I believe that our relationship was never over; it was just on hold until I felt strong enough to move forward with my life.

My bulimia had become a thing of the past now that I was happy. Gone were the days when I would make excuses and grab every chance I could get to stick my fingers down my throat. I had struggled with bulimia for the past seven years, day in and day out. Bulimia had robbed me seven years out of my life, but I had managed to take control of my life again.

No longer was I a slave to bulimia. I was now free. I don't know how I managed to get through that difficult time, but now that I had regained my life back and was about to pick up from where I left off, I felt that I had overcome some of my demons.

I had to learn to love myself again and soon learnt that bulimia did not have any place in my life anymore. Gone were the days when I walked with carrier bags in my handbag. Gone were the scales. I never ever bought another scale again. Gone were the calorie-counting books. There was no darkness in my life, just pure light, and I could now see where I was going, and I no longer focused on what I ate. I was free to eat whatever I wanted, and I still do today.

Gone were the days when I would just eat a packet of crisps or an apple. Some days I could go through the whole day with just a glass of water. Gone were the days of looking frail, drawn, and feeling tired. I had made a conscious decision to start eating properly again, even though it was difficult. Gone were the days when two spoonfuls of food made me feel like I had just eaten breakfast, dinner, lunch, and dessert all in one go.

I can't tell you how my bulimia nightmare started, but I can tell you when it ended, and that's when I chose to live and fall in love for the very first time.

Well, here I was again in Jamaica, explaining my life to Benji, what had happened since we last saw each other. We talked about everything, leaving no stones unturned. I told him what had happened after I had left Jamaica three years ago, what I had been through, how I had reached the bottom of despair, how I had managed to close one chapter of my life and move on.

He told me what had happened in his life over the past three years and that he had always hoped and prayed that I would come back one day. Even though we talked and I told him that I still loved him, and he told me the same, I could see that he was a bit weary of being hurt again. It took me a long time to reassure him that I meant every word I had just said and that I still loved him.

I spent a week in Jamaica with my children's grandfather and his wife. Before I went to Jamaica, Patrick had asked me to take the children to see his family. I didn't really want to go because he had not contributed in any way towards the children going on holiday; not only that but I thought he had no right to ask me for anything.

I was no longer under his control, and he could not make me do anything I didn't want to do, and I wanted to spend my holidays with the people that I loved. I never really had a relationship with his family anyway, and I didn't want to start having one now. They had never really shown any love towards my children when they were living in England or even when they went back home to live in Jamaica, so I didn't see the point in getting to know them now, but to give them the benefit of the doubt, I decided to take the children to visit them.

I wouldn't have minded if the children went alone, but I knew that they would not have gone without me, because they never really knew his parents that well. He had already arranged behind my back for his father to come and take us. It was just like the old times. He was still trying to control my life, even though we were no longer together, making threats that if I did not take the children to stay with his family, I should not return to England.

Well, against my will I packed our bags for the week, while his father waited on the veranda patiently.

I felt a little awkward being around his father. He knew that his son and I were no longer together and that I had left him and found myself another man, but what he didn't know was the reason why, so before I went I had to clear up a few things and straighten out the misunderstandings and the picture that his son painted of me.

I remember him saying to me with a judgmental tone in his voice, "Is it true that you and my son have split up?" I was on the defence and answered back, "Don't go on like you don't know, because you do." He replied, "He told me that you have a man." I replied icily, "I do, and you know why." "Why?" he said. "Ask your son what he did to me. Would you like a man to throw hot cornmeal porridge in your daughter's face? Would you like a man to kick and punch your daughter?"

Patrick always said that there was a reason for why he sometimes treated me the way that he did.

Well, his dad looked at me and said, "Is that what he did to you?" I said yes. Well, that cleared up everything.

The children and I spent a lovely week at his parents' house. The children were happy. I surprised myself by being happy too. I felt miserable on the way there because I had my reservations about going, but they made me feel so welcome, as if I were still a part of their family. It's a pity that they never took the time to get to know me when they lived in England. I should say that we never got to know each other because I found them to be nice people. We all got on like a house on fire, and they treated me as if I were their daughter-in-law. They even told people that I was.

I was even told that I was welcome to come back to their home whenever I came back to Jamaica and that they hoped that maybe one day their son and I would get back together again. I thought to myself, *Not in this lifetime, or the next.*

That was a week to remember, Dunn's River Falls, Portosico Beach, Green Grotto Caves, Fern Gully, Devon House, that's where they sell the most beautiful ice cream, but it was time to go back.

I was happy to get back, because I missed Benji. I couldn't wait to see him again. I felt like I had been away forever.

Having my parents in Jamaica and Benji was hard because it caused arguments between my parents and me. They felt that I spent all my time with him. I was happy and so in love that I couldn't stand a moment being away from him. Even though I spent a lot of time with him, I did spend time with my parents too. It was like my parents and my Benji were rivals, competing for my time. I loved my parents so much, but I loved Benji too, and I wanted to spend every moment of every waking day with him, but I didn't want my parents to feel left out, so I split my time between them, I had to choose between Christmas Eve and Christmas Day. I loved them all, so I spent Christmas Eve with Benji, and I spent Christmas Day with my family and Benji, inviting him along to share the day with us. Well, that was one Christmas I will never forget.

Our Christmas holiday was almost coming to an end. I didn't want to go back home, but I had to. I was so in love, and the happiest I had ever been. I had managed to get back what I thought I had lost, and I knew that this was going to be the start of something special, new beginnings for all of us. The only way was up from now on. Out of all the times I had left Jamaica to come back home, this time was the hardest ever. I had just had the most wonderful ten weeks of my life, and now it was over; however, my relationship with Benji was back on track.

I returned back to England full of hope. While I was in Jamaica a week before I came back, my daughter gave birth to a baby boy. Well, he wasn't due for another week, but I guess he couldn't wait. I was so proud of my grandson; he was so beautiful. I was a little sad because I wasn't there for my daughter, but I was pleased that one of my closest friends at the time was there for her.

Chapter Fifteen

New Additions

1997

As soon as I arrived back in England I knew that I was pregnant. I did have my suspicions whilst I was in Jamaica. I was so happy, but sad because I knew that I would have to face this on my own. Benji was not here; he lived in Jamaica. How was I going to manage by myself with a baby? When my other children were born they had their father here, but my poor baby, she didn't have her dad here, because he was in Jamaica. Well, despite all that I was still over the moon. I was pregnant, for someone that I truly loved. I was going to have his baby. I didn't feel alone, because I had a part of him right here, growing inside me. For some reason, I knew that this baby was a girl.

Patrick was around. He had stayed with Chantal when we were in Jamaica and made sure that everything was all right. I never told him that I was pregnant for at least five months. I guess it was not his business to know. I did not owe him anything. We weren't together anymore. Well, one day he came around, and I was sitting down watching television. As a matter of fact every time he came around I was always sitting down, so he never really noticed. Well, this time I noticed that he was looking at me in a strange way, then he just came out with it. "You're putting on weight, girl." I couldn't hide it from him anymore, because he would soon find out anyway. "I'm pregnant." He went quiet for a while, and then he said, "You better send for your baby's father to help you, because when my kids are opening their Christmas presents, your one will watching mine open theirs." I knew that Patrick was capable of saying a lot of things, but saying something so cruel about a child that was not here yet was unbelievable; however, this never surprised me one bit, because he had said worse, in the past, but this was uncalled for.

Well, I soon snapped out of that one. There was no way that I was going to make anything cloud my happy thoughts of having this baby and having a life with Benji, even though I had never thought about the hereafter.

Benji and I were both happy about this baby; this was something that we used to dream about. I remember us lying down and dreaming about starting a family together. I would say that I wanted a little girl one day and that I wanted her to have his beautiful shiny black hair, then he would reply, "I want her to have your eyes, your mouth, your nose, and my hair." We used to laugh because I would ask him what was wrong with my hair, why we both wanted our imaginary baby to have his hair.

Our imaginary baby had become real, and I just had this strong feeling that it was a girl. I even chose her name from the first time I realized that I was pregnant. It was a beautiful feeling to be so in love with someone and to be having their child.

I felt so special, even though I was on my own; I had never ever felt so special being pregnant until now.

Even though Benji was not here, I still managed to keep him involved; I sent him all of the ultrasound photographs as well as photographs of myself from the first month to the last. He was able to see my belly growing bigger and bigger each month from the pictures I sent. I looked great. I still had a figure, probably for the first time since my pregnancy days; however, I suffered terrible morning sickness.

I was told that my morning sickness would soon come to an end. Day after day I waited, but it just got worse. Foods that I loved, I now hated; foods that I hated I now loved. Smells just drove me to the toilet to heave. It was awful. I was so frightened to eat because everything made me sick. I lost so much weight. This was the first time that I had ever experienced morning sickness in my life.

Well, I told myself that it was all for a good cause and that there was a first time for everything, even morning sickness.

I wrote him letters every day, and I received letters from him by the score. I used to lie down at nights reading them over and over again. His letters kept me going. I used to go to bed each night thinking about all the good times and the special times that we shared. I would spend at least an hour thinking about us. I always fell asleep thinking about him and our baby. He was always the first thing on my mind in the morning when I opened my eyes and the last thing on my mind before I closed my eyes at night.

I felt sorry for Benji because he wasn't here to share any of this with me. I used to wish that he could feel the baby kicking away and see her moving around, and he missed out on all that.

I wrote him letters every day. I always had so much to say, and each letter was so different from the last one. I spoke to him occasionally on the telephone; he sounded so near yet so far.

My daughter Lourdes was born on the twenty-seventh of August 1997. She was the most beautiful little soul. She had the most shiny jet-black full head of hair I had ever seen on a baby's head. She was absolutely gorgeous. I could not believe she was mine, ours. I was so proud of her. She looked like a little china doll. Her eyes, her little mouth, her fingers, everything was perfect. She meant everything to me. Everyone fell in love with her. She was so precious.

She needed her dad, we both did, and I was going to make sure that we were a family. This child did not deserve to grow up not knowing who her father was. I couldn't keep on taking her to Jamaica for a few weeks, once a year. I didn't want him singing happy birthday to her over the phone, across the Atlantic, or receiving birthday cards in the post, with a Jamaican postage stamp stuck on it, and I didn't want her to have a different life to her brothers and sisters. I wanted them all to spend their school holidays together, not me packing her off to Jamaica every year in the six weeks holiday by herself, to spend time with her dad. I had to think about our future now. I had travelled to Jamaica for the past years, but something had to change. Now that we were a family it just didn't seem right anymore, me going and coming.

A week after I had my baby I finally got to ring him and tell him the good news even though my mother had told him that I had given birth to a baby girl. Benji did not have a telephone, so we had to arrange for him to go to my parents' house, where I could ring him at a certain time.

I would be sitting down in a phone booth inside the Internet café; it was difficult for me, especially after just having the baby.

I sat in the booth describing the baby to him, telling him how much she weighed, how many times during the nights she woke up, what colour of hair and eyes she had, and who she resembled; she looked exactly like Benji. No one would guess that she was mine. She had nothing from me.

I felt so distant. I was happy but so sad at the same time. Here we were talking, but on different sides of the world. I wanted to be on the same side as him, so the only way to do that was to go back to Jamaica and take the baby to meet her family. It took me four months to do that because I didn't want her to go without her immunisations, so I had to wait. In the meantime I sent him photographs of his daughter.

We spoke about getting married. It seemed like the right thing to do at the time. I loved Benji, and I knew that he felt the same about me, and now that we were a family, it was the respectable thing to do, to make an honest woman of me. I had never wanted to get married to anyone else in my life before now, only Benji.

I remember the first time that I met him. For some strange reason I thought about marrying him. It's like I had a glimpse into the future, and here we were now, discussing wedding plans. My dream of becoming his wife was about to come true.

We had all these big plans but no money. I had stopped working after Chantal had her son and I had Lourdes, so I decided to stay at home and look after both babies, giving my daughter Chantal the chance to go to college and make something of her life. I didn't want her to be a stay-at-home mum like me. I wanted her to be able to afford to provide for her son and not struggle through life like I had done.

So here I was at home with an eight-month-old baby and a newborn. It was hard coping with the two. I used to think that it would have been easier if they were both the same age, both lying flat on their backs. I couldn't go outside with them both at the same time, because I couldn't really afford to buy a double buggy, so I stayed inside most of the day, until Chantal got home from college. I wondered to myself, how did my mother cope, having me and my sisters and brother a year apart, all four of us. I could not imagine. My respect went out to her for doing the great job she did, day in day out, and it made me look at all the other mothers out there coping with more than one baby at a time, and giving them the uttermost respect for coping.

People would often stare at me when I did get a chance to take the babies out, probably wondering how I managed to cope with two babies of different ages.

They would look at me with a look of disbelief and do maths in their head, to work out how I managed to have two babies both under one-year-old.

Well, I had to try to save some money. More to the question was how to raise money, to make money, and that's what I did. I discovered knitting. I went out and bought myself a pair of knitting needles and a bag of brightly coloured wool. I had never knit anything before. I taught myself how to knit.

I spent all day and night knitting away, sitting on buses and walking on the streets. Every chance I could get to knit, I took it. The speed of my knitting was amazing. Orders were coming in one after the other, and so was the money. I would be at the baby clinic and see a baby with one of my designs on their head. Well, I managed to save enough money to start thinking about getting married. Even though I knew that we could not afford a fairy-tale wedding, that didn't really matter to me.

It was not about spending money that we never had, just to have the best, and possibly getting myself into debt. Even though that would be every girl's dream, including mine, to have the best wedding ever, it really didn't matter at this stage. I did wish that all my family and friends could be there.

We planned our wedding, and I managed to put together the essential items for a bride. I remember me and my friend walking into a bridal shop and trying on a veil. I really wanted to try the dress on, but wow, that was way out of my league. I never dared look between the rails at all the fairy-tale bridal gowns which hung neatly and looked so beautiful without a bride in them. Well, I couldn't even begin to imagine myself in something as beautiful as one of those dresses.

Well, here I am, me and my friend Francis, standing in the middle of the small bridal shop floor, looking in the mirror, me with a pair of jeans on, and the veil covering my face. I must say it was a beautiful ivory veil with little diamantes sewn all over it. I asked the lady how much was the veil. Well, that was within my remit, so I paid a deposit and left the shop happy, and my friend and I were singing "Here Comes the Bride."

Even though I could not afford to buy one of those fairy-tale dresses, I still had the most beautiful dress at home. I had bought that dress a few years ago, around the time when I was discovering myself again, the awakening of the new me. I had bought that dress to go to a New Year's Eve party, and it was stunning.

The dress was made out of velour, with little diamantes sewn all over it; and to top it off, it was ivory.

I remember the night when I wore that dress, all the brave men in that room came up to me and complimented on how beautiful I looked. I felt like a princess in that dress, and I believed in myself that night, and I always told myself that if ever I should marry one day, that would be the dress that I would wear. I even told myself that if it made me feel like a princess that night, it would make me feel like that again, but this time on my wedding day. Well, everything came together after that.

We planned to get married on March 14, 1998. I couldn't wait to get married to Benji. I couldn't wait to become Mrs. Jacqueline Johnson.

Chapter Sixteen

For Better, for Worse

1998

I arrived back in Jamaica with my baby. I was so nervous and excited at the airport. Our daughter was now five months old, and she was about to meet her dad for the very first time. They both would be meeting each other. How would he feel? I had not sent him any more photographs since the first one, because I wanted to surprise him with how much she had grown and how beautiful she was. I did feel a tinge of sadness, because he had missed out on five months of her life, and we would never get those back. In his mind was he expecting a little baby? Even though time had passed, were they going to be able to bond? Would she know that this was her father? All these questions I asked myself.

It would be very hard for him to believe all this, but here I was in Jamaica, just about to present this baby to him. When he last saw me my tummy was flat, and now he was about to see me again, and my tummy was still flat. He had missed out on everything.

My worries were all in vain, because as soon as I walked out the airport and I saw him standing there, he took the baby right out of my arms. She did not make a sound. That was so hard to believe because she never went to anyone she never knew. It's like she knew who he was, but she just couldn't say it. Well, he held her all the way home.

They became inseparable. He did everything for her. He was at her beck and call. This was something new to me. I had never seen any man so dedicated to his child. I had never seen any of my children's fathers even change a nappy, and here was this man waiting hand and foot on this child.

I felt happy. I couldn't fathom any of it. I used to just sit down and watch him with her. I even started to feel a little left out, because all his attention became focused on this child. I now understood that it was because he thought that I was going to take her back home, and he would not see her until she was walking, or even worse, going to school, but I promised myself before I went to Jamaica that things had to change, that this was not going to happen. I could not do that to them.

Everything seemed perfect. I was in Jamaica with my new family, and I didn't want it to end. I couldn't bear to think about leaving. I didn't want to go back home feeling empty and alone. I had made up my mind about what I wanted, and we both wanted the same thing, and that was to be together. We wanted to be a proper family, and there was only one way for us to do that. We both felt the same way about each other and wanted to spend the rest of our lives together, so we were getting married.

Everyone was happy for us. At last we could move on and be together, for better or for worse, in sickness and in health, till death do us part.

March 14 was the happy day. Our families helped to organise everything, and I got married in my father's church. I didn't have all my children there, just two of them. I had one sister and one brother there at the time, but it would have been great if all the others were there to see me take this step, but I was so in love that it didn't matter. I felt that it was just about us, and it didn't matter if the whole world was or wasn't there. As long as we took our vows that was all that mattered to me.

That was a day to remember. I wore my ivory dress with pride, standing at the altar waiting to become Mrs. Johnson.

We didn't even have to go on honeymoon, because we were already in Jamaica, the beautiful island in the sun. What more could I ask for?

I spent few more weeks in Jamaica, then my time came to an end. Even though I felt sad about leaving, I was positive that our lives would be together, not apart. I had plans for us, and I couldn't wait to come to England to start the ball rolling. I was going to miss my husband but not for long because he would join me sooner than he realised.

Back in England I was a woman on a mission. First thing was to get myself a job. I hadn't been able to hold down a permanent job because of the lifestyle which I had adapted, going to and from Jamaica. I had known Benji for seven years before I married him. At first some of my friends did not approve. I guess they thought that he was after my money. Fat chance because I was broke like the Ten Commandments, so if that's the reason he married me then he was going to be in for a shock, but it wasn't.

He never once asked me for anything in all the years I had known him. To be honest having a long-distance relationship is one of the hardest relationships to have because it was never easy saying goodbye at the end of the holiday. There were always tears. Leaving behind someone you love is one of the hardest things to do, and not knowing when you will see them again or if you will ever see them again. Everyone thought that it would not last long, but I knew deep down that it would. All I had ever wanted was to love and be loved in return, and I was so positive about everything. Things were going to be different now. I had a future with a husband that I loved, and I had hope for a better future. I could now see light at the end of the tunnel.

I was a woman on a mission, to find work to support my husband to come over to England in order for him to support us.

I would do whatever it took. I would clean toilets, sweep floors, clean people's houses, whatever it took, just to get him here. I didn't have any qualifications or any skills to get myself a decent job, but I did have many years of experience in cleaning. As a matter of fact I had a degree, cleaning was my life. That's all I had ever done. Especially with having a big family I was forever cleaning up after them, so yes, that's one thing I could say that I was really good at.

I limited myself to doing cleaning jobs. I used to try to fill in application forms for other types of jobs but only got as far as filling out my name, address, and date of birth. When it came to the rest of details, like my experience qualifications and what I had done, I couldn't go any further. What was the point? No one would want to employ someone like myself, who was unskilled and had enough experience as a baby. Over the years I had never given myself a chance to really discover my full potential, even though I knew that I was capable of doing so many things. I guess that there was nothing to focus on to bring out my hidden abilities, talents, and gifts.

Well, I got myself a job working in a health and fitness centre. I was now officially the lady of the Manor. I was a cleaner, not something I could say that I was proud of, but it was a job.

I told myself that at least I was a cleaner in a nice establishment; at least I wasn't cleaning toilets in Burger King or McDonald's, but it was still the same because I was still cleaning toilets. I took any and every cleaning job that I could get my hands on. I wasn't partial to what and where.

I loved working at the Manor. Even though I was a cleaner no one treated me any different. I did think that I put myself down for working there, but no one really cared except me. To feel better about what I did, I would always try my best to look good. I even managed to look better than some of the people that worked there. I just wanted to prove to people that because I was a cleaner I didn't have to look like one; it was just me being proud.

No one outside knew my occupation, and if they did ask what I did or where I worked, I would always say that I worked in a health and fitness centre. That was good enough for most people.

As time went on, I was offered more and more cleaning jobs. Everyone wanted me to come and work for them. Altogether I now had six cleaning jobs in one day.

I would sometimes do three jobs in three different areas. God knows how I did it. My job at the Manor started at 6:00 a.m., so I had to wake up at 4:30 a.m. and get ready to go, leaving my children behind, but making sure that everything was sorted out for them. Chantal was still living at home, so that helped.

I worked really hard to save money to pay my husband's fare to come over to England, and I finally did it.

I managed to get all the money together just in time for him to come for Christmas and for good.

It was all happening. I couldn't believe that he was going to be here in England for Christmas, our first as a family, and within the next forty-eight hours it didn't seem real. Even when I paid for his ticket it still didn't sink in. The only time that it was going to be real was when I saw him at the airport, but even then it still wouldn't.

This was always something I had dreamt about but could never imagine happening, but it was about to happen.

I had everything ready for my husband's arrival. I had even made sure that he had a wardrobe full of clothes for when he arrived, shoes, trainers, winter coat, and a woolly hat. He was well prepared for the winter weather, especially coming from a hot climate. I worried about that too.

I had even decorated the house and bought new furniture. I wanted everything to be picture perfect for him; not that he would have noticed the difference, but this was a new beginning, and I didn't want any reminders or traces from my past life with Patrick.

Everything was new, just how I had wanted it. I had worked my fingers to the bone over the past eight months to get this far, waking up out of my bed at ungodly hours of the early morning and working late evenings just to make all this happen, and it paid off.

I was so excited. I kept on telling myself that soon he would be leaving Jamaica to come here to start a new life with me and the children. I couldn't wait. I had it all planned out, what I was going to say to him for the first time and what I was going to wear to the airport. I felt like I was meeting him for the very first time, and I felt nervous thinking about it. Well, it did feel like the first time because I hadn't seen him for eight months. Lourdes was now one year old and walking around, not the baby he last saw; she was a toddler now.

The following day I woke up bright and early. I had so much to do that day, not forgetting that I had to go to work too, but I was so excited. I didn't know if I could concentrate on cleaning the toilet bowl properly. My head was in the clouds.

Going to the hairdresser's and having my hair down was the first thing on my list. I wanted to look as good, no, I wanted to look even better than when he last saw me. I wanted him to see me and say, "Wow, that's my wife."

Well, I went to work that morning and rushed through my work. My mind wasn't on cleaning. It was somewhere else. My eyes were on the clock counting the hours, but counting five hours back, to Jamaican time, wondering what Benji was doing, was he packing, was he excited, did he feel like I did, or was he on the way to the airport.

I finally finished work. I couldn't wait to get out the place. All the time I had worked there I had never got dressed to leave as fast as I did that day. I always had time to have a little chat after I finished my shift, but not today. I had loads to do.

I got dressed and just about told everyone that I was leaving and then fled from the building like it was on fire and straight to the hairdresser's.

I felt on top of the world when I came out the hairdresser's, new hairstyle, new husband, what more could a girl want?

I was walking home on a cloud when my phone rang; it was my sister Patsy. "Jack, I got some bad news, Mummy collapsed, and she's in the hospital, and it's serious." My sister Patsy was living in Jamaica at the time, but she was coming over for a holiday, and she was due to come back with my Benji.

Well, I stood in my tracks just listening, not being able to say a word. "Jack, Jack, are you there? It doesn't sound good." I was dumbstruck and couldn't believe what I just heard. "Jack, I don't think we will be coming tomorrow because of what has happened to Mummy."

Well, if the news about my mother wasn't bad enough, this made it even worse. God knows how I got home. I was so weak from the news that my mum was very ill in the hospital, and no one knew what was wrong with her.

My whole world fell apart there and then. I cried and cried, *Please, God, don't let her die.* I had never begged anyone as much as I begged God that day to make my mother live.

I cried so much until my head throbbed, my eyes were swollen and red, my voice was gone, and so was my hairstyle. I didn't care anymore about anything, especially if Benji came or not. The only person I cared about at that moment was my mother, and she was thousands of miles away in Jamaica in some hospital fighting for her life, and no one could tell us why.

The only details that we were able to gather was that she had collapsed after coming home from a nine night, which some people would call a wake.

Someone they knew had passed away, and my mother had gone there that evening to pay her respects.

We were told that she was fine during the day. She also went shopping with my Benji to buy presents to send with him to give to us. We were told that she went to the gathering, collapsed while she was praying, and came home not knowing who and where she was. She didn't even know who my father was, her husband. This didn't seem right. There had to be more to this.

I was inconsolable, and I wanted my mother. I felt like a little child again. I lost control in front of my children, and I couldn't cope with what was happening. My mother was one of my weaknesses.

That evening I walked around my house calling for her and saying out loud, "I want my mum, I want my mum." I was helpless, and the more I felt like this, the more angry I became. I wanted to blame someone, so I blamed the devil. "Why have you thrown heartache into my happiness? You saw how happy I was, but oh no, you've never allowed me any peace and happiness, and now you are trying to bring me down, but I won't let you." I was angry. Everything I had planned for was ruined and never meant anything to me because of this.

My family and friends were with me, but I felt alone like I once did years ago. I was so weak from crying that I collapsed at the front door on the doormat.

Reflection 1976

When I was child, I remember when my mother first went out to work, after spending all that time at home with us. Well, I didn't approve of her going to work now. I felt devastated. I had always been used to coming home from school and seeing my mother in the kitchen preparing something nice for the evening meal, and now she wasn't there anymore.

I used to cry myself to sleep at the front door, on the doormat, and no one could take me off the mat until she came home and lifted me upstairs to my bed.

Well, I didn't want to get off the mat now. Oh, how I wished that my mother could come right now and take me off the doormat and put me to sleep, just like she once did.

Throughout the evening the news got worse, and no one thought she was going to make it. They had discovered that a blood vessel had erupted in her head, in medical terms "aneurism," that's what they called it. Bleeding to the brain sounded more serious. They had also discovered a lump. Well, this news totally made me lose it.

I had to do something, but what? How could I help my mother when she was thousands of miles away lying in a hospital bed fighting for her life? Well, the answer suddenly came to me. I knew how to help my mother, and that was by praying.

I got up off the doormat. I could just about walk. My legs felt like jelly, but I managed to make it to the kitchen, and I gathered everybody together, even the youngest child, and I asked them all to get down on their knees and close their eyes, joining hands together in a circle. I knelt down on my knees with them, and I started to pray. The words just flowed from my mouth. I felt as if someone had taken over.

God knows how long I prayed for, but the room stayed silent while I pleaded and prayed. The power of prayer had become my only tool over the past years, and it had never let me down. I knew that God had heard my cry and took into account every word that I had said and wiped away every tear that I had shed, once again.

I felt so strong when I returned to my feet. I realised that I had just taken everything to God in prayer. It was out of our hands, and in his hands now.

That evening my friend Heather took me out for a drive, to clear my head. She even made me go to the supermarket to get some shopping. She said to me, "You never know, Benji and Patsy might still come, and there is no shopping in the house, and the children are hungry." I had planned to do a big shop, but now food was the last thing on my mind.

I remember saying to my friend, "I don't think so. They can't leave my mum in that condition. I don't want them to leave her like that." My friend put her arm around me as I walked down the aisles. I was so weak from crying, and I hadn't eaten all day, so that contributed as well to how I felt. I felt like I was floating in a nightmare. This didn't seem real; none of it did.

I didn't even know what to pick up in the supermarket. When I got home I realised that I had just spent £100 on shopping, and most of it was things that I did not normally by. My head was all over the place. It's a good thing that my friend did come with me because if I had gone by myself I would have bought a load of rubbish. Heather was like family, she was initially my sister Mary's school friend, they had grown up together, but then everything changed as we got older, I and Heather became friends too. Every Friday night without fail, we would all be together, planning what we would eat that night, fish and chips, Kentucky, Chinese, we all took it turns to decide, we were all very close, we would all end up buying the same clothes, clothes, shoes, bags and hat, even if we were not together, After my separation from Patrick, and the realisation of a new beginning for me, Heather became my raving partner, we went to parties and clubs together, every week. Heather had been there from the start of my relationship with Patrick, and right to the end. And here we were walking around in the super market, late at night, and me feeling lost and confused again.

When I got home my sister told me that Patsy had called and said that they were still coming and that they would arrive back in England tomorrow morning. My father had persuaded them to leave. He told them that there was nothing they could do and that the doctors were doing their best. He told them that they should not lose their ticket to stay behind, and if anything happened in terms of improvement he would let us know.

I didn't know what to make of it all, because I knew that my father could not manage because he was not well himself. He was totally dependent on my mother. She did everything for him. I often wondered how she managed on her own, because looking after him was a full-time job, and even worse than looking after a baby. I knew my father's illness took its toll on my mother.

My mother was not exactly a young woman anymore. It was hard enough for me looking after him when he stayed in England for six months, but my poor mother had to look after him full time, so how was he going to manage without her? She was his rock.

Oh well, if my father thought he was going to be okay, who was I to argue with him? After all I was just his daughter, as he used to call me, and right now I didn't have the strength to argue about right or wrong.

I was too tired and weak from crying, and I wanted to go to sleep. I couldn't even think about Benji coming tomorrow. I wanted to go to sleep and wake up in the morning and find out that it had all been a terrible nightmare, but when I woke up in the morning, I remembered that it was all so very real.

Well, it was one big rush to get dressed to go to the airport. I didn't care about how I looked. Boy, what a difference a day makes. This time yesterday I was planning to go to the hairdresser's, and what to wear, and now here I was with my new hairstyle looking like I had just put my head in a socket, and as for the clothes I had planned to wear, I was now reaching for an old baggy jogging suit that had seen better days.

Chapter Seventeen

Prayers Equal Miracles

1998

That morning we were late for the airport, and no one seemed to mind. Everybody had adapted my attitude which was "when we reach we reach, they can't leave us anyway."

When we arrived at the airport, Benji and Patsy had already come through arrivals. They were greeting us like we were the ones that had just come through, because we had just arrived, while they had long since come out and were waiting for us. It was just as I had said, "They can't go anywhere." This was not the vision which I had for the day when Benji would arrive.

Everything I had imagined about the airport scene was not the same. I had imagined running into my husband's arms and crying because I was so happy to see him, but here I was just saying, "Hello, Benji, have you lot been waiting for us long?" I couldn't even cry whether I was happy or sad, because I had ran out of tears from the night before. My voice even sounded like I had a grater stuck to my vocal cords. This was a far cry from what I had imagined; this was a nightmare come true.

On the way back home I tried to be happy. This was the moment I had always dreamt about. I even used to imagine being carried over the threshold. Well, now that was way out of my mind. I was happy to see my Benji, even though I couldn't show it at the time, but sad to know that my mother was left all alone by herself in a hospital bed in Kingston, Jamaica.

How were we going to get through Christmas? What was going to be the outcome? The one thing that I appreciated was that my Benji and Patsy could fill us in on what really happened and what condition my mother was in when they left.

Well, she was in a really bad way because she didn't even know who she was; she didn't know who anyone was. Benji told me that he had carried her to use the toilet, but she never knew who he was. He couldn't believe what was happening, so he asked her again, "Ms. Gat, you really don't know who I am?" She replied no.

Christmas Day came; I wasn't really bothered even though I had been well prepared for it. For the past few years Christmas had now become a big occasion in our home. It hadn't always been that way, but that seemed like another lifetime ago.

For the past few years I had always pulled out all the stops to make Christmas special for everyone. All my family would gather at my house for the big event of the year. It was always a grand occasion. There was a feast fit enough for a king, presents fighting for space around the beautifully decorated tree, and music that filled the house with Christmas spirit. Yes, it was all happening in our home, but this year there was something missing. Worrying about my mother, and not knowing if she would make it, and worrying about my father, being alone on Christmas Day, just took all the Christmas spirit away.

Christmas Day came and went, and it was now January. My mother was still in hospital, and there was no progress, and the hospital was now saying that they wanted to operate; however, they needed my father's consent to do so.

My mother was moved to a private hospital because we felt that she might have a better chance and be looked after properly if we paid. We had started to communicate with the hospital in Jamaica. We wanted to feel like we were doing something instead of just sitting down waiting to hear from my father what her progress was.

It was difficult for my father because he had to rely on someone, anyone to ring and hold the phone for him while he spoke.

Well, my father asked us what we thought about the operation. He even said that he would agree to whatever we decided, so my mother's life was now in our hands.

It was a hard decision to make, but we decided against the operation, and I remember saying to him that it was out of our hands and in God's hands now. I was against it because it's like deep down I knew that if they operated on her, I felt that we would lose her.

I never gave up hope for my mother for a second. I told my brother and sisters that we had to get her here someway, somehow, because if we left her in Jamaica she would surely die. Well, we all put together; and my sister Patsy,

who had just come, went back to Jamaica to bring our mother back to England
to see if there was anything that the doctors could do for her here.

My mother came to England; God knows how my sister managed to get
her here especially the state that she was in. I was at work the day my mother
arrived. I didn't want to go to the airport with my family to receive her because
I couldn't bear to see my mother in that way. My mother had always been a
healthy and fit, always-on-the-go type of woman, and very strong, in body
and mind; so this was hard to accept. I had never known her to be ill, just the
normal things, like little aches and pains.

I remember telling someone at work what had happened to my mother and
the circumstances that caused her to end up like she had. My friend listened to
every word I said.

Rose was a very religious lady, and very spiritual too. I had grown up
in church, and I believed in God. I had faith, but I did not attend church
anymore, apart from going to christenings, weddings, and funerals. I hadn't
been to church since I was sixteen years old when I had my daughter Chantal
christened; however, I still believed in God, and I always prayed.

Reflections 1975

Maybe the reason for not wanting to go to church was because when I was
younger I was made to go whether I wanted to or not. I never really had much
of a choice where my father was concerned, mornings, evenings, during the
week, and to church conventions, all around the country, we were woken up
every Sunday morning and told to get ready for church. This made me rebel
against going. I was glad that I didn't have to go anymore when I was fifteen
years old and pregnant. Well, after I had the baby my father didn't bother to
force me to go to church anymore. But I found God again when I had no one
to turn to.

Well, my friend Rose looked at me and said, "Jackie, by what you have told
me it sounds like your mother has had a spiritual attack." Spiritual attack, what
was that. Well, she explained a little about it to me. I was shocked; but then
nothing surprised me anymore, not after what I had been through with Tony,
all those years ago, when I was eighteen years old.

Well, my friend Rose said to me that she wanted to get someone from her
church to come and pray for my mother. She asked me if it was okay to do
that. Well, I felt that I didn't have a choice. I didn't want my mother to die, so
I would welcome anything right now. Prayer had seen me through some tough
times and had always helped me, and besides my father had always told me that
prayer could move mountains, so yes, please send someone to pray for her.

That evening for the first time since I last saw my mother in Jamaica, I was
about to see her again, but this time I didn't want to see her. I couldn't handle

it, but I had to try. I arrived at my sister's house. She greeted me at the door and shook her head. She said, "Mummy's upstairs, but she's not the same. She's just lying there helpless."

My heart sunk to the bottom of my feet. Well, I walked up the stairs, but I could not go into the room. I was scared of what I would see, so I just walked past the room. I could not face my mother in that condition.

Well, it took me forty minutes before I finally plucked up the courage to face my mother, praying to God to give me strength to go into the room and to take away my fear of the unknown, just like how I had prayed that Sunday morning, before facing my father. This was my mother, the woman that had always loved me, and I never feared her once in my life until now; only God knew what I feared.

Anyway, I got up without thinking anymore, and I walked to the door of the room and gently opened it. As I stood there looking at my mother in the bed, I couldn't believe that the woman lying in the bed was my mother; she looked completely different.

Her eyes looked glazed and so far away. They looked like they belonged to someone else, empty, vacant. My mother's eyes had always shone. Everyone commented on their colour. She had hazel eyes, tinged with green. Her hair which was once shiny and jet black was now brown, and her face looked different. I told myself no, that can't be my mother.

I walked over to the bed where she lay. She looked like a rag doll. There was no life in this once-vivacious woman that I called mummy. I said, "Hello, Mummy," but she didn't respond like she used to. I don't even think she knew who I was at the time. She just lay there mumbling away, laughing, and pointing to the corner of the wall. She started to pick up things off the bed that weren't even there, and she kept on calling out for someone we didn't even recognise. She didn't even recognise her grandchildren whom she loved so much.

After a while we tried to put her to sit up, but she was helpless. She couldn't even sit up. What had happened to her, and why?

The doorbell rang, and I ran downstairs to open it. The two women that my friend had asked to come and pray for my mother had arrived. They asked me where she was, and I told them that she was upstairs. Well, the two women led the way, and I followed right behind them.

As soon as the two women walked into the room, they started to pray. They held my mother's hand as she lay there. She just kept on smiling and mumbling away as they prayed so deeply. I remember one of the ladies praying so hard and telling my mother to get up out of her sickbed, and then she turned around and said to me that there was nothing wrong with my mother and that she was going to get better. She told us that our mother had suffered some kind of spiritual attack.

The two ladies asked to see the medication that my mother was taking. One of the ladies, who I later found out used to be a nurse, looked at the bottle and read the label then asked us why my mother was taking these tablets. To our horror, the tablets were for someone who had a urine infection, and the other tablets were for people who had depression. It was only then that I realised that this was the reason for my mother's trancelike state. These tablets were to calm her down resulting in her falling in and out of sleep.

The women walked over to the bin and threw the tablets away. I believed that there would be a change. There had to be. I wasn't going to give up on my mother without a fight. I told the two women that I believed that my mother would overcome this because I had got down on my knees in my kitchen and held hands with my friends and family and prayed for her and that I didn't know how the words came about but just did, falling off my tongue one by one. Well, one of the ladies looked into my eyes and said to me, "You know that when you got down on your knees to pray for your mother, well, God heard your despairing cry, and the heavens opened up for you, and that's why your mother is still here today. It's because of the prayer that you sent for your mother. God received it." Wow, powerful stuff.

After they left, we managed to lift her out of the bed. She could not walk. She had lost the use of her legs. Whilst in hospital in Jamaica, they made her lie in bed and gave her medication that had no relevance to what had happened to her.

I held on to her right hand, and Benji held on to her left. My sister held on to her right feet, and my brother held her left. She had to learn to walk again. After walking her around the room, we then undressed her, and we all lifted her into the bath; she mumbled all the way.

After taking her out the bath we then laid her down on the bed like a baby. I thought to myself, *Look at this, this is what she used to do to us, and now the role had been reversed again, first with my father and now with my mother.*

I dried, moisturised, and powdered my mother, just like I had done to my father; and then we put her back to bed and tucked her in. I felt strong and full of hope that she would recover, and I did not shed one tear of sadness again.

Well, the following day I went to visit my mother. I knocked on the door; and to my amazement, lo and behold, I heard, "I'm coming, wait, I'm coming." When the door opened it was my mother, standing there saying, "Hello, Jack." You could have knocked me down with a feather.

I walked into the house not believing what I had just seen. I followed my mother into the kitchen where she was cooking a pot of soup and chatting away like nothing had happened. I couldn't believe it because yesterday when I saw her she was so far away, and today she was here with us. My mother had come back.

I was so happy. I just stood there silent, thinking that this was miracle. It had to be; there was no explanation for this.

I sat down with my mother and started to ask her questions. "Mummy, don't you know what happened to you?" She replied no. She asked me how did she get here and what had happened to her. I asked her again in disbelief, "Mummy, don't you remember anything?" Well, that was when she told me that the only thing that she remembered was not wanting to go to the nine night because she was tired. She had just come back from shopping, buying Christmas presents for Benji and Patsy to bring for us, but because my father couldn't go, he asked her to go and represent him at the nine night, so she went, and the last thing that she remembers is kneeling down to pray.

I told my mother that it was now January 6, because she spoke like it was still December 15, the day when this happened. My mother started to cry. She couldn't believe that she had lost almost a month out of her life and could not account for it, no recollection whatsoever, not even about the time she spent in the hospital. She didn't even remember coming on the aeroplane. She even asked me who came to Jamaica to get her, and this was incredible. She then started to cry. "So what happened to Daddy? What did he eat at Christmas? You know he can't use his hands. Who fed him? How do I know if there was any food in the house? How did he manage without me?" My mother bombarded me with questions after questions. I couldn't even answer one, because how did he manage without her? But he did. I found myself walking around at work, praising God and thanking him over and over again.

That day when I picked up the phone and rang my father to tell him about the miracle was a great day. He asked me where my mother was, and I told him that she was standing next to me. Well, he started to cry, and he said, "No, not that woman that left here. She was half dead. Well, this is like Lazarus who rose from the dead. You're telling me that she's better." I said, "Yes, Daddy," and I told him everything, that my mother could not remember, then she spoke to him. I wish that I could have seen his face at the other end of the phone. I could only imagine that he must have felt that he had lost her, but now he had got her back.

Well, she got better, and it was like nothing had ever happened. That was a nightmare that I would never forget but was finally over. My mother was back to her old self again. We did take her to the hospital to have a checkup, but they said that she was as fit as a fiddle. We also told them that we brought her from Jamaica for medical treatment and told them that she was in hospital for three weeks in Jamaica, with bleeding, and a lump on her brain.

My sister had brought the scan pictures, which the doctors in Jamaica had given to her. The doctor looked at the photographs, with a puzzled look on his face, and then told us that he could not see any form of lump or nothing to indicate that my mother had any of the following things that we had just told him. We explained to him the state that she had come to England in, and we even went as far as telling him that we had got someone to come and pray for her.

The doctor was amazed and told us that in all the years that he had been in this profession, he had never heard or seen anything like this in his medical career, and if he ever lived to see a miracle it was now. I remember looking at the ultrasound photographs when my sister first showed me, and there was a shadow on them, but now they were clear. The lump had gone.

The doctor asked our permission to send the photograph to another hospital, for them to look at it. Well, up until this day that photograph has never been seen again. It just disappeared; and no one, not me or the hospital, knows what happened to it.

My mother was returning back to Jamaica in better health than she had ever been. She had recovered very quickly, and we spent the rest of time she had left enjoying her company. Just being able to have my mother around and in the best of health was the best thing ever. She even managed to help us with the children and then after a few months went back home to my father, who was eagerly waiting for her return.

Chapter Eighteen

Confessions and Betrayal

2000

Benji had not been in this country for a month, when he hit me for six with his devastating confession of fathering another child. I couldn't believe what I had just heard. I had to ask him to repeat what he had just told me. I even told him to say it slowly so I could take it all in.

I felt as if someone had just slapped me in my face a thousand times. Here we were, in the kitchen washing up the plates, and enjoying each other's company, talking, laughing, joking, and sharing the chores, and all of a sudden, it was decided by him that this was the right time to break my heart. Well, it's not the first time I've thanked a man for opening up my eyes. "Thank you very much for being honest with me. However, your honesty has cost me my faith, my belief, and my trust in you." From that day, our lives were never the same again.

I tormented myself questioning our love time and time, over and over again. If he loved me, why was he not honest and man enough to tell me before we got married that he had this secret? Why was he not man enough to take the chance on losing me, instead of deceiving me? He should have taken hope and put it forward in his mind that maybe if I tell the woman that I love that I had made a mistake, would she not love me enough to forgive me, so that we could still have honesty left between us and try to mend the bridges that were burnt.

I had put on my trust in to this relationship. I never once thought for a second that something like this would happen. I was always honest with Benji, right from the very start of our relationship. Even when I was confused about what was going on in my relationship with Patrick, I had always taken the time to let Benji know everything.

I found this very hard to live with. I had put everything that I had into this relationship, struggled to get him here, working ungodly hours and doing menial jobs to get him here. He had been unfaithful to me. I hated him for putting me through this, while I was over here pregnant with his child, having morning sickness, day and night, waking up to go to the toilet every minute during the nights. He was in Jamaica, making another baby with someone else. I just could not get past the thought of it. All the letters we had written to each other declaring our love for each other, and here I am thinking it was all a charade. Even our marriage, that was a lie too. I felt so deceived like I'd never been before.

Thoughts of us standing in my father's church saying our vows raced through my head. "How could you," I screamed, "how could you stand in front of me, my parents, and God and know that you had this big secret?" I felt like a fool. "Oh my god, your family knew this, and they all sat down in the church quite happily, while we said our vows. How could you do this to me, to us? You've ruined everything that I thought was honest between us."

My bubble of happiness had just burst. I felt the bottom had fallen out of my world. I shouted and swore at him. I even slapped him in his face. At the time, I hated him for hurting me. Well, he tried to explain to me why this had happened, but I couldn't see beyond the reasons why. He told me that it was a mistake and that it was just one of those things; bad luck he called it. I was hitting out with so many questions, but the more I asked why, the more silly answers I got in return: "I was helping her out," "I was lonely." How was I going to live this one down? How could I ever trust him again? More to the point, how was I going to tell everyone? What would they say? What about my friends, who had thought that this would not work? What were they going to say? When I told them, were they going to say, "I told you so"? Patrick would probably laugh at me too.

I couldn't get over the fact that there was a child involved. If there was no child involved, then I would never have found out, because he would have kept that a secret just like he tried to do with this.

I tried my hardest to understand why he went with someone else, but no matter how hard I tried to justify the reasons why he did this, it still made no sense. I thought about all the letters which he wrote, declaring his love, and how much missed me, and that he would never look at another woman again. All of these letters written around the same time of his betrayal. When I thought about the time leading up to our wedding, when I arrived in Jamaica, and there were no preparations on his part, because he had no money, I now realised that his money was spent on hospital fees and items for this baby, who had just been born, the daughter that I knew nothing about up until now.

Well, I tried to get on with my life and put it behind me; but it was difficult because every time I looked at him, I wanted to hit him. Our relationship became a love-hate relationship. I still loved him, but I couldn't get past what he had done, and I told myself that if Benji truly loved me, he would not have looked at another woman, and I wasn't going to make another man hurt me like before.

Family life took its toll on our relationship. As the children grew bigger, problems grew bigger too. The boys became the everyday topic in the home. Drugs, alcohol, gangs, suspension, expulsion became a part of their lives. I became a victim fighting a battle with teenagers.

Benji worked at nights. He had been doing this for a few years since he arrived in England. I used to remember as a child hearing my mother and father talk about night work and how it can slowly destroy your relationship. My parents both worked, and at nights they both went to sleep at the same time.

At that time, I think that Benji preferred going to work than staying home and arguing with me. We had chosen to stay in this relationship. I couldn't throw him out. He was in a strange country, far away from his family. I had brought him here, so he had no one or nowhere to go, and I still loved him.

Well, everyone whom I told about his infidelity said to me, "Benji is a good man. Give him a chance. Just put it behind you, and try to move on. His baby's mother is not here in England, so that makes it easier." Well, that's what they thought, but it wasn't easier, and it still caused a lot of arguments. Sometimes we would not talk for days, so working at nights helped him to escape the battlefield we called our home. Benji hardly spoke about his infidelity. What little he said, I always had to prise it out of him, I guess he was ashamed and didn't know what else to say, or he was fed up of going over it again and again. He must have told me sorry a thousand times or more.

Even though this had happened, I couldn't imagine Benji not being here with me. We had come so far, so maybe in time things would get better between us, and I would learn to forgive him for his mistake. I figured that we all make them and should be forgiven for them. Well, that's how we learn.

Well, for the next few years I spoke to Benji about this night work and how he should give it up and find alternative work during the day, just so that we could spend some quality time together, and maybe that would help to heal the rift between us. I wanted us to do things like families do together, but that never happened. I remember him once saying to me that jobs are not easy to find and that at least he had a job that helped to support the family. Well, he was right, at least he had a job. I told myself, maybe I was being too hard, maybe I was a little ungrateful, and should be grateful coming from the life I had left behind all those years ago. Well, nothing more was said.

Anniversaries were vacant in this relationship. Valentine's, birthdays, and wedding anniversaries were just other events we celebrated with other people. Well, it became the norm, going out together just did not happen in this relationship; spending an evening sitting down in a restaurant enjoying a meal did not happen. Years passed, still no cards, no flowers, no romance, no chivalry existed for me.

Many nights I remember lying alone in my bed, thinking about the good times that we shared in each other's company, wondering if they would ever come back again. Feeling alone, I would tell myself that it was better to be alone than to be with someone and feel alone.

I suddenly realised that I had been feeling alone from the day my husband confessed his conscience.

The distance grew between us, like a malignant tumour, and silence did not feel so golden and dwelled in the midst of this relationship.

Arguments were petty and caused mostly by me. I sometimes felt resentment, trapped. That's what I used to say, "You should have given me a choice to stay or go. You deceived our love." Feelings of hurt and anger haunted me for so long. Letting go was slow and took its time each day to manifest to the next, then letting room in for forgiveness, however, not forgetfulness. I learned to move on quite a bit from how I felt when it first happened.

Chapter Nineteen

My Purpose

2000

Life became a lot more comfortable for us. We could now afford to buy whatever we wanted, within reason. There were two wages coming in, my cleaning work and his night work. Our relationship was stable. We didn't really argue much. I guessed I accepted what Benji had done and moved on. I was tired; we both were. I started to welcome back into my life the good things about Benji, the things that I had fallen in love with him for, and his kind and loving ways towards me and the children.

Benji was a good man. Despite everything that happened I knew that did not make him a bad person. He tried his best to make me happy.

Benji was a godsend. My life became so much easier with him in it. I didn't struggle anymore. I had his full support, and we helped each other in every way that we could. We were a team. We depended on each other, financially, emotionally, physically, and spiritually. I couldn't imagine my life without him, not ever. I would always say to him that I didn't want him to die first, because I could not live without him. I had to go first, then he would say the same back to me. It sounds corny, but that's just the way that it was between us.

I enjoyed working at the Manor. The Manor was a health and fitness club. I met so many people there and made so many friends. I didn't really think about the reasons why I got myself a cleaning job. I never really thought about the money anymore. Sometimes when the end of the month came and it was pay day, I didn't even realise because I enjoyed working there so much. To be honest I can't say that it was the job that I enjoyed, but it was the people that I met along the way.

Every day was different at the Manor. I would leave home at 5:30 a.m. to get there for 6:00 a.m., because that's when the members would start to arrive.

I was always on time. It wasn't easy to wake up at 4:30 a.m. and get ready for work and go out on the streets in the pitch-dark winter mornings, especially when the snow was thick on the ground. I had to learn the timetable for the busses in the early morning. I had to be really organised to do that, and I was. I would make sure that everything was in place for the children when they woke up to go to school in the mornings. All their clothes were prepared and folded neatly on the back of the chair, socks, shoes, underwear, coat, comb and hairbrush, cereal left in bowls, and their money for school left on the windowsill in their rooms. Everything was in place for the day.

I felt really bad leaving them at that time and not being able to see them off to school, not knowing if they had eaten or woken up on time or brushed their teeth. All those little things I would worry about. I remember picking Lourdes up from school with her jumper on the wrong way. Benji had to get her dressed and comb her hair in the mornings and take her to school then sometimes pick her up at the end of the school day. He used to tell me that he was one of the few fathers that he saw at the school each morning.

It was hard for him coming home from work at that time of the morning and only getting a couple of hours' sleep before he had to get up and get her dressed for school. Well, the other children were much older now and could help themselves, so they were okay.

My work at the Manor became more than a cleaning job. I loved being around the people, and they loved being around me too. I would always find the time for a little chat with them whenever I could. They brightened up my day, and I would do the same for them.

I became more and more confident around people, and everyone was comfortable around me. We were all like one big happy family at the Manor.

I began meeting people from all walks of life at the Manor. It was a private gym, so you didn't get any and everybody going in there.

While working at the gym I was able to meet a few celebrities. The first celebrity I met was someone from *EastEnders*, the TV soap. I always thought that if I had the chance to meet someone famous, or someone from the soaps, how would I react? Would I be starstruck, or would I treat them the same as everyone else? Well, I treated everybody at the Manor equally and with respect, whether they were famous or not.

I became friends with everyone. It didn't matter to me about colour, sexuality, gender, race, or whether they had a disability. We were all friends and respected each other. They never once called me Jackie the cleaner; it was always Jackie our friend.

Things at the Manor started to change for me when I realised that there was more to this job than met the eye and that I was here for a purpose.

Everyone started to open up to me in a way that I would never have expected; sharing their lives with me became the norm. People were strangers to me before, and now here I was supporting them in whatever way that I could. I became an agony aunt to them. Sometimes I used to laugh to myself because members would send other members to come and share whatever they were going through with me. Whether it was for advice or just a friendly chat I was always there for them. I remember one member asking my advice about having plastic surgery. She had just taken out a £5,000 bank loan to pay for a face-lift and wanted to share that with me, and what I thought. I would always try my best to be open and honest with everyone that would share their thoughts and feelings with me.

The first thing in the mornings if they came in, and I wasn't there that day they would inquire at reception if I was coming in today, and if I wasn't they were always so concerned, wanting to find out if I was okay.

At the Manor I was faced with anorexia, bulimia, cancer, and murder, people having to chose between lives. I knew what it was like to have bulimia, also being on the verge of anorexia.

I met a lovely lady called Jasmine. The first time I saw her was when she came walking down the stairs in her swimming costume. I stood their shocked by her body; however, I was able not to show it.

Jasmine had the most amazing pair of blue eyes that I had ever seen. They were so blue. It was almost like looking into a river, but her body was ravaged by an eating disorder. I don't know how she had the strength to stand up and walk, or even fight, to stay alive.

I met people with cancer who shared their experiences with me, and I thank them for that because they inspired me by their strength and courage of dealing with this disease. This made me look at my life and thank God that I was fit and healthy and able to come out to work and meet these people who had inspired me with their courage and determination to get well. They did not let their illness control their lives and stop them from coming to the Manor or doing things that they loved.

I was happy working at the Manor, coming home looking after my children. I still had my other four jobs, but the Manor was my main job. I felt that my life was now under control. I was earning money. I could afford to eat the best food and buy my children whatever they wanted and not what they needed. For once in their lives, I could now afford to buy the best clothes for my children. I could afford to shop in nice shops, and I could finally afford to treat myself to nice things.

The days of me wearing shoes with Kellogg cornflakes box insoles were behind me. I remember having only one pair of shoes, which were red. Well, they had to match everything I wore, even if my feet didn't want them to. I wore the red shoes so much until they had holes in the soles. When it wasn't raining it was fine, but when it was it wasn't. I couldn't really afford to buy many clothes, because I always put myself last and the children always came first. I made sure that they never went without; even if it was something small each week, I would buy it for them.

I even remember the days when I would look forward to when it was bank holiday, and they would pay us double money that week when we cashed our benefits. That was the only time when I was able to buy big, but the following week, I would pay the price for buying big, because I would be broke.

Well, now I could afford expensive price tags. I was living the poor man's dream, splashing out I called it.

I became a bag alcoholic, shoes mad, clothes crazy. I acquired a smell for expensive perfumes and shopped in the West End, Bond Street, Selfridges, Debenhams, and Karen Millen. All the expensive shops became my haunt. I even noticed that I spoke differently, socialising with people from different social backgrounds. This began to have an effect on how I spoke, and for me this was a positive thing. I found myself adapting to different people and adjusting to different situations. I spoke intelligently, and well spoken. I spent so many years hidden away. I became a victim of my own circumstances through no fault of my own, and now I was out of my shell to stay.

Seeing another side to life, I wouldn't have had that experience if I never worked so hard in my five jobs, running around from house to house, doing jobs I hated, sometimes standing at the bus stop in the early hours of the morning, crying my eyes out, saying to myself, "Look what I have to do to have a better life," waking up out of my bed at some ungodly hours of the morning and leaving my children at home to clean toilets, but as soon as I would walk through the doors of the Manor and see someone's smiling face, I would remember how lucky I was to be there, because if it wasn't for the Manor, my life would not have changed in the way that it did.

Chapter Twenty

Saying Goodbye

2001-02

Working took my mind off my father's illness. My father's health had deteriorated over the past few years. He was now eighty-three years old, and it was hard for me to accept that he was going to die one day soon. As a child the thought of him dying had haunted me for so long. My mother and father had started a family quite late, after being married for quite a few years. My father was much older than my mother, so I never ever thought about her dying. It was always my father that I would lie down at nights and cry about.

As a child you associate death with old age, so my father was older than my mother, so that meant that he would die first. Well, as I got older, I soon realised that this was not the case and that we all are not exempt from it. Death is not prejudiced. It just doesn't come to people that are old. It is not partial. Well, I cried myself to sleep counting how many years he had left before he died. No one ever knew that I used to lie awake torturing myself, telling myself that he had at least twenty years left.

My father wasn't getting any better. It was hard to hear about how much weight he had lost and that he could not really walk anymore and was now confined to his bed. He couldn't really eat that much anymore, and now he had become severely incontinent. It was horrible to hear those things about my father. He was wasting away, a shadow of his former self.

I couldn't cope with all this. It was stressing me out so much until I started to lose my hair, and I didn't know what to do, who to tell, where to go for proper help, and I didn't want to worry my family, so I kept the full extent of my hair loss to myself.

I was devastated because my mother always told me that a woman's hair is her beauty, and now I was losing my beauty.

Well, I tried all different types of lotions and potions. Tablets, vitamins, and hair products filled my bathroom cupboard. It wasn't about money anymore. I had lost a lot of money buying hair loss products, but I didn't care. I would rather lose the money than lose my hair. I became clever at concealing my baldness. I used to comb my hair in a particular way so that no one could notice except me. When I was at home I would wear scarves to hide it and right through the night. I couldn't bear to take it off. Looking in the mirror was the hardest. Benji never knew. He was the last person I wanted to know that I was losing my hair at the front of my head.

I became obsessed with looking at everybody's hair, on the streets, on buses, and everywhere. I just wanted my hair back. I was even jealous of my Benji's hair because he had a full head of it, and I didn't. I tried not to stress myself out too much over my hair loss, but it was easier said than done.

My father was ill, and I believed that played a big factor in this.

I had wanted to go to Jamaica to see my father. My sister Mary had gone earlier in the year to visit him, and she came back with a full account of how ill he was. She told me that he had lost so much weight and that his mobility was becoming less. He didn't really walk around anymore; he just sat in the same place that he always sat, on the veranda, just looking around and not really able to move.

I could just picture him sitting there. My father had always had his favourite spot on the veranda. He used to sit there for hours, just whistling away to himself or singing or playing his mouth organ. I inherited my father's musical abilities, because I could also sing, and I taught myself to play the guitar and the piano, but I never really got round to learning to play the mouth organ.

Well, it now made me sad to know that my father could not help himself anymore and now depended on all of us.

I decided that I had to go and see my father, whether I wanted to go or not. I didn't want to face him like this, but I never had a choice. I had always been a big coward when it came to facing things like this.

I remember my father as this big strong man, and now he was no longer the same.

One of my big weaknesses is my parents. I always fell apart when there was anything wrong with them. Well, I had to be strong and think about seeing my father. Right now it was not about me and how I felt. I had to stop being selfish and go to Jamaica and see my father for the last time, because his health was deteriorating at a rapid speed.

When I would speak to my mother on the phone she would always try to protect me from the truth. She never really told me the full extent of how ill my father was, because she knew that I would fret, and she was right.

I never really asked her how he was anymore because I was scared of what I might hear, and when I did pluck up the courage to ask, she would always reply that he was no way worse. No way worse started to sound bad. My mother said that he didn't really come out of his room anymore; that said it all.

With the help of my sister Mary sorting out our bookings, Benji and I were able to go to Jamaica.

This was the first time that I was going to Jamaica and felt apprehensive about it. I had always been excited about going to Jamaica, but this time was different.

The long flight to Jamaica made me manage to take my mind off everything, even my father; but as we got closer and closer to Jamaica, I begun to feel nervous, especially when the plane landed. It was a different feeling to the one I had always known, and loved. My favourite part of my Jamaican journey was always the ending, when the doors would open and I would walk out.

Well, this time when the doors opened, I didn't get that nice feeling that I knew; and when I walked down the steps of the aeroplane, the atmosphere was so different. It didn't feel magical. The warm air that embraced me always brought a huge smile from ear to ear. The smell of Jamaica that once embraced me when I smelt all the different types of fruits, mangoes, sour sap, neesberry, passion fruit, and coconuts all rolled into one, didn't smell so nice. I could hear the crickets and not forgetting the little flies that lit up the night. They didn't sound so loud or shone that bright anymore. I was scared.

In the airport I didn't have time to think about what was going on outside, because I had to concentrate on what was going on inside, so that took my mind off how I felt.

After checking in at immigration and finally getting our luggage and checking out, we were now free to get on with our holiday. Outside everyone was happy to see their family. There was hugging and crying, and there was this old man who had returned back home after living in England, after arriving there in the '50s. Being at the airport can be a right tearjerker and a real heartbreaker, because it can affect some people in a way they never thought could affect them.

It always made me feel sad and happy for them at the same time, because it reminded me of the first time that I saw my parents after they went back home to Jamaica. That's a day that I will never forget. I was filled with tears of happiness, even though it made me feel sad, because I had missed out on so many years of having my parents around me. Everybody looked older, all the children looking at me and wondering, *Well, that must be the lady in the picture. You know the one mums always going on about, Grandma.*

Well, my parents had always come to the airport to meet us and brought along everyone with them. I knew that my father's health started to affect him, because he stopped coming to the airport with my mother and now stayed at home sitting in his special chair in his favourite spot on the veranda. Just waiting for us to arrive at the house.

This time I looked around for my mother, but I couldn't see her. Where was she? My mother was always the first one we would spot when we came out of the airport, shouting our names, calling and laughing; but this time, she wasn't there. I didn't hear my name being called, "Jackie, Jackie." She hadn't come. Well, she sent someone to collect us instead. I was so disappointed, and scared because I knew that something must have happened for her not to come.

Reflection 1992

The airport journey was always like going on holiday. I remember as a child I used to love going to the airport. It was a wonderful experience, because the airport was not like the park where I went to play every day. We only went to the airport when someone was going or coming back from holiday, which was also rare. Just like being invited to weddings. How many friends do we know that get married every year? None. It's more like every five or ten years, if not at all.

It was a long journey in my mind, because I was lost in thought all the way, but a short journey. Because I was thinking so much, I didn't even realise that we had reached our destination. I was definitely going to face my father whether I wanted to or not, just like when I was a child if my father summoned me to do something. Well, I had to do it; and even though I was not a child anymore, I felt summoned to be here in Jamaica. This was something that I had to do. I had to be here for him because he needed me now, more than ever, just as I needed him.

I looked way up in the distance at the big white house that my father had built with those same hands that could not work for him anymore. The veranda lights were shining so bright. I don't know why, but I half expected him to be sitting in his favourite chair in his spot, looking down into the yard, waiting for us to come up, but I really knew that he would not be there.

I looked at his dream. This was one of the dreams that had taken him to England and had brought him back home, his church; he had also built that too.

I thought to myself, *Jackie, here you go*, and then I started to walk up into the yard onto the veranda and into the house.

My mother came out the house to greet us. It's like she was relieved to see us, as well as happy. My mother was my father's sole carer. He had no one else but her. She did everything for him, just like I had done when he came to stay with me, but that was only for six short months. Well, this had been for six long years without a break. Well, she didn't have to worry now, because I was going to take care of him the whole time that I was there.

There was a solemn atmosphere in the air. As we sat down, on the veranda, and spoke, I asked how my dad was, and my mum said that she could not leave him to come to the airport because he had taken a turn for the worse and that she was so worried about him, and she hadn't slept all night.

After we spoke without thinking I just got up. I prayed to myself and asked God to give me strength, as I walked into the house, with Benji and my mother following behind me. I walked towards my father's room, and I opened his bedroom door and peered my head inside before I walked in. I wasn't shocked at what I saw, but I was a little taken aback because my father looked different. He was definitely not the man that I remembered. He looked like a skeleton, just lying amongst the sheets. It was sad to see him this way, lifeless, a former shadow of the big strong man that I used to know.

For some reason I didn't feel frightened anymore. I didn't fear my father anymore. "Hello, Daddy, it's me Jackie. I've come to see you." I stood there looking at him. His eyes were closed, and he was talking to what I thought was himself. He stopped talking then opened his eyes and looked over to the right where a chair sat next to him. He paused as if he were listening to someone, and then he started to talk again.

My father had not acknowledged that we were there. "Daddy, I've brought you a present." I always used to bring presents for him when I came on holiday. My father loved presents, especially anything that was religious.

I had brought him a ceramic Bible which had the Lord's Prayer written on it. I had wrapped it up specially and kept it separate in my hand luggage so that I could give him as soon as I got there, but I didn't expect this. I then presented him with the gift, but he just stared at it as if it were nothing; he was not interested in my ceramic Bible with the Lord's Prayer written on it, because he was with the Lord. I now realised that my father was travelling far away. He suddenly looked up at me and asked me where was my uncle, his brother. He then asked me why did I leave him outside and that I should tell him to come in. I didn't know what was going on and why he was talking like this. I replied, "Daddy, don't you remember that your brother died two years ago?" He didn't even answer me back. He just looked away and carried on talking to the chair as if someone was sitting next to him. I felt despaired; my father didn't know that I was there or who I was when I spoke to him. I knew that he was on his way.

I sat down next to him, and I held his hand and looked at him. My father was in there somewhere, but was he?

His features had somewhat changed. I found myself resting my head on his chest. I could almost see his heart beating. I lay there for a while, praying that if my father was going to pass away, please God let it happen now while I am there. It's like I was willing it to happen. I couldn't bear to see him just lying there lifeless anymore.

I pulled the sheets from off his legs. Oh god, those big strong legs that used to chase us around the garden were gone, replacing them with what looked like two sticks. I didn't want to see him suffer anymore, because we were all suffering. Along with him we were all going through this together.

While I was lying down next to him I was also praying. Well, at this very moment, all my fears of him dying had gone.

I thought back to the time that I nursed him when he stayed with me, how I had felt honoured by God to be the one to take care of him. The last honour that I would have wanted was for me to be there when he did pass away. I got up from off the bed and left his room.

All night I couldn't sleep because I could hear my father having a conversation with the unseen guest which had invited himself into his room, and guiding him on his way.

This went on all night. Well, my mother came into my room, and she started to cry. "Jackie, how am I going to manage without him?" I said to her, "How are we all going to manage, but we will."

That morning I prayed again before I got out of bed, because there was no way that I could spend three weeks in Jamaica and listen to this. My father had not stopped talking. I listened right through the night.

He still didn't know who I was when I brought him a cup of coffee in the morning. He shook his head, looking at me really perplexed, and then he said, "Who is this woman giving me sweet soup to drink? Get out of this room." I couldn't believe he was telling me to get out. My father never ever spoke to me that way before. Maybe it was wishful thinking on my part that he would drink the coffee, and everything would be the same way that it used to be.

My father had always loved when I made him a cup of coffee. He always used to say to me that no one could make his coffee like I could. I was making coffee for my father from the age of years old just the way he loved it, with a pinch of salt.

That day I spoke to my brother Perry on the phone and told him what I had witnessed, and I even told him that I believed that our father was on his way out. My brother lived in Miami, Florida, which was only an hour or so away, so he was able to get on a flight and come over straightaway. Perry was my father's first son, from another relationship. He was much older than us, My father had him when he was a young man, leaving him behind to start a new life in England, however sending for him, once they had settled into their new life in England,

My mother took Perry as her son, she loved him just like he were her own, funny thing was, she was not that much older than him herself, I use to think to myself that they looked more like husband and wife than my father did. My father was much older than my mother,

Perry was the most gorgeous looking man, in those family snaps, and he had the sweetest voice, all the women loved Perry, all different nationalities, Spanish, Italian, Indian, Morrocan. Perry was the man, that that they all loved at the same time, I couldn't blame them, especially when I looked at his photographs., not only was he a pretty face, he had the most amazing speaking and singing voice that I had ever heard, such a gentle beautiful tone, which mesmerized you. Perry lived in Florida, so we never really got a chance to really see him any more, only when we went to Jamaica, that's where we would all meet up, just like now, I needed him here in Jamaica with me, not in Florida, I needed his support, and after all, I felt that he had a right to know how ill his father was. So on the plane he jumped.

Well, my brother arrived that evening. I hadn't seen him for years, so meeting him in such circumstances was not something I expected. I always thought that when I would next see him it would have been like the first time when I came to Jamaica and all the family was there, and we were all happy.

That evening my brother and I sat in my father's room. He sat on the chair, and I sat on his bed and held his hand. He still didn't know that we were there. My brother and I just sat there staring at him, lost in our own thoughts. Well, something happened which really shocked me. I could not believe what happened next, but my father looked at me, then he looked at my brother, and he said, "Perry, Jack, is that you?" and then he started to cry. My father had just realized that I was there, and from that moment everything was okay. My father came back to me. I couldn't explain what had happened to him, but I now truly believe that if I had not gone to Jamaica to visit him he would have passed away, because I felt that he was on his way out, and something brought him back. My brother was happy to leave him after spending three days; he had to return back to work, in Miami, Florida.

For the next three weeks I did everything for him. I washed, fed, and cleaned him; I made sure that my mother did not do a thing. I would sit in his room, and we would talk for hours, until my throat was so dry. There was nothing left unsaid; we covered everything.

We talked about the good old days. We talked about the bad times too. I remember my father asking me to forgive him for whatever wrong he may have done to me when I was younger, for the way that he treated me when I was pregnant with my first child, for punishing me when I was a child. He then added, "You were all good children and didn't deserve some of the punishment that I gave to you all." My father was confessing and asking for forgiveness.

We spoke about everything. We left no stone unturned. We laughed, and we cried, and my father asked me about everyone he used to know back in England. He wanted to know what had happened to them. Were they still alive or dead? He wanted to know everything. I didn't want to leave him for a second. I wanted to spend all the time that I could with him, because I knew that I may not get that chance again, and this could be the last time that I had this special time with my father.

My husband, Benji, was a great help to me and my father. He would always come into the room and take over so that I could get a break. We would share looking after my father. Even though he had lost so much weight he was still heavy to lift. God knows how my mother managed to lift him. I had the highest respect for her, not only as a mother but also as a wife. If ever there was a woman who practiced and preached her wedding vows, in sickness and in health, till death do us part, it was my mother.

My mother was seventeen years old when she married my father, and she loved and respected him, even now. My father was seventeen years older than my mother, and he respected and worshipped the ground that she walked on; they were inseparable. He was her right arm, and she was his, so you could imagine how difficult it was for her seeing this big strong man that had always loved and protected her just lying there unable to even move, just a shadow of himself.

I remember my father asking me what day it was. He had lost all sense of time. He didn't even know what day or year it was anymore. He didn't even know if it was day or night, because he had not left that room for a long time.

Well, our time in Jamaica was coming to an end, and I started to feel really sad, because I knew that this would be the last time that I saw my father. I didn't know how to tell him that I was leaving the next day. It was so hard. Every time I tried to, I couldn't tell him, because he was so happy that I was there. How could I tell him that I was leaving tomorrow?

The next morning we started packing. I found that so hard because not only was I thinking about leaving him, and not seeing him again, I was thinking about my mother too.

Sometimes when I was caring for my father I used to wonder to myself how in God's name did she cope. I could see that my father had now become a burden on her, something that he would never have wanted to be.

She was suffering so much. My mother had always taken pride in the way she looked. She was a very elegant woman, who was always well dressed and very coordinated, and her hair had always been nicely combed. That was not the case now. She hardly left the house. Her hair was out of place. She never had the time to even have a bath during the days because as soon as she woke up she was at my father's mercy, from morning until night. She never cared about the way she looked anymore. She would have the same old dress on, walking around the house, with sadness in her eyes.

My mother never used to be like that. She was always laughing, but now there was nothing to laugh about.

It was time to leave; all our cases were packed and waiting outside for us, but there was one last thing that I could not get myself to do, and that was to tell my father that I was leaving. The words couldn't come out. Benji saw that I was finding it hard to tell him, so he came into the room, and he said, "Father, we are leaving. We're going back to England." Well, my father looked at me and said, "Are you leaving already? You've only just come." I replied, "Daddy, we have been here for three weeks now, and even if I was here for three months, Daddy, I would still have to go." Because my father was bound to his room for so long, three weeks was just like one big long day, and he didn't realise that.

I didn't expect my father to say what he said, "Take care, daughter, and I hope to see you again one day, but not in this life but the next. I know that I will see you again, but until then take care of yourself." My father was telling me goodbye for the last time because he knew, just like I knew, that I wasn't ever going to come back to Jamaica and see him lying in that bed again.

I stood there with a lump in my throat, trying to be brave. I replied, "Daddy, I love you," and I bent down and hugged him, knowing it was the last time that I would ever put my arms around him. I turned and walked away, without looking back, as the tears started to fall. I didn't want him to see me cry, because knowing my father he would say, "What are you crying for? I never came here to turn into stone. You know that one day I would have to go home to my Lord." I was used to that way of talking from him. My father's outlook on death was always blasé. I used to wish that I could be like my father and have the same outlook on life as he did.

I walked out of the room with tears cascading down my cheeks and walked out onto the veranda, where someone was waiting to take us back to the airport. As I was just about to get into the van, I turned around and went straight back into the house to see my father for the very last time. This was something that I would always do whenever I was leaving Jamaica. I would walk from room to room just gathering up all the good memories of time spent in those rooms.

But this was a different kind of memory, good and sad. I peered my head through the door, before I walked in. I then bent down and whispered in his ear, "Goodbye, Daddy," and then I left.

After arriving back home in England, it wasn't that long before his health deteriorated again. This time my sisters were with him, but he had gone back to how he was when I first saw him. He did not know them, and he had started to talk to the unseen visitor again.

My father passed away on February 28, 2002. It broke my heart when I heard that he had gone. I was devastated, but in a funny sort of way I felt relieved. He was gone from this world but not from my heart.

I thank God that I was able to be there for him when he needed me. This was the second time that I had felt honoured to be a part of my father's life when he was ill. Someone had brought my father back to me, and I had him for three whole weeks. We laughed, we cried, and we said goodbye, and I am happy to know that I had the opportunity to do that.

Chapter Twenty-One

Feelings of Gratitude

2002-03

My life changed again after my father died, for the better. I began to realize that my father wasn't just my father. He was everyone's. People looked up to him in a way that amazed me. They spoke about him with the highest respect. They spoke about the qualities which made him the person that they had known and loved.

My father devoted his time to helping people. My mother always used to say to him that he would take the shirt off his back or give his shoes away, and he did.

One of the greatest things that I saw my father do was to give a pair of his shoes to a young boy, who didn't have any shoes to wear.

Reflection 1998

It was the morning after my wedding. A little boy who lived across the road had come up to help wash up the pots. Well, I remember asking him if he came to the wedding. He told me that he was there; however, he stood outside the church. I remember asking him why he didn't come into the church. Well, he told me that he didn't have a pair of shoes on his feet, and that he couldn't come in the church barefoot.

At the time, my father's feet were swollen so badly. My father was a man of many shoes, which he could no longer wear, because they could no longer fit his feet. The shoes were stacked neatly on top of each other, gathering dust, so my father called the boy and gave him a pair of shoes. This made my father feel sad. He said, "Imagine I have so many pairs of shoes, and not one can fit me, and this boy didn't have a pair of shoes to come to church." Well, my father even said to him that he didn't have an excuse not to come to Sunday school now. You should have seen the look on this little boys face, when I presented him with my father's brand new shoe still in the box, well that was the first time in his life that someone had given him a pair of shoes, something great as a pair of shoes, to wear on his feet, it never mattered to him if they never fit properly, as long as his feet could sit in them, then that's all that mattered to this boy.

Well, a few years later, and the morning after my father's funeral, I looked out the window and saw someone standing at my father's grave. I put my slippers on and walked down to the church to see who it was. It was the young boy whom my father had given his shoes to. He stood there with his head bowed. We both stood in silence as we looked down at the grave. He then said to me, "Ms. Jackie, I remember when I didn't have any shoes, and your father called me and gave me a pair." I will never know another man like Father. I felt so proud to stand there and hear someone say that about my father.

When my father was alive he supported people in so many ways. They would always come to him for help, whether it was financial, or just to tell him what they were going through. My father would always listen, and they would even ask for his advice.

I loved and respected my father even more now than when he was alive, just like when we grow to respect an artist like Bob Marley or Eva Cassidy, through their music; but only after they die do we realise how influential their music really is. Well, that's how I thought of my father now, and I wanted to be just like him, and I told myself that all the time from then on.

I found out great things about my father after his death, and I believed that helped me to move on and be strong. I even found myself thinking like my father. I dedicated my time to helping others as much as I could, and when the opportunity did arrive where I could help someone, I never turned it down.

I adapted a new positive attitude to my life and everyone, especially at the Manor where I worked.

I had changed. I spoke openly about my father's death. I told them about the wonderful and unexplainable experiences and confirmation that I had encountered after my father's passing, which made me know that my father was always with me. Even though he was no longer here I could still feel his presence around me. I felt special because my father had now become my guardian angel.

I found ways of coping with my loss. One of them was watching programmes about mediums coming into contact with loved ones. That helped me so much because I wanted to try and understand more about death. I wanted to know where my father was. I was anxious to hear his voice. I just wanted to know if he was okay. I would get comfort from speaking to my father each morning. I would get off two stops before and walk up the long road. I just wanted to let my father know what was going on in my life, but I guess he knew that anyway.

Walking along and talking out loud, if anybody heard me they would have thought that I was crazy. Having this relationship with my father even after he had died helped me in a way that I never ever imagined. I did this for one year. One day I realised that one day had passed and I never thought about him that day; however, I felt guilty.

That one day turned into two, then three, and that's when I realised that I was moving on.

I attracted members at the Manor, who were going through their own loss. They admired me for my strength and the courage that I had shown all around. I became someone that they could share their loss with, no matter if it was recent or happened years ago. They felt that they could come and share their experiences with me.

That was healing for me and also made me realise that I was blessed and that I was able to have that time with my father.

I was empathetic towards strangers who were coming up to me and just sharing their loss with me. I couldn't believe how these people were standing talking to me after everything that had happened to them. They inspired me in a way that I had to thank God for what I still had, because having to choose between your mother and your son when your car is on fire is something that you could never imagine going through, but someone had to choose between the two people she loved, her mother and son, and she was standing right in front of me, talking about it so openly. I admired her even though she suffered at the time because of the choice that she had to make. I was in awe. How do you make a decision like that: your mother who gave life to you or your son whom you gave life to? God knows how she got through that, but she did, and she now was able to share her loss with me. Another person also shared her loss with me. It was such a terrible tragedy, and a terrible loss. Her brother went on holiday and was found murdered on Bondi Beach in Australia. Her parents were so distraught they could not go to identify him, so she had to do one of the saddest things that no one wants to do, identify your loved one's body, which was badly decomposed and left in lying on a secluded part of the beach. The only thing that he could be identified by was a bracelet that they had found on his wrist, which she had given him for Christmas.

After arriving back in England, her sister could not handle the pain of losing her brother and later committed suicide. Hearing what had happened to other people helped me to move on. I felt privileged that they would do that for me. We both shared our losses and helped each other in different ways.

I became happy, and I just couldn't understand why. I had embraced my father's death in a positive way. Even though I still missed him terribly, I had accepted everything.

I walked around with a smile on my face, and I found myself singing all the time. I never really used to sing that much in the past because of everything that I was going through. I forgot how to sing, but I was singing again, and it felt good. I didn't feel alone anymore, I always felt that my father was with me. I just couldn't explain the joy that I felt inside. I became positive about everything, and I soon discovered two hidden talents that I never knew I that I had, performing and writing.

I started to perform as a comedian, and I wrote my own jokes. I had discovered another side of me that I never knew that I had. I created a character out of my imagination, and I named her Ms. Meryl Brown.

I have often been asked by people what made me want to dress up as an old lady and tell jokes. My answer to that question is I don't know. It's not something that I had ever wanted to do, getting up on stage and dressing up as someone else to make people laugh. It's not something you get up and say that you're going to do, but this was different.

When I was dressed as Ms. Meryl I was no longer Jackie. I loved making people laugh, because laughter is one of the best medicines there is.

As Ms. Meryl would make people laugh, as Jackie I was now going through some personal issues with my eldest son, Michael. Amidst everything that I had gone through with my father, I had a serious problem with my son. I never really spoke about it to anyone. I don't think that I ever confronted this problem. Maybe it was because I didn't want to feel like I was a failure, so I just carried on as normal and didn't confront these issues.

My son Michael began drinking at the age of seventeen years old. He would come home with cans of beers and go to his room where he would sit down by himself and drink. He had also started to smoke cannabis. I didn't approve of his lifestyle, and I spoke to him about this on numerous occasions. He would always say, "This is my life, and if I want to drink, then I will." He also had a lot of issues going on in his life at the time that may have contributed to his drinking problem, but he would not talk to anyone in the family about what was going on in his head.

He was expelled in the last year of going to school; it wasn't that long before he found himself a job, as a welder. Going to work was a positive thing for him at the time, after being kicked out of school.

He became independent, and he was able to buy his own clothes, trainers, television, and his stereo. Michael always took pride in his appearance, and his room was always spotless. He was always a private child. He never really liked anyone going into his room or touching his belongings, so we always respected that. Michael was my second son. After me and his father separated, Tony never really bothered about him anymore, that was such a shame because Michael was the carbon copy of Tony, just like Raymond was the spitting image of Patrick.

Reflection 1993

Michael had the darkest complexion out of all my children, no one believed that he was my son, there was no resemblance at all. all I was proud of Michael's complexion, I had always admired dark skin, maybe because mine was so fair, I was always asked by the other children when I was younger, if my father was a white man, even if he came to parents evening, and they saw that he was black, they would still ask, Michael had the look of an apache Indian, complimented by his darker skin, he was a beautiful child, mischevious, and grew at a fast rate, he sat upright unaided at the age of two months old, and he walked at 7 months old. Growing up, he had a coolness about him, he was well respected by all the children in the area.

They all looked up to him. Even the adults respected him as a little youth, we would be walking along the streets, and people would be calling to him from across the road, hailing him, he was only 10 years old

Well over a period of time I noticed that the drinking escalated, and so did his use of cannabis, and he was now spending his wages on his habit. Well, it wasn't that long before he got sacked for turning up for work drunk; this was a recurring thing that I later found out.

It was hard for his boss to let him go because they had always got on very well together, and he did have a soft spot for Michael, treating him like a son, but the drinking was affecting his work and his attitude towards people around him. He became very aggressive and offensive towards other people, so there was no choice but to sack him. His boss was very apologetic to me for sacking him, but he had to.

After Michael got sacked, I watched his life deteriorate right before my eyes, and there was nothing that I could say or do for him; he would not accept my help.

It was so hard for me watching my son's life go down the drain. He became withdrawn, and he hardly went out anymore. All he did was stay in his room playing rap music, drinking alcohol, and smoking cannabis. I wanted to help him, but I didn't know how, and furthermore he was in denial about his alcohol and drug addiction.

For the next few years I watched my son's life get from bad to worse as he became withdrawn and depressed and often spoke about suicide. He blamed me for bringing him into the world, and he would always throw it in my face, like it was the worst thing that I had ever done to him.

He would shout at me, "It's your fault why I'm in this world; I wish that I wasn't born." It broke my heart to hear him talk like that. It's like he hated me for giving him life.

Things were so bad in the household, and everyone had become affected by what was going on. As a family we tried to deal with it, but this was something that was bigger than anything you could imagine going through with your child.

I felt like I was losing my son, and I didn't know who or where to turn to; we both became victims.

His friends started to disappear one by one until they were all gone. All he did was just drink, get aggressive, and hurl abusive words at me and his siblings. He became angry at us all, especially me. What had I done so bad to make him hate me like this? I felt that I had failed him as a mother. He never really knew his father that well, because we separated when he was a baby. I was the one that had always been there for him, and now he hated me for it.

The years passed without me really telling anyone how big this problem was. Not even my sister Mary knew the full extent of what we were going through, because I never really told her. I guess I was too ashamed and didn't want to accept this.

After everything that I had gone through in my life, I never thought that I would have to deal with something like this, and from my child, whom I had always been there for.

My life seemed to be on track. I didn't have the best jobs in the world, but it paid the bills, and I was happy because I could afford to treat myself and my family to whatever they wanted. I had always done without so that my children could have, so what did I do wrong? I asked myself, was I being punished for something I had done in the past?

Well, I tried to carry on as normal; going to work was like a release for me. It took me away from what was going on at home. I would go into work with a smile on my face, but inside I was crying. I found going home very difficult because of what was happening there. I always wished that I didn't have to go there. I remember standing outside my home wondering if I should go in or not. I wanted to carry on walking past my house. It didn't feel like home anymore.

Well, things couldn't have got any worse, that's what I thought until I found out that I was pregnant. I was so distraught. How I could bring another child into a home like this one? When all this was going on, I saw how my younger children were being affected by it, and now this baby. How could I cope with a baby when I was coping with all this?

All my energy went into trying to help my Michael, worrying about his health and what drugs and alcohol were doing to his health, but it became a no-win situation. I felt like I was fighting a losing battle, so finding out that I was pregnant was the worst thing that could have ever happened to me at this point in my life.

I was happier in my relationship with Benji. Things were much better than they had been, and we only had one child from our relationship. It would have been a blessing to have another one, but I told myself that I couldn't. If our circumstances were different, then I would have welcomed another baby into our lives, but no, not while this was going on.

I had always wanted to have another child with Benji. Even though this baby was unplanned he would still have been loved and wanted very it just as much, but how could I? So I made up my mind that I could not have this child. I remember my husband pleading with me not to have a termination. He said that we couldn't murder this baby because of my Michael.

I found every excuse there was in the book not to have the baby. I even told him that the house was too small, and we didn't have enough space or room for this child. I even said that I couldn't give up my job, because I didn't want to go back to having nothing, and I had become independent. I was also doing my comedy act with Ms. Meryl at the time. I tried to convince myself that it just couldn't work, but deep inside I was hurting, because I did want my baby.

I thought back to when I was a sixteen-year-old and pregnant for the second time around and having to make such a big decision at a young age, to terminate my pregnancy because I was scared of what my parents might say. Well, here I was again, twenty-three years later, the same situation, pregnant, however different circumstances. This time it wasn't my parents; it was my son.

I agonised day and night over a decision. I was confused, and no one understood how I felt. I remember sitting in the waiting room, waiting to be seen by a doctor. I didn't tell my Benji where I was going that day. I had read loads of information about abortion, different types and procedures. I was now at the hospital waiting to see a consultant to find out how many weeks pregnant I was. Well, if there was one thing that I remembered from that appointment was the nurse saying to me that I was making the right decision, because I already had six children. She also told me that she had three children herself, and that was enough for her. Looking back she was wrong to giving me that advice. Who am I to choose who lives and dies? That's what I told myself.

That day I really didn't expect to have a scan, but I did. That made it even worse. Seeing my little baby swimming around made it all real. I had tried to convince myself up until now that it was only a bunch of cells, not a real baby, but I was only fooling myself because it was a real baby. I left the hospital feeling deflated. I felt even more confused than when I arrived. There was now a date set.

That night I didn't really sleep. I just lay there thinking about everything, but oh so very still confused, termination, and it was only a week away.

I walked around feeling in a complete daze just thinking, *God give me a sign. Let me know what is the right thing for me to do.* I truly believed that he would, but I was running out of days and time, and I still never had the answers that I so needed.

I prayed that night and asked God to help me to make up my mind. Just show me a sign, any sign would do, because deep down in my heart, I really wanted this baby, but I was scared that having another baby would just add to my problems and hold me back from doing things that I was now doing.

Well, it was a Friday morning, and I decided to go shopping. I was still looking for answers or a sign from God. I decided to go and have a look at some baby clothes; this would confirm that I wasn't really interested in babies anymore. Only three days away from having this operation, and I was still looking for answers. Where would I find them? Would they be in a Mothercare, amongst the baby clothes, prams, and beds? No, it wasn't in there, because I was not interested in looking at anything that related to babies.

I walked out of the shop feeling nothing; I had to distance myself away from how I really felt, but I was really crying out inside for help. I needed someone to help me now. I walked along the high street, I just wanted to get on with my shopping and go back home. I came to a bookshop. Well, for some reason I just had to go in.

I walked along the aisles of books, just browsing the covers. I can't even tell you what type of book I was looking for, if any.

I walked along until I came to a shelf with some books. I pulled out one of the books, and it said on the front cover *Journey of the Souls*. Well, I opened the book and skimmed through it. I was captured because it was the type of book that I often read. I was always very much drawn to reading books on life after death, reincarnation, return to heaven, and many more.

This book was written so beautifully, and I wanted to explore more, so I decided to buy it. Well, I turned around to go and pay for this book, and I noticed that the shelf behind me was stacked with pregnancy and baby books. Without really thinking I just pulled one of the books out, and for some reason I just opened the book randomly, and it read due dates. I just could not resist looking at when my baby was due. Well, I scanned down the page, and I pointed my finger to the date when the baby was due. I could not believe what I saw. To my surprise my baby was due on the day that my father had passed away. I was gobsmacked. My baby was due on February 28, 2004, two years to the date my father died. Oh my god, that was the answer that I was waiting for, but I never thought that the answer would come like this.

What a coincidence, I thought, but no, I never believed in coincidence. I believed in fate, and I believed in God, and I always believed he would not let me down. I stood in the shop, shocked by what I had just seen, but happy. At that moment I had never felt so happy being pregnant. There was no way that I was going to get rid of this baby, especially now. This was a sign; but was it a sign from God, or my father, or was it a coincidence, as some people might say?

I remember that day standing in the shop in disbelief at what I had just read. I had to ring my friend Christine. I always told her everything.

Well, I told her what had just happened in the shop, and she was just as shocked as I was. We spent a long time on the phone trying to figure it out. This was amazing, a miracle.

I went home happy. I never even went shopping after all. I was too shocked. I just wanted to get home and take it all in. Maybe I was just imagining it. Maybe it was what I wanted, or I saw the wrong date, 28, instead of 23, but I knew I didn't.

I couldn't wait to tell everyone that I had decided to have the baby, or had that decision been made for me from the very start?

Well, I continued working at the Manor; I worked for a man called Vincent. Vincent always referred to me as his housekeeper, and he always said to me, "Jackie, what would I do without you?" He always made me feel special, nothing less than that.

Being a cleaner at the Manor wasn't the right thing to do anymore, but I needed the money, and there were people there that had become my friends. We were like family, so it was hard for me to just hang up my duster and say goodbye to the people that I had grown accustomed to seeing their faces day in and day out for the past six years.

They felt the same way too. It was hard; and I always wondered to myself what people at the gym thought of me when they saw me on my hands and knees cleaning the treadmills, showers, and toilets and mopping the floor and lifting the heavy Hoover upstairs. It didn't look right as I started to get bigger and bigger.

Waking up early in the morning and going to work in the cold winter morning with snow on the ground, God knows how I did that. Waiting at the bus stop heavily pregnant sometimes I could just about walk, but God only knows how I got through those days.

When I would leave the Manor, I would go straight to Vincent's house to do my second cleaning job. I would be so tired that I could hardly keep my eyes wide open. Well, before I could lift a bucket, I had to find a quiet place to sleep, in the bathroom on the floor, that's where I would sleep. I used to get a pillow and the duvet from the cupboard on top of the stairs and lock myself in the bathroom, next to the toilet curled up on the floor fast asleep. I couldn't help it. I was exhausted from working, but I never stopped.

I managed to work right until the end of my pregnancy. I remember at the beginning thinking to myself that there was no way on earth that I would pass the first trimester and that a miscarriage would be inevitable.

When I think about how hard I worked, I know that this baby was meant to be, because no one that I have ever known had ever done anything like this before. I also know that it was not the money alone that kept me there. It was the people, my friends that I didn't want to leave behind.

Well, I ran out of time, so I had to say goodbye. It was so hard because I knew that I was not going back after I had the baby. I couldn't. I had to move on. No matter how much I missed everyone, it was now time to move on. My friends at the Manor believed in me so much, more than I believed in myself. They always said to me, "Jackie, you shouldn't be here. You should be further than where you are. You are a very intelligent woman. You have so much to offer." No one had ever called me intelligent until then, but it was hard to believe because if I was so intelligent, what was I doing there cleaning the toilets? I never thought that I was capable of doing anything more than that, but everyone knew and believed in me more than I believed in myself.

Chapter Twenty-Two

New Chapter

2004

My son Marley was born on the twenty-first of February 2004. I was so proud of him. He didn't look anything like his sister. He was white, with blue eyes and dark hair. I couldn't believe how beautiful he was. Everyone was mesmerised by him. My blue-eyed baby boy.

Marley was my seventh child, but it felt like he was my first. I had always felt that way about all my children. I had never adapted that thought all babies are the same and that I have been through this before. I always felt like each baby was my first. The only difference was now I was a lot wiser, confident, and patient, not like I was all those years ago.

I was always proud of my babies and treated all of them like china dolls. They were special, but Marley, there was something different about him that stood out from the rest, and it wasn't just his blue eyes and ivory skin; it was much more than that, and it all became apparent to me.

I remember one evening sitting down holding this baby, his little eyes fixed to my face, while he guzzled down his milk, I held him so close to me. I knew he felt safe and happy. I could just tell by the way he wrapped his little fingers around mine and by the way he stretched out his little toes as he concentrated on finishing his bottle.

I remember being deep in thought just thinking about how my life was at this time. Yes, I was happy because I had just had my baby. Everything that I had gone through during my pregnancy, the feelings that I had at the beginning about having this child, and here he was. I asked God to forgive me for the way that I felt at that time in my life, and I just looked at my son with tears in my eyes, and I asked him to forgive me too. This wasn't the first time that I had asked for his forgiveness. I had asked him to forgive me the night I lay in my bed thinking about what different methods of abortion there were. I had been given information on various types that women could choose from.

I remember talking to my baby and telling him how much I loved him, but I couldn't have him because of the way that my life was at the time. My eldest son was abusive in the home. The house wasn't big enough. *Please forgive me,* I thought as I looked at this perfect little baby boy.

It was very difficult for me to even sit down at that time and to choose what method of abortion that I was going to use, or even my options, because I wasn't trying to get rid of the flu. This was a child. I remember the nurse at the hospital explaining to me what methods there were. "Oh, we can give you two pills, one you would take that day, and then two days later you would take the other one, and then it would be over." Well, she didn't exactly say it in those words, but that's what she meant.

I remember at the time thinking to myself that was a good way, because it sounded easier than going into hospital and having the operation. DIY, that's what I told myself; but when left alone to my thoughts, I realised that it was the hardest way because I would be alone, by myself, after I took that first pill. Walking home alone, lying down in my bed, and waiting for it to happen, wondering what was going on inside my body, is my baby dying yet, waking up in the morning, and thinking is he dead yet, no way could I go through that, knowing that I was going to swallow a little pill that could take lives.

I was responsible for this child, I was his mother, and I had a responsibility to protect him, not endanger his life. That's how I felt. Now I had to be sure about what I was doing because there was no turning back from this. No second chances, only one life, and when that life cycle ends no matter how long or short, I could not turn back the hands of time.

I could never live with regrets; that's one of the hardest things to do, to look back over your life and say I wish that I had done this or I wish that I hadn't. Your choice, your decision, has to be the right thing for you at that time; and whatever you choose to do, remember that you have to live with it forever. Good or bad, there is no right or wrong. Whatever I decided at that time was the right decision for my life.

Well, my son was here now, and there was no doubt in my mind that I had made the right decision to have him. Because of what I had been through I felt even more protective towards him and an overwhelming love for him, mixed with a little guilt. I wanted to make it up to him, and the only way that I could do that was by loving him, unconditionally.

All those thoughts came to mind as I sat holding this child. Well, something amazing happened at that moment. I looked at him, and I couldn't believe what I saw, my father's face. Yes, for a second I saw my father's face gazing right back at me through my son. I couldn't believe it. I thought I was seeing things. Maybe I was imagining what I saw, but I wasn't. I know that my son was due to be born on the day that my father had passed away, even when I had my first scan. The date was accurate as well when I first saw the due dates in the book, which confirmed to me that I was going to have this child.

Well, even though he did not come on that day, he came in between Valentine's Day and the day that my father passed away, three special dates, 14 Valentine's, 21 my son's birth, and 28 my father's passing. Seven days apart, I could celebrate Valentine's, I could celebrate my son's birthday, and I could remember my father, all special dates to me.

Well, after what I had just experienced I didn't know what to think. Maybe that's what I wanted to see, but no, that's the last thing that I expected to see. I couldn't even explain to myself, let alone anyone else, what I had just seen or thought I saw; so I kept it to myself.

I still missed my father terribly; after all it had only been two years since he passed away, so it was still early days. In the early stages of his passing I had thought about him every day. I dreamt about him all the time. My dreams were so vivid sometimes I even thought they were real.

One dream that I remember so clear was after my father first passed away. I dreamt that I walked out of somewhere into this beautiful garden. The trees were so green. The sky was a deep blue just like the sea. There were flowers everywhere, and the only sound that I could hear was the sound of silence.

I walked along until I came to a hilltop, and then I stopped in my tracks, because there I saw my father. He was sitting down on top of this green hill, just like he was taking in the scenery. My father had always sat, sometimes for hours, just looking out at the sea, at the trees, in the distance, when he was alive; and in my dream he was still doing the same.

His back was turned towards me, but I knew it was him. It was then that I remembered that my father had lost the use of both arms. I started to run towards him, shouting, "Daddy, Daddy, what are you doing sitting up here? You are going to fall," but it's like he didn't hear me. I called out to him again, and this time he heard. Well, he turned round, and he looked at me. I couldn't believe how well he looked. He didn't look like how I had last seen him, on his deathbed. He looked big and healthy and happy. I said, "Daddy, remember your hands can't work," and he looked at me smiling, and he said, "Look, daughter." He held both his hands up, and he said, "Look, daughter, my hands are all right now," and with that he started to wave them around for me to see, and then he got up, and he started to levitate off the ground and floated toward the deep blue sky, waving to me. I waved back at him, and we never stopped waving to each other. The farther away he went, the smaller he got, until I could no longer see him. He was out of sight, but not out of my mind.

I woke up feeling fulfilled, feeling happy, and at peace just like how I knew my father felt. It felt real. That was an awesome feeling and experience to have, and one that I still remember so clearly just like it were yesterday, and still feels so real.

Well, I had to take my baby out for his first visits, so I stopped at one of my neighbours. She invited me into her home and couldn't wait to see the little bundle that I was unwrapping for her to hold. She sat down with arms outstretched waiting for me to hand the baby over to her; and when I did, she looked at him and said, "Oh my god, this baby looks just like your dad. He is the spitting image of your dad. Can't you see that?" I said out loud, "Thank God, I know he does." Then I began to tell her what I had seen that night when I was feeding him, how I thought I had seen my father's face in his, how I hadn't told anyone because I didn't want them to think I was crazy or think that's what I wanted to see.

Yes, my neighbour had confirmed what I thought I had seen, and she was very serious about it too.

"Jackie, I can't believe it," she said. "No, this is spooky. Why is he the only child you have that looks like your side of the family? None of your children really look like your family. They look like their father's side. He is the only one, and he looks just like your dad. I'm not being funny, but that's your dad." Well, I smiled.

It wasn't long before everyone who knew my father started to say the same thing. I could see the resemblance in my son, even his facial expressions, the shape of his head, his nose, his hands, everything about him was my father. He was a peaceful, loving baby; however, there was one thing that I found strange. When it came to changing his nappy, he would always cry and try to stop me from putting it back on. He would twist and turn and kick. He just didn't want his nappy back on.

I remember one day I was telling my mother that I had a problem changing his nappy and that he always tried to stop me from putting it back on. Well, it was then my mother told me the story of what it was like for her when my father was ill and had to wear incontinent pads. My mother said that my father would cry because he realised that he had no control over the way his body functioned anymore. She said that he could not accept this at first; and he would always say, "Look what I, Bob La-Touché, has come to. I never imagined the day would come when I became a child again." And here it is, as they say, once a man twice a child.

I could hear the emotion in my mother's voice as it crackled, then she composed herself and started to laugh. "That's just what your father used to do. He never wanted to wear a nappy, and when he used to see me coming he would screw up his face. Even when your father was young, he used to say to his brothers all the time that he was going to kick them. That was his favourite thing, kicking."

My mother knew so much about my father because she had known him all her life. They had grown up together. Both their mothers were best friends, and they all lived in the same district. My mother married my father at the age of seventeen, so even though they had been married for fifty-six years they had known each other most of their lives.

Chapter Twenty-Three

Fighting Demons

2004

My life was a lot happier after I had my son Marley, but it was short lived because the problems with my eldest son, Michael, got worse. The drinking had slowly spiraled out of control, and I was also losing control of keeping it in the home.

I wanted to help him so much, but at the time I felt as if all the doors were closing in my face. Life seemed impossible. Who would help me to overcome this?

I had to try to help myself and Michael. I went searching for answers, through books and the Internet. I needed to get some answers. Not even the doctors could help me. They would tell me to bring him to come and see them. "Come and see us" would echo through my mind, because how could someone who could not admit to themselves that they had a problem with drugs and alcohol go and see a doctor willingly? The biggest letdown I've ever heard was "We can come to the home to see him, but we cannot promise to help because you do not come under our area. However, we can refer you to somewhere else." I was never referred to anywhere.

My home became a war zone. I battled every day to keep my composure, but things became so transparent to my family and friends, even the neighbours. I had become my son's enemy. He hated me for some reason, but I couldn't understand why. What had I done to him that was so bad that now he hated me?

I would always know when he was not drinking because he would be quiet and would not abuse anyone, but as soon as he got that pound to buy that cider, he was a different person.

I told myself that it was the drink talking most of the time, and not my Michael.

Drink and drugs had robbed me of my son. The demons of alcohol and drugs had crept into his life and stolen it away and were now controlling him. Now I had to find a way of justifying what was happening to him.

I was threatened, cursed, fought, and spat at. He bullied everyone that lived inside the house. It got so bad that I could not have anyone round, because I was scared of what they would think or say. I noticed that my friends had stopped coming around to see me, but to tell the truth, I was more focused on what was going on in my life rather than think about why they had stopped coming round. I never blamed them because I always thought that if the shoe was on the other foot, I would be scared too. Yes, scared, my friends were scared. I don't blame them. They were probably too embarrassed to even say anything, when I never once told them about what I was going through, good old me, always smiling through my tears. I remember sitting down with a friend, we were in the middle of a conversation that had now stopped, when he walked in. My eyes followed him around the room, praying that he would just leave, begging God not to let him start.

My son had become violent to everything and everyone in the house. The rap music that he religiously played inside his room now controlled his mind. The derogatory words and lyrics that came out of his mouth were so disgusting. He broke things inside the house and blamed it on accidents. Plates and cups would break, each day, to the tune of "It's an accident, what could I say." I stopped believing that because of the sound that they would make when they broke. It sounded deliberate, the sound of someone who sounded very angry.

His mind was plagued with suicide thoughts, and he now blamed me for bringing him into this world, and now he was punishing me for giving him life. I blamed myself for everything that happened to him, the drinks, the drugs, the suicide thoughts; he was punishing me.

Every time there was a confrontation he would always come out with "You watch, you're going to come in my room and find me dead one day." Oh god, I lived with that fear, because I felt that he meant it. How did it get this far for him to be contemplating taking his life and telling me that he would be better off dead? That way I wouldn't have to put up with him again. How could my son think that I would feel that way if he was to take his life, because if he did take his life, then half of my life he would take with him.

His behavior was out of control, and we were all at risk. I now had to choose between letting him stay and letting him go. As much as I loved him, I had now started to hate him and what he was doing to the family. I couldn't face him. The communication was gone. We never spoke to each other apart from when we were hurling abuse at each other.

We walked past each other on the streets, him on one side and me on the other, like two strangers. I had lost my son, and I felt that I would never get him back.

I used to imagine him standing next to me, at some family function, or going shopping together. I became jealous when I saw other mothers with their sons. I wanted my son back, but how was I going to get him back? Had it gone too far for him to turn back? I felt cheated and robbed. Was it my fault this had happened? Was I too busy focusing on other things to even realise that my son had started to drink?

Well, it was Sunday evening, and it was no different to any other Sunday evening. Everyone was on tenterhooks, just waiting for him to explode. Even the younger children in the home lost their voice.

Even the youngest children in the home lost their voice when he was around. They were quiet as mice. When he came in, they dared not look at him. They had become frightened of him; so had I.

That evening we were all sitting downstairs, apart from the baby who was upstairs sleeping. Michael got up and went upstairs.

I had become wary of him around the baby. I didn't trust him anymore. I remember one time he asked me to hold the baby. Michael had always been good around babies and younger children. They all loved him, and he always found time to sit down with them even if it was to have a go on the PlayStation. He always had patience with children. Well, that had all gone.

I handed the baby to him, but with doubt. I stood in arm's length waiting for him to hand the baby back to me, standing there anxiously counting the seconds, which felt like a lifetime; then he gave the baby back to me. He then said, "This baby is evil, and it was the devil." I never took what he said seriously, because he wasn't drunk, but then I started to think maybe there was something worse than the drink. Maybe he had schizophrenia. I even started to read about personality disorders, anything, everything I could find on the Internet.

It had got to the stage where the police were often called by me to the house. I can remember an incident when I had to call the police. My son was drunk and was threatening everyone in the house, even the baby. It all got out of control. He fought me for the telephone. He grabbed it out of my hand whilst I was talking to the police. "My son is getting violent!" I shouted down the phone. Well, I never got the chance to finish what I was saying, then he put it down. It wasn't long before they rang back, but I told them everything was okay.

That was just one of many incidents that carried on over time. Another incident that clearly sticks in my mind as if it were yesterday was when I locked myself in my room and called the police, whispering to them that my son was drunk and violent. I even whispered the address on the phone, like it was some secret. My son was standing outside the house, shouting and swearing and throwing stones at the window. I was so scared. I didn't even want to look out the window, just in case he saw me. I was alone. Benji was at work. I can remember my daughter Lourdes crying and begging me not to let him in, because she saw that I was going to go and open the front door. Well, it's not that I wanted to let him in. I was scared what he might do if I didn't let him in, and I didn't want the neighbours to witness this. I felt ashamed of him.

Another incident was when he threw a brick through the window, glass flying everywhere. Thank god no one was hurt. That night the police were called, but he got away again.

He had always gotten away from the police, about seven times that year. Every time they came, he ran out the house when I told him they were on their way. Looking back, I always deliberately gave him the opportunity to get away. How could I let the police capture him and lock him up? How could I do that to my own son? But I was left with no choice.

Well, it wasn't long before the police were here, running up the stairs. I could hear a clutter of footsteps and shouting as they reached the top. Michael was standing there with a bottle of brandy in his hand.

One of the policemen could see that this was breaking my heart, and he said to me, "My son used to drink, so I know how you feel, but there is nothing you can do for him. He has to want to help himself."

As the police handcuffed him, I asked them if it was necessary to do that, reason being was that my son had in no way resisted.

The police stood in between us, as I heard my Michael say, "Mum, are you really going to make them take me away?" Words could not form in my mouth. "Come on, son," I heard the police say. "Mum, Mum, what are you doing? I haven't done anything." Those words rang like a bell in my ears.

Things just got so bad, there was no escape from the drugs and alcohol which took control in our home. I just could not have him around any longer.

When I had first started my relationship with Patrick, Michael was just a baby, so you could say that Patrick was the only father he had ever known. He never had any contact with his father, Tony. I did try to contact Tony on a few occasions to ask him for his support. We were desperate, and maybe Tony could help, but it was a waste of time, because he always made excuses. Michael was this stranger to him, and I guess that he could not bring a disruptive influence into his home to be part of his family.

Well, Patrick decided to take Michael to live with him. It was after another argument. I had reached boiling point and wanted him out. My fear of Michael had now turned into anger. I was no longer frightened of him. I had lived with a bully in the past, and there was no way I was going to take this from my son. He had to leave, and now.

That night Patrick came to get him. I could hear Patrick saying to him, "Son, pack your things. Your mum can't live with this anymore. Your brothers and sisters are scared of you. You can't stay here." I could hear Michael telling Patrick that he didn't want to go. "Come on, son, you have no choice."

I watched Michael walk down the stairs with black bags full of his things. I wanted to cry, but I had to be strong. I didn't want him to see me cry, because then he would probably start begging to stay. I watched them get into the car and drive off, then I sat down and cried.

Well, it was only a matter of time before Patrick got fed up with Michael's behaviour and his drinking and then told him that he had to find alternative living arrangements. He had stayed with Patrick for almost one year, and that was a real struggle to keep him there. Patrick would always threaten to kick him out. He even said to me so many times, "Jack, he has to go. I can't have him here with me anymore. It's just not working."

My biggest fear at the time was that Patrick would eventually kick him out, and he would have nowhere to go, so he would have to come back home. I couldn't allow for that to happen. I never realised how bad things were at home until he left, and we got some kind of peace back in the home.

Well, I resented Patrick for saying that, but I couldn't blame him for feeling that way, because I had felt like that for the past few years, with no one to help me. No one was interested; they only talked. It was my problem, not theirs. I often thought to myself, at least they could go home and close their doors and forget about it, but me. I had to live with it, day in, day out. I couldn't escape from any of this. Where I would escape to?

Michael had to leave Patrick's flat, and he didn't have anywhere to go, or no friends to put him up. There was only one place to go, and that was the YMCA. I had always seen the YMCA as a place where down-and-outs lived.

Well, my friend had a sister who worked in the YMCA, and she was able to put in a good word for him, so he now had a room at the YMCA.

There was not a day that passed where he didn't come around. I used to think that he deliberately came round to cause trouble. The neighbours and their children felt intimidated by him. The children would scamper into their house when they saw him coming. "There's Michael," they would say, "let's get inside."

This is how everyone saw him now, a laughingstock. I even had to take out a written injunction, just to keep him away from the estate where we lived, because of the trouble he would cause when he was drunk. When would my son get some help, so this nightmare could be over?

Chapter Twenty-Four

In the Deep End

2004-05

I needed some change in my life. I couldn't just sit down and let problem after problem get me down. I missed going to work at the Manor. I missed everybody there. I remember working at the Manor, when my son first started to drink. I would always worry about my problems; however, soon as I got to the Manor, I had forgotten what it was that I was worrying about.

My friends at the Manor all loved and respected me. They did not want to see me go back, only forward. I remember my friend Jane saying to me, "Jackie, as much as we love you, and we'll miss you, and you make the place so lovely and clean, for us, and we thank you for that, well, we don't want to see you back here because you are a very intelligent woman, and the world is your oyster after you leave this place."

Jane was right, there was no going back. It was forward all the way. I walked through the doors, eight months pregnant, never to return; but I didn't really know what I would be doing next apart from being stay-at-home mum again.

I had gained my independence by going out to work, meeting people, and making a new life outside of my home. I loved the freedom which being independent gave to me. I had been working for six years now, and it was very hard for me to give that up, to stay at home again. I had spent so many years at home looking after my children, living off state benefits, and not being able to provide for my children in the way that I wanted to, so going to work opened up a lot of doors for me, and it also gave me a peace of mind, so staying at home all day was something that I had done before, gotten out of it, and created a working life for myself, which I did enjoy.

Well, Marley was now four months old, and I had started to think about my life again. Staying at home was starting to get to me. I had gained my independence out there in the world of working people. I had joined the workforce. Maybe I might not have had the perfect job, but I had a job that was putting food on my table, and my children were a lot happier in terms of being able to have things which they wanted.

I felt proud for that alone, to see my children smiling, knowing that I could afford to buy them what they wanted, and not just what they needed.

So here I am again a stay-at-home mum, with ironing up to my eyeballs, plates up to my elbows, and housework coming from all four corners of the house. As much as I loved staying at home and looking after my baby, I needed more.

I cried when I had left my cleaning job. Can you believe that? But it was more than just a cleaning job to me; it was a learning curve too, meeting people from different social backgrounds, races, cultures, and genders. We all became friends. I never really saw what was on the outside of a person anymore, only what was on the inside of the people that I had met and now called my friends. I missed everything. I was always a people person and always enjoyed good company. I had to make a new start, in my life. Having a baby didn't mean that I had to stop and wait until he started school. That would be almost four years from now. What would I do until then?

Well, one day I just woke up and without thinking just rang the college for a prospectus. I wanted to go to college, to be a midwife. The more I thought about it, the more it became real.

I had so much to think about, but that was after I had applied for a prospectus over the phone.

It wasn't that long before it arrived, and I filled it out, with my questions again, "Who would look after the baby? But the baby is too young for you to leave him. You won't be able to spend time with him. I might miss his first tooth. Maybe I should wait until he goes to school, but I could have qualified by then for something."

Throughout all my questions I still continued to fill out the application form and sent it off, waiting to hear my fate.

I could not believe it when the college told me that they had given me a place, after interviewing me and me telling them that I had just had a baby, and I had been out of education for over twenty years and did not have any other qualification. I thought that I would not stand a chance.

Well, here I was enrolling on a level 3 access course, which I later found out was the most demanding, rigorous, stressful course to do, especially at that level. It was later on after I applied that I found out that I could have done a preaccess course to prepare me back into education. Well, I was here now and could not turn this opportunity down, even with a baby, and no proper child care arrangements made. I remember saying to Benji that I had to find a childminder. I don't think he really understood what I had just said to him, because when I did repeat and elaborated on it, he said no way. He did not want me to leave Marley with anyone. He told me that he would not be able to sleep during the day if he knew that the baby was somewhere else.

Benji was adamant that Marley should not leave the house and that he would take care of him during the days while I was at college.

Well, my first day at college, I felt so proud of myself as I approached the gates. I felt like a child starting school for the very first time, happy but a little nervous and scared. The only difference was that I was a mum now, with no mother there to hold my hand and reassure me that I was going to have a good day and that they would be waiting for me at the gate at the end of the day.

As I stood there looking very much like the student but now an adult, very nicely dressed in college-type clothes, and my satchel, across my side, I wondered to myself, would I be able to cope with going to college, looking after my family, and a new baby? How would I manage to do my assignments and everything else? This was all new to me. What had I done? But those thoughts soon faded.

As I walked through the door, I couldn't help but find a little pride amongst all my emotions. Me Jacqueline La-Touché, going to college, seven children, who would have thought that, eh? Well, not me for one; sometimes I could be my worst enemy.

Well, here I was wearing my identity badge with pride, my face beaming with pride in the photograph. Jacqueline La-Touché was written across the top of the card. For the first time in my life, I felt like I was somebody. I felt like proud of myself for reaching this far and being brave enough to move forward for some kind of change in my life.

Having a young child and studying was the hardest thing to do. I don't know how I managed both, studying different subjects, reading different books at the same time, taking in a variety of information, and doing assignments by deadline.

I remember once having seven assignments to hand in all at the same time. I would come home from college, do the housework, cook, feed the baby as fast as I could, put them in the bath then bed, and glue myself to my computer. Evenings turned into nights and then to morning and I would still be glued to my computer. I used to be awake for the night feeds; that was not a problem waking me up, because I was wide awake.

I had something to prove to myself. I was eager to learn. My brain started to feel like a sponge soaking up water. I absorbed information in so many ways. I would even record myself reading, so at nights when I was lying down in my bed, I would listen until I drifted off to sleep, and when I woke up in the morning everything that I had taken in was in my head. I would be walking round in the morning telling the story of Florence Nightingale or how one man's dream, of the NHS, came into existence. I would even be talking about how the heart, ventricles, arteries, blood vessels, veins, and capillaries work. I was gaining knowledge of the medical world; it was amazing.

There were times when I did feel like I had got in too deep and was sinking; meeting deadlines stressed me out, until I would sit down crying. Thoughts of giving up came to my mind, but then I would fight those thoughts and feelings, then I would say to myself, "Jackie, you can't turn back now. You will regret it. All the hard work, all the commitments, and sacrifices which you made to do this would all be a waste of time."

I couldn't live with regrets. I didn't want my family and friends to see me as a failure. Most of all, I didn't want me to see myself as a quitter.

I now had the chance to make something of my life, and because the going felt rough at times these thoughts came to mind.

I'd never seen myself as quitter, but this was getting more intense as assignments after assignments started to come my way. My bag started to get heavier and heavier with books.

Over the next few months as the work poured in the pressure was on for everyone. I began to see my college friends quit the course one by one. It was really hard seeing that because I knew how they felt because I felt exactly the same way, but I had to go on. I had reached this far to turn back.

The access course was for one year, but the amount of work which we had to do, we were told that we had to cram in two years' worth.

Level 3, I made sure that I never got any less than that; I made sure that I never had my work resubmitted. I made sure that my work was of a very high standard. I did a lot of research and presentations and most of all learnt to use a computer, finding my way around the World Wide Web.

I couldn't believe it when I was one of two in my class who passed their IT exam first time round, considering I was the only one in the class who came across as computer illiterate, because when I heard the word *mouse*, I wanted to run.

I remember the first day when I walked into the college and realised that it wasn't pencil and paper anymore; it was computers. It was even worse when my teacher told me that we had to use Word. She wanted all our work word processed. I couldn't understand what she was going on about, "I don't want work handed in that is written by hand." That's what she said. Well, this was the way forward. "Word," that's what it was all about.

Well, I didn't let on that I was not familiar with a computer. Even though I had bought one a couple of months before I started college, I didn't get much chance to practice at the time, because everyone wanted a turn on the computer, and then when it was my turn, I discovered Amazon, for the music. I felt like a kid in a cookie jar. I rarely found time to learn to use Microsoft Word and learn to copy and paste, but when I did, I just exhaled. I taught myself how to do PowerPoint presentations and a lot more.

As my confidence grew, the months just seemed to fly by. The course was coming to an end, and there was so much work to be done in preparation for the coming exams, but fate dealt me a cruel hand, right in the middle of it all.

My son Raymond was arrested and charged with murder. The word *murder* still rings in my ears today, and I guess it always will, because that was the day my life changed forever, but not only my life, so many other lives too, including my closest friend Christine, because it was her nephew whose life ended that fateful night.

Raymond was guilty of not listening to me when I spoke to him. He was guilty of defying me when I told him to stop hanging around on the streets with the wrong crowd. You see, I had struggled to bring him this far, and I only ever wanted the very best for all my children, just like mothers do. I had gone without for them, and I taught them right from wrong. They were not without manners and respect too.

My parents had taught me from an early age about manners and respect, and how far it can take you, so that's what I always tried to portray to my children.

I can say that all my children had manners and respect for everyone, especially their elders. No adult had ever told me that they had sworn or been rude to them in any way. I laugh when I say that, because they say that we cannot vouch for our children, but if I am wrong for vouching, then please come forward and prove me wrong.

I remember my mother telling us that she knew each and every one of us inside and out, and our capabilities. Even when we became adults she would tell us, "I knew that you could do this. I could see it in you from when you were a child."

Well, she was right because here I knew that my son was not capable of such an unforgiving act, but he was still guilty by association.

That night when lives were changed forever, I was sitting down around my computer, right in the middle of my psychology assignment, a deadline to meet for Monday. As I sat down typing away deep in thought, the phone rang; it was my closest friend Christine. She was screaming down the phone. I had never heard her like that before. It was so frightening. She was hysterical. All I could hear was *murder*.

My friend Christine was my closest friend. I had known her from the age of thirteen years old. School days were the best days of our lives. We would look back and reminisce about the things that we used to do, or didn't, the places that we used to go, the clothes that we used to wear, even the boys we used to like. Me and Christine, had it going on, as teenagers, we had the look, we were the fashionistas of Tottenham County, second school, well that's what we thought, , we even had the personality to match, we knew it, so did the other girls. We were both popular, we got on with everyone especially with the boys, we had very good platonic relationships with the them, and they loved being in our company, and that's why some of the girls were jealous. School days, the best years of your life well that's what they say.

Well my life changed when I became a mum. I never saw any of my school friends again; we had all gone our separate ways.

Many years later Christine came back into my life, and from that day on, we never left each other.

We were like sisters, you could say. People even thought we were sisters. I guess they could see and feel sisterly vibes going on between us.

We always looked out for each other, clothes, ornaments, and food. If we both saw something that we knew the other would like, we would buy it without hesitating. Our homes were each other's. We always shared our tables together, our children were together, our families were together. Not only was I friends with Christine, I was also friends with all her family, and her family with mine. I remember her brother Curtis was so caring towards me. Well, he bought me my first shopping trolley, so concerned about my back. He would even buy clothes and bags. Every time he bought Christine something, he would buy the same for me too.

Christmas, birthdays, and weddings, we would all celebrate together as one big happy family. We spoke so highly of each other, and Christine was so supportive of me, and very proud too, especially when I did Ms. Meryl. She was always a step behind me. She was my biggest fan. She would always make sure that Ms. Meryl was in her full glory. That's how much we meant to each other until that sad night.

Well, that night when Christine's nephew was murdered, Raymond was at home with his girlfriend, sitting on the couch where they had spent most of the day wrapped up with each other; but now he was locked up, a category A prisoner, rubbing shoulders with the likes of murderer Ian Huntley.

I had to get him out of there because he was not guilty of the most horrendous crime ever committed, murder! You cannot justify taking a life, and you cannot get past the word, because that's all that rings in your head, so I can't blame my friend and everybody who turned their minds and backs against me when this happened. How could they not, when I was now known as the mother of the murderer. Well, that's what I was told.

The three Cs came back to haunt me again, charged, convicted, and condemned. According to some, my son was a product of me; so if he was guilty of such sin, then so was I. Well, I can tell you that I paid the price for such sin.

I missed my friend Christine so much. A day would never pass without us speaking to each other, even if it was just for a minute to say watch that film, documentary, or comedy at nine o'clock, even the adverts, or listen to the radio. How was I going to live without her in my life? I wasn't even given that chance to explain to her, because she didn't want to listen, and I don't blame her. She had lost a nephew, her sister had lost her son, her nephews and nieces had lost their brother, her parents had lost their grandson, his cousins had lost their cousin, and his friends had lost their friend. Even a teacher would have lost a pupil. I saw this as a chain of hurt; everyone was affected by someone else's mistake.

There was no way we could ever get past what had happened, and I had to accept that I had lost my friend, because she had lost her nephew.

Visiting Raymond was one of the hardest things that I had ever done.

I remember standing in the queue waiting to be searched for weapons and drugs, taking off my shoes and putting them into a tray, having my hair searched, and being scanned, before they would let me through. I hated being treated like I was a criminal too, because that's how I felt, week in, week out.

Because my son was a category A prisoner, he had to sit in a small room behind a screen. It was so hard seeing him like that looking defenseless and sad. There was no proper communication between the screens, and I didn't feel free to talk to him. One thing that he always said was that he was one hundred percent innocent. At the end of every letter, he would use that as his logo, 100%, etched in black felt tip.

I had to fight for him because I could see that he had become vacant. He hardly spoke when we visited, and his eyes looked distant and empty. They didn't shine anymore, and he had this weird smile on his face.

I remember Patrick coming back from visiting him and telling me that our son didn't look well. I asked him what he meant, even though I knew what he would say. Not well was his way of saying that he was losing it, in better words, "depressed."

No one could help him, not even the people he called friends, because they were locked up too. You see, they were all charged with the same murder, the same place and the same time, and my son was said to have been there, but how could he be, when I had seen him at home all day, sitting on the couch, wrapped up with his girlfriend. I even started to ask myself, did I really see him that day, and if I did, why was he here?

I began to question God, "Why did you do this to me at a time when I was starting to find my feet, when I was trying to make a name for myself, and a life for my children?" I asked that question over and over again, but I got no answer.

Over the next few weeks my life became a living nightmare, day and night, and there was no way of me wakening up for now.

I used to walk along the streets wishing that the ground could open up and swallow me. At the bus stops I used to wish that I was invisible, but the worse thing for me was that people whom I had spoken to before this happened were crossing the road or not looking in my face anymore; they were walking past me like we had never met before.

I remember standing in a shop, looking through the clothes rail, and opposite me was a lady that I had met at Christine's sister's house on the night of the wake. We were all standing in the garden just chatting away like old friends, and now here we were, standing opposite each other and looking through each other. I found those days very difficult to get through.

Christine was Marley's godmother. She was there when he was born. Well, she had to be; she was the only person that I had rung that day when I stood in the bookshop, just staring at his due dates, February 28, 2004, the date when my father passed away, my confirmation. Christine adored Marley from the moment he was born; she was the proudest godmother ever, always boasting to everyone about her godson.

I used to surprise her with visits to her workplace, baby all nicely dressed to see her, because I knew that she would be ready to show him off. "Here's my godson. Come and have a look at him." She even wanted him to open his eyes so that her friends could see his blue eyes. "See, I told you," she would say to her workmates, "I told you he had blue eyes." They all used to gather round the buggy peeping in at him.

Now here was my friend walking past me and Marley in the street with a blank expression written on her face. I felt so sad and hurt by this, but when I remembered that night, and the screams down the end of the phone, my heart fell to my feet again.

I had to move on and admit that our friendship, which we had built for thirty years, was over. I could not dwell on the past. I had to move on, and I could no longer punish or allow myself to be punished for my son's mistakes, even though he was innocent.

"If he was innocent, then why did the police arrest him? Why was he charged? Police don't get things like that wrong." Well, that's what I heard people say. "There's no smoke without fire." Well, guilty by association was the crime.

I had to learn to forgive Raymond, because I blamed him for more reasons than one; losing my friend was one reason.

I never got to go to university after I had left college. All my friends that I had studied with had all left for university to fulfill their dream of becoming whatever it was that they wanted to be. This took everything out of me. There was no room for anything else. University was out of the question for now, maybe ever.

My dreams of becoming a midwife was no longer my dream anymore.

Well, Patrick saw how Raymond and I were being affected by all of this. "Jackie, I know you love your friend, but you have to forget about her and focus on your son. We know our son, and we know that he is innocent, and we have to prove it because all of his friends are saying we know you weren't there, but we can't speak for you. Well, Jackie, we have to speak for him, so right now, you got to stop thinking about what people are saying and stand up for your son. We're going to do whatever it takes to get him out of there before he goes mad." I felt like I was losing myself all over again.

Patrick was a great support to me at that time. He would stay with me while Benji was at work. You could say that our relationship was now on an even keel. We both had something in common, our son, and we had to stick together, no matter how we felt about each other. I needed him around at that time, and he knew it, and he was there for me. For some reason, I felt strong when he was around.

I found that I always called on Patrick for support, with Michael and Raymond. Benji was at work most of the time, so I was always at home by myself in the evenings dealing with them, and the police.

Raymond was bringing a lot of trouble to my front door; people were coming to warn me that he was going to get into trouble.

There was not a day that passed without me giving Raymond a lecture. Every morning before I left to go college, it would be the same thing. I wouldn't leave the house until I spoke to him.

People were telling me what he was getting up to no good on the streets. Well, I was at the end of my tether, scared and worried for him every time he was out on the streets.

Two months before he was charged with this murder, he got beaten up really bad, to the point where he blacked out in the middle of the road. They had put him there and just left him. Well, he came round just in time to a car right in front of him.

That Sunday afternoon, I was in the kitchen cooking the Sunday dinner. Well, I heard when Raymond came in and lay down on the sofa. It was only when a neighbour came over and alerted me that she had seen him staggering home with a missing trainer. She then asked me if he was okay. After telling her yes, I looked at him lying in the sofa then noticed that he was about to lose consciousness. His eyes were glazed and slowly closing. I called the ambulance, and he was rushed to the hospital. If that didn't slow him down, what would.

Well now, Raymond could not understand why he was guilty by association; all he could see was that he was at home all day with his girlfriend. He couldn't understand how he ended up here, but we could.

My son had always been a good child growing up. You would never hear his teachers say a bad word about him. He was happy go lucky, just like most kids his age were, and I rarely ever told him off about anything.

For the first few years everything was fine when he started to attend secondary school. Waking up for school and coming home from school was not a problem, until now; where it was once easy to wake him up for school, it was now difficult. He was coming home from school later and later. Staying out with friends got more and more frequent.

When he was younger I used to know where he was, because I would look out my window and see him there, but now, I had to walk the streets to find him, sometimes late at nights, getting out of my bed to do this, ringing his father to help me find him. We would knock at his friends' homes, disturbing their peace; his friends were all at home.

I realised that the friends that he now had were friends that he had met on the streets, not some of the friends he had grown up with.

Raymond dropped out of playing football. He was a great little footballer. He had a lucky left leg and always scored a goal. We could see that he was destined for a great future if he continued with his football, but that soon changed. Gone was the football, and some of the friends he had grown up with.

Bunking school, smoking cannabis, dropping trousers from his waist, sitting under his bottom, and having unsavory friends were his new thing. I remember sitting in the headmaster's office and pleading with him to change; we all were. I was there that day because instead of my son having pencils in his pencil case, he had cannabis seeds in there instead. As I sat in the headmaster's office crying, just looking at my son, he wasn't even five foot tall, and his attitude was starting to smell.

His teachers could not believe how much he had changed from the sweet little boy they had all spoken about at the parents' evening. No one could believe that this was the same boy, sitting here with an attitude, and no regard for his mother. I couldn't believe that it was my son Raymond. It's like he didn't care if they expelled him or not.

Well, as I sat there begging him not to throw his life away, he just sat there with a smirk on his face. I wanted to wipe it off, but I couldn't give them anything to say about me. They would probably have blamed me for Raymond rebelling.

By now he had lost all interest in going to school; getting him there was so stressful. Every morning before I left to go to work, I would be giving him the full sermon. This became an everyday thing.

I worked at the Manor Gym, just round the corner from his school, so I would always see him. Well, one day I was on my way to another job; and I saw him walking up the road, so slow, without a care in the world. It was 11:00 a.m. He had just left home.

Sometimes I blamed myself for going to work. Maybe if I was at home all the time, then I would have more time for them. I would be there, and he would not be able to go out that much. I blamed myself for everything. Blame had become my middle name from ever since.

That day the headmaster gave him an ultimatum. "Raymond, you can either leave the school grounds now, never to return, or you can go back to your classroom to join your friends." My son sat there with his smirk still on his face and his attitude. "Well, can I go and get my stuff and say later to my friends?" "No, you leave now. I'm giving you an ultimatum. That means to choose your education or a life of crime." Well, at that moment my son looked over at me. I looked at him pleadingly, with tears in my eyes. That day my son chose to stay at school.

Raymond had started to hang around on the streets at the age of fourteen years old, and I blamed myself for that, even though God knows that I was dealing with so many things at the time, one of them being my eldest son, Michael, who was battling with alcohol. Maybe I had focused too much on him and didn't have the time or energy and mind to fight with this on my own. Why didn't I see this coming?

I had no support with Michael; everyone had turned their backs on him, because they could not handle it. As a family we all became victims of this, in some way or another.

I remember once having a conversation with Raymond and his friends, asking them why they chose to hang around the streets, getting into trouble. "We have nothing else to do," one of them said. "We have no father around to take us out and do things with us, that's why we hang around together. We're like a family, we stick together." Well, they all nodded their heads in agreement. I remember feeling like I wanted to cry with the answer that they had given me, my son included too, because at that time his father had abandoned him too.

Well, this is what these young boys were saying, "If we had our fathers in our lives, our lives would be different." As they say, you heard it from the horse's mouth, meaning I heard it directly from the boys that go around causing disturbances in people's lives, blaming their fathers for forsaking them.

I started my campaign to prove my son's innocence. I walked through alleys, up and down the streets looking for cameras, even hidden ones too. I needed to get proof that my son was not on them, because these alleys and roads that my son had supposedly travelled should show if he was there or not.

I had to think of more things to do. One of them was printing leaflets and organising meetings with the people that believed his innocence and supported me, and I thank God for each and every one of them, because their support gave me the strength to fight each day and to wake up and get dressed to go to college. God knows how I passed my exams, but I did. Sitting in the exam hall, you could hear a pin drop, and probably my thoughts too. I muddled my way though all of the questions which I had spent so long revising and getting mentally prepared for, all those assignments that I had stayed up until early hours of the morning finishing to meet the deadline the following day, and here I was just muddling through. Well, God must have rescued my thoughts and made me focus enough to pass.

I had passed my exams. I had studied so hard for this, and now it didn't mean a thing, not even the certificate, proof that I had achieved. I just couldn't believe that I had done it, especially throughout all this. What was the point, because nothing mattered anymore.

That evening on my way home from college, I passed one of the neighbours standing at her door. Well, I never really spoke to her that much before the day she came over to tell me that Raymond was hurt. I guess I had no reason to, until that day.

For some reason, I walked up to her gate and asked her if she had heard what had happened to Raymond. Well, she said yes, and then she said, "Jackie, I saw Raymond sitting outside on the wall, at ten o'clock."

"Ten o'clock," I said.

"Yes," she replied. I asked her if she was sure, and she told me, "Yes, because I remember that night we were unloading the car, because we had just come back from a day trip. The younger kids were in the back of the car sleeping. We were carrying them in when we saw Raymond on the wall, and my daughter even walked past him and said hello." My neighbour even told me that she remembered looking at her watch, and it was ten o'clock. She was so sure. I couldn't believe my ears because if this is what she was saying, then Raymond was innocent.

Well, it took another few months before he was found innocent and free to go home. The supposed CCTV image of him standing at the phone box turned out not to be him after all.

I was happy that he had been freed. I felt like I had been set free as well.

I felt tired, drained of everything, my emotions and my health. I had cried so many nights. I got angry with God, with myself, and with my son, for getting caught up in the wrong company, and making me lose my closest friend Christine. I don't think he realised the devastation he caused by not listening to me, going around and forging a name for himself as part of that life. Lessons were learned by him.

The day before his release, we received a telephone call from his solicitor Mark, telling us that they would be going for bail. We had spoken about going for bail over the past months. We all wanted him out because we knew that he was innocent, but we feared that if he got bail there might be repercussions, so we chose to let him stay inside, because it was safer, and we wanted him to be proven innocent before he was released completely, so we didn't opt for bail, due to those reasons.

I can even remember us asking the solicitor after he had met my son for the first time to give us his honest belief. Did he think our son was guilty? We even said to him that we know that solicitors have to do their jobs to defend their client, guilty or innocent. I even wondered what they thought about their clients, did some of them think that their client was guilty but still did their job to defend, or did they fight harder when they knew that their client was innocent? Well, Mark worked so hard to prove Raymond's innocence. He told us that from the first time that he met with Raymond and spoke to him he had no doubt that this boy was innocent.

The morning of Raymond's release was just like any other morning, washing plates, hoovering, and getting the house in order, before we left to go and collect him from the Old Bailey Court. On the way there, I didn't really say much. I was excited that he was coming home. However, I had mixed emotions. I was happy in one sense, and in another I was sad. I was sad about the circumstances which caused my son to end up in a place like this, and I was happy that his name was cleared.

We arrived at the Old Bailey, and his hearing had just finished; he was now free to leave. My son was free, after four months.

As we walked outside I wondered how he must be feeling at that very moment. My son walked tall with his head held high. As we made our way back to the car, I couldn't help but feel sorry for him. As he chatted away about his time spent in prison, he stopped to tell us that his arm was hurting him, then he told us why. He said that the prison guards known as screws stripped and beat him up the night before his release. They held him down, twisting his arm, as another guard lay into him. I was horrified at what I had just heard and found it very hard to believe that this happened to my son.

On the way home he chatted away about his experience of being in prison. He spoke about being locked up for most of the day, pacing the floors of his cell and spending his time just looking out of the window surrounded by bars, wishing he was a bird and that he could fly home. When he said that, I remembered the big bag of letters that I had kept in the bottom of my wardrobe.

I had so many letters that Raymond had written to me, and I wrote him every day too. Well, that was the only positive thing I felt that could help him at the time.

Writing to him would help me to express to him how much I loved him; and it would help him to stay strong, keep hoping, and have faith. Most of my friends supported me in writing to him, even sending him money. He responded to all their letters. He had a lot of support from everyone; they even visited.

For every letter sent a letter was received. I really began to look forward to hearing from him, and when I did, I would end up feeling more sad after reading his letter. I kept him in touch with everything that was going on. He always wanted to know about his dog. We couldn't tell him that we had given it away. We had to give him some kind of hope that his puppy was there waiting for him. He spoke about his little brother Marley and Lourdes. He really wanted to see them, but I didn't want them to go to that place. I couldn't bear if Lourdes asked me the reason why he was there, and Marley was too young to know what was happening. Anyway I just kept him updated with pictures of them and drawings which Lourdes would do for him.

There was not one letter were he did not protest his innocence, and at the end of each letter, he would write boldly 100% Innocent. Seeing the word *innocent* written boldly always gave me hope. I think it gave him hope that one day the truth would come to light. Well, that's what he always maintained in his letters.

Well, here we are almost home. As we got closer, I realised that this was not easy for him as I had thought. I remember thinking about this day, how we would all be happy when he was freed, but it wasn't as I had imagined. Come to think of it, I don't think he imagined it either. I didn't realise that it would take him time to adjust back into the real world. I thought that he would come out and wouldn't be affected by prison life that much, but he was. I had spent the past four months trying to cope as best as I could, which was very difficult. One of my hardest moments came when I had to ring my mother and pretend that everything was fine. I was good at pretending. I'd done it for so long that it came like second nature to me. However, that day it took me hours to pluck up the courage to ring her because each time I picked up the phone to dial the number I put it down. I even managed to eventually make the phone ring several times but then put it down fast, almost as if I could hear her walking towards the phone. I wasn't going to tell her. I couldn't. There was no way I could do that to her. You see, my mother was the biggest worrier I had ever known. I guess that's where I got it from.

Well, I couldn't hold out much longer. I felt like I was torturing myself. I had to hear her voice. I needed my mother, even if I wasn't going to tell her. I just needed some motherly love.

Before I dialed the number I said a little prayer and asked God to give me some strength to do this.

As I waited for my mother to answer the phone, I tried to think of something nice and funny, then I heard my mother's voice, then in my happiest voice, I answered her back, "Hi, Mummy." Well, she asked me how I was and asked about all the children individually, then it came to Raymond. "How is Raymond? Where is he?" I stopped for a moment, and without thinking I said, "Mummy, he was just here, but he's gone out now." Well, can you imagine how it got easier after that. I never felt like I was lying when she asked me where he was each time she rang. For me it felt like I was protecting her from feeling like I did.

My mother was learning to live without my father, and her life was getting back on track. She had thrown herself into the ministry, taking over from where my father had left off. She was carving out a life for herself gain. She had spent the past years looking after my father. She had become his mother, wife, and nurse, all in one. I had experienced the same thing when I was nineteen years old, being a nurse to Tony and a mother too, so I knew how she felt.

My mother dedicated each day to looking after my father, feeding, bathing, tucking him in at nights, even waking up in the middle of the night, to lift my father from the floor when he had fallen out of his bed. Now she was free from all of that. My mother was my father's carer without no break, no one to release her from that.

I remember looking at my mother and thinking that I had not seen her in a nice dress for the past few years. She did not see the point in putting on a nice dress, even around the house. No one would believe that she was the lady of the house, more like the housemaid, but she never cared.

So you see this is why I could not tell her, because this would break her heart, and she would worry about me so much, and I couldn't bear that, so for the next four months, we told jokes and laughed a lot over the phone.

Well, my mother was the first person I wanted to ring when I got back from picking Raymond up. I couldn't wait to tell her what I had been through, and before she even had the chance to say, "Lord Jesus," I would shout out that he was free and innocent. Well, when I did ring her and tell her the news, it was just like I had thought, but then she asked me, how did I get through it? She even said, "Jackie, you mean to tell me that every week you phone me, this has been going on for four months, and you gave everyone instructions not to tell me?" Funny thing is that I never needed to give instructions to anyone because we all knew our mother; and there were no ifs, buts, or maybe's about this.

All the neighbours who had supported me for the past four months, well, they all came round. This was a celebration of freedom. We wanted to play music and dance, but for my son it was different. He just wanted to talk about the past four months locked up in a cell.

As he spoke about his experience, he unknowingly paced the floor, from one end of the room to the other, and looked at the clock, telling us what he would be doing now if he was locked in his cell. It was sad to see how being locked up for four months had started to institutionalise him.

It took a few months for him to readjust back into his life. His experience had changed him. No one ever came to my door again and warned me that he was hanging around on the streets and in the wrong crowd. Being locked up and knowing that you are innocent must be one of the hardest things to come to terms with while you're there. He was facing twenty-five years if found guilty.

His lifestyle changed, and so did his friends. The negative impact which it now had on his life was that because he went to prison, no one would employ him. I remember once saying to him why don't he go out and get himself a job. Well, his reply was "Do you think it's going to be easy for me to get a job now?"

All the letters he wrote, I still kept them in a bag in the bottom of my wardrobe. I don't really know why I kept them, because when I think of it now, it seems like I was holding on to what had passed.

I have never read any of his letters since the day he was released and don't think I ever will.

It took the hard way for my son to learn. What were the chances of this happening to me? Well, I thought never, until that night.

We read about murder every day in the newspapers, but none of us would ever think that we would be affected by it, or it could happen to us, or anyone we know. I used to feel so sad for the families in the newspapers. You would only read their stories, and you couldn't imagine their pain, but when you're affected by it, you can feel the families' pain and see their grief.

Never in my life would I ever imagine that I would be part of a story like this, my best friend's nephew, and my son, only this could happen to Jacqueline La-Touché, that's what I told myself, problems waiting patiently in line for their turn one after the other, still plaguing my life.

I had got used to life without my friend Christine. I had seen her a few times on the streets, but we just walked past each other like the strangers we'd now become.

Chapter Twenty-Five

Vocational Thinking

2005

After a while everything calmed down. However, the backlash of what had happened to Raymond came to destroy me yet again. I thought I had gotten over it all, but that was not the case. I became depressed. I felt like my life was passing me by; everything and everybody was moving except me. I didn't know how to get myself out of these feelings. I stopped believing in myself and everything that I had done. I just stayed inside the house and wallowed in depression. Why was this happening to me? Everything was over, and you thought that I would be happy and continue where I had left off, but that wasn't the case for me at that time. I wondered to myself, *How did I manage to get here again?*

I needed to get out of this, and I knew that no one could get me out, unless I wanted to. I could sit down all day feeling sorry for myself or get up and start living again; so with all my strength and determination, which I had put to the side, I managed to pick them up and start again.

I decided that I wanted to carry on with my midwifery. I had worked so hard, and because of what happened to Raymond, I had lost the will to continue, but I felt ready to move forward, so with the help of someone I had met at the mother and toddler group, who was also studying to be a midwife, I was able to get a voluntary placement working at the Whittington Hospital, on the maternity ward, doing administration work, behind the scenes. For all the years of having babies and attending the antenatal clinic, I had never realised all the hard work which went into arranging the appointments, filing all the documents, taking blood tests, and everything else. I loved working there. I even worked on the wards, supporting the mothers, sitting down, talking to some of the young mothers, just like myself, when I was sixteen years old. That took me way back. I even saw the way that some were treated by some of the nurses. I remembered the three Cs again, charged, convicted, and condemned for being a teenage mother. Well, I understood exactly how they felt, so I would take the time to sit down and talk to them, listening to how they felt. They looked forward to my daily visits. I hated the way some of them were treated by the professionals who had adhered to this vocation. I promised myself that as a midwife I would be different.

My voluntary work was very important to me. I wanted to be able to see the joy on mothers' faces when they held their baby for the very first time. I wanted to be able to support and guide them through that journey. My first experience of childbirth, at the age of sixteen years old, was a far cry from my experience of having my other children over the past years.

It should have been one of the happiest moments of my life; but because I was too young to understand what I was going through, or how I was supposed to feel, I was burdened with what everyone thought about me. I didn't really live my pregnancy to its full potential.

Well, I became very passionate about being a midwife; that's all I ever thought about. Well, my daughter Sacha was pregnant at the time whilst I worked at the Whittington, and she was due to have her baby around that time.

One of my greatest experiences of working there was when my daughter came in to have her baby, she was actually on the ward where I worked, I can even remember sitting in the admin, office filing the patients hospital maternity files, and coming across my daughter Sacha's file this was amazing, I couldn't believe that I was holding it in my hand and filing it away with all the others, that was a special feeling. I felt like I had come a long way from where I had been, especially from my time as a cleaner, here I was sitting in a hospital sorting out important files, and one of them my daughter's.

Well, my grandson was born, while I was there, I was a proud grandmother again, and felt like I played a big part in helping her in the hospital, not just as her mother but as a volunteer, I had dedicated my time to helping the mothers, and the overworked staff at the hospital, even though Marley was still young, I had dedicated two days a week, leaving my baby at home, to come here and support mothers with their babies.

Well, as a volunteer I was not allowed to do any practical work, like bathing babies. However, I was able to do that with my grandson, I thought to myself "Well, Jackie, you must be the first volunteer to ever work at Whittington Hospital and bath a baby, and what are the chances of that baby being your grandchild, to me that was a big chance, to others it might have been slim, I thanked God for putting me in that position, place and time.

Well, I worked at the Whittington for four months, my work there was now limited, no more babies to bath, and I had conquered, and mastered the admin, I could now do it all with my eyes closed and I felt that it was now time for me to move on, I had gained my experience on the admin side and the supporting people side of things.

I felt ready to apply for university again and I did. However, I was turned down for the University of my Choice, I couldn't understand why.

I had applied at the right time, and I had all the necessary qualifications, to get in, I even got a fantastic reference from the college, and I had applied within the three-year limit, before my certificate was invalid.

Well, I rang the university to find out why I had been turned down, only to be told that they could not offer me a place there, because I was a student from abroad. Well, that was the reason why I was turned down, they had made a mistake, I was British born, but according to them, I was not. Well, this knocked my confidence very much, they told me that I would have to apply again next year, I was ready for this. However, now I felt that the stuffing had been knocked from out of me again, I felt that I had no more fight in me, I had been fighting from the age of fifteen years old, and now when I thought that I was finally reaching somewhere, someone had pulled the rug from under my feet.

One year what could I do in that time, did I really want to go through all this again, I was confused and I didn't know what to do next. Well, I had no choice but to stay at home and look after Marley, he was getting older now, and needed my attention. Benji had been there for him more than I had been.

Marley relied on Benji for everything, when he wanted food, he would go to Benji, when he needed his nappy changed it was Benji, when he was fell asleep it was Benji who made that happen, by rocking him until he was out. I felt a little jealous of their relationship, but not in a bad way, sometimes I wished that Marley would come to me, he always cried when Benji left for work.

Well, over time things got a little better between me and Marley, I spent more time with him, taking him to play groups, and parks, Marley was enjoying socialising with other children his age, he had not been able to do that before, because I was at college, and Benji was just too tired to take him anywhere during the daytime, he did try sometimes, but not that often.

I felt like I was a bad mother, and it was my fault why Marley had grown to love Benji more than me, so staying at home now, was not such a bad thing, when I looked at it in that way, this was our bonding time, and I began to enjoy looking after my son I got to know him more, over the past year I had spent so much time engrossed in studying that I never had time for anything or anyone, not even my son, circumstances had taken over my life to a degree, where things that mattered never seemed to anymore, but now I wanted to focus on spending this time to have more of a relationship with Marley.

Marley amazed me, with unexplainable things, especially when he would point to the photograph of my father, and say "that's me maary" you couldn't tell him that it wasn't him otherwise you would never hear the end of his crying, or he would just keep on repeating "me maary, maary its me" I found this amazing, because not only did Marley look like my father, he was looking at my father's photograph and saying that it was him, I thought, how could a two year old look at a photograph of an old man, who he never knew, and said that this was him. He would even point to photographs of his brothers and sisters, when they were babies, way before he was born, and he would tell me exactly who they were, and he always got it right. Just like he had seen them they were babies.

Marley was a special child, I always believed that, from the moment in the book shop, right up until now.

Chapter Twenty-Six

Letting Go

2006

Well, fate dealt another cruel blow when I heard that Christine's other nephew was terminally ill with cancer. I had got on very well with Daniel before that fateful night. We were one big happy family. He was always driving me around, whenever or wherever I wanted to go, even to play Ms. Meryl. The most memorable moment was performing as Ms. Meryl at the Hackney Empire, at an audition, and my friends sitting in their seats clapping away and laughing as I stood in front of the audience. They always supported me in everything that I did.

Hearing that Christine's nephew Daniel was dying was another shock for me. I just couldn't believe when I heard. I was worried about her and how she must be feeling, because it wasn't that long ago that she had lost her other nephew. I thought about all her family and how they were all coping with yet another devastating blow.

It was not that long after hearing that he was terminally ill that he died. I wanted to pay my respects from the moment that I heard, but how, because memories were still fresh in everyone's mind.

Well, I heard that it was going to be his funeral, and I really wanted to go, but then I thought about what might happen if I showed up. Would the family not want me there? What would they say when they saw me? Will they want to argue? Well, all these thoughts came one at a time through my mind.

I thought about the good times that we had when he was alive, and that made up my mind for me. I was going, and I would be prepared for whatever was in store for me. I was going to pay my last respect and would not be intimidated by people who threw the book at me for being my son's mother, the three Cs, all over again.

The day of the funeral came. I felt sad and a little apprehensive, but that didn't stop me from getting dressed to go. We all met at my friend Linda's house, and we all left together. My friends supported me in a way, which gave me strength to deal with many things; they knew that I had some reservations about going; however, they all assured me that they were looking out for me.

Well, I thought that I was prepared for whatever was in store for me that day. Well, I wasn't because that was the day when my friend Christine and I became friends again. As we stood in the graveyard crying and hugging each other, I could hear my friend saying, "Jackie, I missed you so much." I hugged her even more and cried I love you too.

I couldn't believe what had just happened; one minute we were standing at either end of the graveside, and now we stood embracing each other, as people walked past or stood there and watched us. Well, they knew what had happened previously, and they knew that she was my closest friend.

As I looked over I could see another friend of mine with tears in her eyes. They were all touched by that moment. One of my friends, whom I had come with, had helped in bringing us together.

While my friends and I stood there chatting away, my friend noticed that Christine was walking by on the other side. Well, the least expected thing she did was to call Christine over to where we were standing.

As Christine got closer to us, I stood there quietly, tilting myself to the side. I felt awkward as my friend spoke to her. Fiddling with my thumbs, I tried to distract myself from what they were talking about, when all of a sudden I heard my friend Linda call my name and Christine's too. "Jackie, Christine, I know what has happened cannot be changed. This has to stop now. I know that you both love each other." Linda spoke to us in a raised voice like we were both two little girls in the playground fighting over a doll. Christine and I stood with our heads bowed, as she demanded that we put our arms around each other. "She's your friend," she shouted at us both. Well, back at the reception, everybody gathered, celebrating his life in the way that he had loved. Music, that was an important part of his life. Daniel would always take the time to record music from me, he knew that I loved music just as much. Christine and I were inseparable that evening, wherever I was, she was there. I could see the stares, and glances of people that walked past us, even her family, they were looking as to say what is she doing talking to me, but Christine did not care what they thought, she had forgiven me, something that I thought would never happen. However, I thought to myself, that I had done nothing wrong to be forgiven for, it was my son's mistake and not mine. Well, that was water under the bridge, and I accepted my friends forgiveness, hoping that we could move on from that tragedy, which changed our lives.

Well, from that day on we were friends again, I knew that some of Christine's friends and family did not share the same views as Christine, and must have thought how could she get past what had happened, to become my friend again. Well, only God knows how we both overcame that. It is difficult to lose someone you love to murder. I know that this has changed my friend forever, even our friendship, because even though we talk and laugh on the phone, a lot has changed, our friendship is different, you could say that we have both moved on. However, we are still there for each other and will always be.

As much as I started to enjoy my time at home with Marley, I had become stuck again, I felt like I was going around in circles, one minute everything was fine, and the next it felt like I was back to square one.

My son Michael was still drinking, and there was nothing any of us could do, he had become his own worst enemy, and was intent on self destructing, he became paranoid about everything and everyone. He was now walking the streets drunk and disorderly, sitting on benches with other alcoholics, everything was out in the open, he had lost all his dignity, he just didn't care anymore, even about his appearance. Well, that was very hard to see, Michael had always been nicely dressed, he used to pay a lot of attention to how he looked, and took a lot of pride in himself, he spent so much money looking good, always the best for Michael, the latest trainers, clothes, hat, jeans, jackets, and he always had his hair neatly cut.

I used to complain about the amount of time that he used to spend in the bathroom, getting dressed, now all that did not matter to him anymore, he now looked disheveled, his clothes looked unclean, like he had worn them for weeks, he didn't smell fresh anymore, he started to grow a beard, and his hair was also overgrown, even his trainers were dirty and old, and he just didn't care about his appearance, or even about the bottle of cider that he used to cleverly disguise with a carrier bag. Well, all that was on show for everyone to see, it was no longer a secret, it was all out in the open.

He would come around to the estate, drunk out of his mind every day. He now started on the neighbours. Everyone felt sorry for me. "Poor you, I don't know what you're going to do about him. He is disturbed. You need to get him sectioned for his own good." God knows I felt like that. I couldn't take this anymore, the embarrassment of everything. It had spilled out of the house and now on to the streets. He had now become a mockery to everyone. I remember an incident where I had to shelter in one of the neighbours' house. I was scared to go home, because Michael was waiting outside the front door for us to come back. My neighbour even told me that the children and I were welcome to sleep at her house that night and go home in the morning when Benji came back. That's how bad it had gotten.

Well, rock bottom came one day when he tried to pick on some of the youths around where we lived. Michael was now twenty-two years old. He had been drinking for six years now. Well, for the past six years our lives became a nightmare which we thought would not end, up until that day, when he fell to the ground drunk and surrounded by these youths, ready to beat him; even they had put up with him for so long.

There was no respect there anymore. Funny thing is that they had always looked up to him as the older boy. Now he had come down to their level, and they were not going to put up with his drunken disorderly behaviour anymore. Well, just in time I came to his rescue as he lay on the ground. I stood there looking over him and shaking my head, as I watched him on the ground just laughing away.

I felt so angry and hurt by him. Without even realising it, I lifted up my leg, taking it back, as far as possible, to give me a good chance of kicking him. As I moved my foot forward towards his body, my leg stopped right at his side. I could not do this. I wanted to, but something stopped me.

I could hear myself shouting, "Get up get up, you fucking idiot! Look at you, you're a disgrace to this family." The YMCA had told him to leave, because they had found him smuggling alcohol into the building on more than one occasion. They had even warned him. Well, he never listened to their warnings and was now blatantly bringing it in with no disguise, so they had to tell him to leave.

I remember begging them to give him a chance. One of the workers wanted to, but the other lady whom he had been abusive towards felt scared and very much intimidated by him and could not work there as long as he stayed there, so they couldn't lose their staff because of him, so he was now sleeping ruff on the streets.

Well, I continued to shout at him, as everyone stood there watching. They had stopped laughing and now stood there in silence. As I reached down to pick him up, he held on to my hand and eased himself up from off the ground. I continued shouting, "I can't take this anymore. If it kills me you're going to get some help. Even if I have to drag you to the hospital to get you sectioned, I'm going to do it."

I took him into the house and sat him down, and that's when he finally asked me for my help. "Please, Mum, can you help me. I need help. I don't want to drink anymore."

Well, that night he didn't have anywhere to go, so I let him stay with us. He was my son, and he was in a very vulnerable state, so leaving him on the streets would make him more susceptible to everything.

The next day I made a few telephone calls, and I managed to get an appointment with a drug and alcohol counsellor. I also managed to get him into rehab.

Michael was now admitting that he had a problem with drugs and alcohol and needed our support to get through this.

The biggest test came for Michael when the counsellor told him that he was not allowed to consume any drugs or alcohol for the next few days and that they would do a drug and alcohol test before he entered the rehab, because they did not want him to come there and jeopardise the other patients' recovery.

I wondered to myself how on God's earth was I going to keep him away from his demons for the next few days.

Well, I spoke to him and told him that this was his only chance to get help from us and that we could not go on like this anymore, and if he messed up, then he would be on his own.

The weekend passed with great surveillance by everyone in the house. We watched him like hawks, looking in his pockets, bags, anywhere we thought he would stash his drink. We even followed him to the shops. I felt sorry for him. This could not have been easy for him, or any of us, but he was trying with our help.

Knowing that we all wanted the same thing for him, and that was to get better, gave him the courage to accept help from everyone.

I remember the day when he went to live at the rehab. It was a nice homely place full of all recovering alcoholics. Even the doctor was in recovery. We even met a man by the name of Roy, who told us that he once was a successful businessman with a huge bank account. He also told us that he lost his family along with everything else. Alcohol had robbed him of the grand life that he used to have. This man was twice Michael's age.

Michael listened to this Roy's story and could not believe that this had happened because of drink.

Well, this was Michael's new home for the next year. I felt sad leaving him behind, and he looked so vulnerable. I felt scared that the other men there might bully him. He now reminded me of the little boy that I once knew.

As I hugged him and told him goodbye, he held on to us and told us that he would be fine. He even said to me and Patrick if it was not for us, supporting him to get here, he would still be out there on the streets drunk. He even asked me to forgive him for all the things that he had put us through, most of them he did not remember doing. That part of his memory was just a blank space in his head.

This was the best place for him right now. Even though I felt sad leaving him there, I knew that there was no other way apart from this way, and I actually felt very relieved that he was now in a safe haven and would get all the help and support he needed to fight this. I knew it would not be easy, but he had made the first step, and that was to recognise after six years of fighting with his demons that he did have this problem.

Visiting Michael was very pleasant, because he always had some story to tell us. They were pleased with him, and his recovery was positive. However, he still had a very long way to go.

While he was there it's like I could see the Michael that we once knew. I had forgotten how funny he was. He was a joker, but we had not seen the funny side to him in so many years.

It took a lot out of me supporting Michael. I had all the other children to think about as well, but it's like there was no room for anyone else.

I started to forget about myself again. I hardly went anywhere. My friends had all stopped asking me to come out with them, because I always said no, so eventually they stopped. I lost interest in myself. I just could not be bothered to do anything.

I would question myself about why my life was always an uphill struggle. Why is it when I think that I had gotten over a hurdle, another one was always right in front of me?

My relationship with Benji had also suffered though the years. I felt sorry for him. I felt responsible for bringing him here to face this nightmare life with me, and the children. He had always lived on his own before now, so he wasn't used to all this, just a quiet life. Well, this was far from quiet.

It was always one thing after the other. The arguments became frequent. We spent more time arguing about the children than anything else. Sometimes I felt like I was alone, without his support, but then I would think to myself that when I met him, he lived alone without a family, and I had brought him into this hellish nightmare, my nightmare.

Depression buried in a grave from my past came back to haunt me, slowly creeping through the years, waiting to put me down on my knees again. I stopped believing in myself. I didn't go out anymore. My confidence began to fall again, like I had seen it done in past relationships. Things I had managed to achieve through the years, going to college, studying nursing and midwifery, and passing my exams, even performing on stage as Ms. Meryl and making so many people laugh, right now, all that seemed a thing of my past.

I could not believe that I had ever done any of those things, how did I manage to do them in the first place, with everything that was going on in my life at that time, especially with my two sons and my marriage, how did I ever have the courage to stand up in front of an audience, and make people laugh until some cried tears, because right now I felt like crying the tears of a clown, here I was forty years old, and I didn't know how I had reached this far, without losing myself, right now I had no thought of where I was going with my life. My marriage was a shambles, and I t felt like we were just going from day to day, with no direction, this was not the married life I had dreamt of, when I first met Benji, all the dreams and plans that we had, when we first met, no longer existed in our life, together. Where were we going, I didn't want us to end up being like the Mr. and Mrs. Browns, from my parents time, who lived in the same house but separate lives, then you would see them at church on Sunday, united in prayers, and so much together. Well, I felt that we had become the Mr. and Mrs. Brown, of our own circumstances.

I remember a friend of mine getting divorced, and me asking her how did she manage to get the courage and strength to do that, I respected her for taking a hold of her life, and being brave enough to admit to herself that her marriage was over, I also remember thinking to myself that, I could not be brave enough to take that step ever. Everyone around me was moving on with their lives, but ours stood still.

Chapter Twenty-Seven

A Change Must Come

2008

I found myself a social life, and beautiful friends to fit into it. My husband always trusted me to go out with my friends, and I always respected that, he cared enough not to put any restrictions on my life, even though our relationship was lacking, we still remained to commit ourselves together, for the sake of our family.

I started to go places, meet people, enjoy myself, so much had held me back from this for years. However, I had began to see a bit more clearer now, I had started to make my own happiness, I figured that no one could do that for me, I had to learn to be happy inside again, that's what I told myself. I had to create my own, and I did.

I stopped begging Benji for his attention, I stopped pleading with him to take me out, I stopped pleading with him to notice me, before someone else did, I used to tell him, one day you are going to let another man walk into my heart and take me away. Divorce became a new word in my vocabulary, sometimes I couldn't take the silence anymore, I would just randomly come out with it" I want a divorce" we might as well get one, we are not living like man and wife anymore, we have not done that for years, sometimes I'd just come out with" one liners like" our marriage is not worth the piece of paper it is written on." All these thoughts and feeling became more apparent as time went on, I wanted things to change for me and Benji, but how. We had lived like this for years, I guess it was easy to stay this way than to change, but this was not the life that we knew when we first met each other.

I needed to start living a meaningful life, I needed a purpose to carry on and move forward with my life, I once read that procrastination is a stealer of time, I didn't really take it in at the time and now that procrastination lay buried in my mind, the years had been slowly taken away, going to college and studying to become a midwife had to be put on hold, because of the daily battles with life which I fought, all that slowly slipped out of my reach. I had studied so hard for this and, now it meant nothing to me anymore, my lost dream.

To stay positive I told myself that it was not meant to be, my sister even told me that midwifery may not have been my calling, she said even though I was passionate about becoming one, it didn't mean that it was for me, and that y purpose probably lay elsewhere.

I started to believe that she may be right, never looking back with regret.

January 2008, that's when my life changed, but this time for the better. Yes, there were still a lot of daily battles that I faced each day. However, I remained positive. Prayer stayed with me throughout those days. As long as I prayed I knew that God would hear me, and just because he never granted my plea, at the same time, it didn't mean that he never heard me, because he did. I told myself that he was a patient and loving god, and just because I was impatient when I called upon him, it never made him any less patient or loved me any less. Well, that's what I would tell myself, "Just be patient, you're loved. Be positive because everything you keep on asking him for you will get, if you believe that it is yours." So I waited, twenty-eight years which seemed like forever, but finally started to feel like I was on the right track.

I started look for things to do, to keep my mind ticking. Well, I told myself that I had lost my chance of becoming a midwife and that if I wanted my life to change, only I could do that. I even told myself, "Jackie, how are you going to meet people if you just stay inside all the time? You need to get out and create a life for yourself. Put yourself in the spotlight." And that's what I did.

I never had any regrets about not pursuing my career as a midwife; however, I needed to do something in the caring profession maybe that would be fulfilling in another way.

Well, I got myself on a voluntary training course, on the Home Start voluntary programme. At the end of the course the goal would be to become a trained volunteer, supporting families. This was something that interested me, and maybe if I enjoyed this, who knows maybe one day I might be able to get a job, in the same field, supporting families, but in a professional role.

Well, I completed the course and was now waiting to be matched with a suitable family. It wasn't that long after the course finished that I started on another course. This was a parenting support group, Strengthening Families, Strengthening Communities. I enrolled onto this course because I felt that I needed some support for my son Steven and also around my parenting. I wanted to try to understand more about my children and to learn new skills as a parent, so this was perfect and came at the right time. At first I was a little dubious about going, questioning my parenting, and the reasons why I felt that I had to attend, but I soon overcame that, telling myself that I would enjoy attending and meeting other mothers who felt the same way that I did, frustrated, and not afraid to admit that they needed help too.

At the time of attending this group, my life seemed to be more on track, and so did Michael's life too. He had since come out of rehab, after spending two years in there. He was so different. I couldn't believe how being somewhere else for the past couple of years could give him a different outlook to his life.

Gone were the dirty old trainers and disheveled look, and back was the Michael that we all once knew and loved. I was so proud of Michael for seeing this through. We were all so proud of his achievements. Everyone who had turned their backs on him was now giving him a chance. My family was no longer frightened of him. He was no longer banned from going to their homes. They now welcomed him back with open arms again. Even his brothers and sisters welcomed him back.

Raymond had calmed down too, since spending that time in prison, and he was now a father to a little girl. That experience of being locked up frightened him into dropping the hard nut exterior he had created around the little boy that he once was. Well, the thought of spending twenty-five years in prison had a positive effect on him.

My only worry at this time was for Steven. I didn't want him to go through the same thing that they both had. I wanted to protect him and myself from facing anything like that again. He was old enough to see and remember what we had gone through, with both Michael and Raymond, so you think that he would know better, but that was not the case, because he now started to hang around on the streets, so here I was again, feeling like I was back at square one. However, I was going to do my damned best to do something about it. As they say, prevention is better than cure. I thought to myself, well, if I try and it fails, at least I won't beat myself up about it, just like I did before, so here I am on this parent course, ready to learn a new way of parenting and trying to understand the dreaded teenager.

My life changed the first day that I walked through the door. I met mothers who were in turmoil over their children, mothers who cried each week when they spoke about their child, mothers who had lost control along the way, mothers who were trying to reach out to their children, mothers who had become victims of our society. Well, I was one of those mothers whose child had become a victim; so that was why I was here, to learn about myself and to try to understand what today's society brings, and how to deal with it.

I met a lot of mothers there who started to look up to me. I felt no way about sharing my life stories with them. I felt no shame. All I felt was the bond in the room between all the mothers, united every Tuesday morning, divided every Tuesday afternoon, to go back home, to their homes which had now become a battlefield for some of them, and to put on their armour and use the tools that they were given that day, knowledge.

I remember sitting down with one of the mothers. Her name was Annette. We would sit together every week. Even if I had turned up late, my seat would still be there waiting for me to fill it.

Each week we all sat in the same place we were in the last time we were there even though we were told to sit anywhere we wanted, but we felt that we were in our comfort zone when we sat in the same place. Well, here I was, expressing to Annette how I felt about coming here each week and listening to all the mothers, talking about what they were going through with their sons and daughters. "Annette," I said, "each week I come, I hear horror stories from the mothers, and I have just realised that my son is a good boy. He has never disrespected me in any way, apart from ignoring my word, when I tell him to come home at nine o'clock and he comes at ten o'clock." "Well," Annette replied, "Jackie, you know what we are going through because you've been there with you other sons. They haven't. They see you here, standing up and sharing your life with them, and they see that you still remain positive. You give us hope, so, Jackie, even if you feel that you shouldn't be here because your son is still within your reach, you are here for a purpose." Purpose, I thought, my mum said I had a purpose, my sister too, and now I'm saying that I have a purpose, and that is to support people in whatever way possible.

From that day, I felt a need for us to start a mother's support group, a place where we could go and be ourselves again, forget for a few hours about our problems, and focus on us. A sanctuary of laughter and fun, where we never had to speak about the parenting group, which was specifically designed with children in mind.

I was even told that I would get all the help and support that I needed to do this. All the mothers thought this was great, especially when I explained its purpose.

I felt for them so much and shared the pain which I had gone through with my eldest son, who had become an alcoholic, ending up with no friends, and almost costing him his family.

I spoke openly and freely, gaining respect and loyalty, badge you receive for remaining sane at the end of all that.

Each week we had professionals sit in with the group. They were mainly there to watch how we got on in the group, but sometimes they took part, which was great because sometimes amidst the tears there were laughter, role plays, creative activities, and more.

One day after the session was finished I was standing outside, when one of the support workers stood outside with me, commenting on the wisdom, knowledge, and understanding that I had. Life experiences. "Jackie, you have so much to offer in a group setting. You have the respect from everyone in there. They look up to you each week for strength. Why don't you apply for a job at Harts for Families, supporting vulnerable families?"

"Who me?" I replied. "They wouldn't employ me, I have no qualifications."

"Well, Jackie, what you have is worth more than a piece of paper with writing, telling you that you had read a book, studied, and passed. You have a degree in life skills, that's worth so much. Well, Harts is recruiting again and opening a new branch in Islington. Why don't you download an application."

"Yeah," I said, but deep down I probably wouldn't have been bothered to do it. What was the point? What did I have to offer them in my application? Come to think of it, I'd never completely filled out a job application. I only ever got as far as the front page with name, date of birth, address, and age; and I only ever applied for cleaning jobs, which you never really needed to fill out an application for. Imagine filling out one. What would they ask you? Or even at an interview, imagine one of the questions being, have you ever cleaned a toilet before? Even worse, imagine them telling you that you didn't get the job because you didn't fit the criteria.

I was afraid of being turned down because I didn't fit the criteria. Well, to my surprise, one morning I woke up to find an envelope on the doormat. I opened it wondering what was inside, and who was it from. Well, I tore it open, and inside was an application form for me to fill in. At the same time the phone rang. With the application form in my hand I answered the phone. To my surprise it was David, whom I had met at the parenting support group. "Hi, Jackie, did you receive the application form that I sent in the post?" Here I was standing with it in my hand and being asked if I had received it. "Yes," I said, "it came this morning, thank you." "Jackie," he said, "if you need any support filling this out, I along with my other colleagues will be happy to help you to do this." "Thank you," I said. I couldn't believe that he was serious and believed that I was capable to apply for this job, just like all the other applicants. Well, I thought, if he and his colleagues believe in me, then I need to start believing myself as of now.

I told David that if I needed his support I would contact him; however, I had to do this myself.

Well, that evening I sat down in my bed, looking through the application. I picked up my pen and started to fill out my name, address, and date of birth, like I had done with previous applications. It seemed relatively easy to fill out. Well, that was until I got to the questions about my professional skills and qualifications. Professional skills, qualifications, how could I complete that part? They were asking me for things that I never had.

I sat there feeling disheartened, and thinking why bother. I was just setting myself up to fail. I just sat there for what seemed like forever. At one point I even put the application form down and closed my eyes to fall asleep. Suddenly it's like a voice started to question me, "Jackie, didn't you finish your nursing and midwifery course? Didn't you complete a Home Start voluntary training course and was now waiting for a family to support? Didn't you just complete Strengthening Families Parenting Group and gained the respect from the mothers and the professionals? Remember that you were also a volunteer on the maternity ward at Whittington Hospital, supporting the mothers? Didn't you help someone who was deaf and experiencing domestic violence to flee that life and support her to get a roof over her head? Don't you remember the hell that you endured for almost seven years with your son who was on drink and drugs, and what about the time when someone wanted to end their life because of their relationship ending? You spent so much time just listening and talking to her. Didn't you see her years later, and she thanked you for saving her life?" That's just a few Jackie. I could name so much more.

Straightaway I sat up in my bed, picked up the application, and started to fill it out without a shadow of doubt. I was positive and now believed that this job was mine; however, there was a deadline. Application completed and signed. I rang David the next day and told him that I had completed it and if he would be kind enough to look through it with me, and he did. Everything seemed fine. It was the day before the deadline, and we panicked because it had to reach on time. We could not delay in sending it. We thought about faxing. We thought about handing it in. We thought about posting. What would be the best way of making sure that it reached on time? Well, testing myself I decided to sent it by post recorded delivery. I thought to myself, if this is meant to be it will. If it gets there on time, then I will know for sure if I was doing the right thing. Well, straight to the post office, and I never looked back.

Two weeks later and application forgotten about, I received a telephone call. I was told that I had been short-listed for the job, as a support coordinator. I could not believe my ears. I went silent on the phone. The person on the other end had to ask if I was still there. She spoke about the job as if I had already got it, working hours, and talking about the job being flexible. She told me that the interview was in two parts, Monday and Tuesday. I could not believe it, me Jacqueline La-Touché, support coordinator. I was short-listed amongst probably one hundred or more people who applied for the post. There were under thirty vacancies for the posts, and I was amongst the short-listed. I was so excited and rang everybody to tell them my good news. I still could not believe it. I was happy, and that's when I started to believe and even spoke like the job was mine. I remember my friend Carol saying to me, "Trust me, Jackie, that job is yours."

I prepared for the interview on the Monday, and I wanted to dress the part, I had never been to an interview for any job, in my life this was my first.

However, I knew what to wear, I wanted to look smart, for myself, because I had never worn interview clothes before.

Monday, the first day of the interview, I arrived feeling little apprehensive, sitting amongst the other applicants, who were suited and booted, some looked like they had spent their lives in an office, for a second I thought to myself "Jackie you are way out of your depths here," and then the little voice in me said no you're not, right now you are equal with everybody in this room, you are all here for the same Job, doesn't matter if they look like they come from out of an office, or qualifications cover their living room walls, you have been short-listed for this job, so you have as much chance of getting it, as they do.

We were all called into a room together, multiple choice questions on support, for me that was a piece of cake, I breezed through the questions, like a kite, I felt confident and sure about day one.

Day two came, interviews took place at another location, it was a bit of a problem getting there because I was not familiar with the area. However, I found it in the end, and I was on time. Quite confident still from the first part of the interview, I was more relaxed, and positive.

Jacqueline La-Touché I heard my name, and I was asked to go into the room, where two ladies sat, with their pens, and note book, and papers with some questions which they were about to ask me.

I sat down, feeling a little nervous, fixing my clothes, and fidgeting with my hands, as I sat in the chair. They made me feel very comfortable, asking me questions, that did not relate to the job, this helped me to feel relaxed, and to open up my mind, for the questions they were about to ask me.

All I remember was just chatting away, and just being myself, open and honest with my questions. They asked me questions relating to the post, as if I had done this type of work in a professional setting, take your time they said, I remember saying to them that I had never supported anyone as a professional, "don't worry Jackie it doesn't matter, just take your time."

I began to feel a little flustered, when they asked me how would I prioritise my cases, if I had twenty families to support, Twenty families, how could anyone support twenty families at one time, I could just about support my family let alone twenty. Well, my answer was "if I had twenty families, I would, oh my god, I began to hesitate, my mind began to go blank, I began to feel stupid as the two women waited for my answer, then the little voice inside my head came to my rescue "Jackie you would prioritise your cases by putting the ones with the most needs in front of the ones with the lesser needs." Before I knew it I was letting it all out, I started to think about all the times I had supported more than one person, in my everyday life. Well, I saw the ladies nodding their heads. Well, that must be a good sign, "So Jackie tell us two occasions where you have supported someone, as I sat there thinking of a time there was so many to choose from, I was spoilt for choice, the two women, were so interested in my story, they wanted to know the end result, and how the person was now doing. Well, I was now in my element.

I spoke about the time when I had supported someone through alcohol and drugs, my son, I spoke as if he were someone else, I had firsthand experience as a mother, dealing with this, and a victim. I sat thinking to myself, that I had come a long way, because three years ago, I once was supported by the Harts for Families organisation. Three years ago, I needed support around the issues that I was then facing with Michael and Raymond, I had referred myself for support. Well, three years on, I am here being interviewed by the same organisation which supported me through a time in my life when I felt most vulnerable. I thanked God for making this possible, I had firsthand experience of all different types of issues faced by families.

Well, I couldn't believe it when they said, "Thank you, that's it, you can go now." "Is that it I thought, don't you have any more questions for me." Well, I guess that I was enjoying the interview.

They even asked me did I have a preference, to working in Islington or Wood Green, for some reason, I liked the look and feel of this newly refurbished office, which was waiting to become, the head quarters for Islington Families.

Even though my preference was to work closer to my home, if I got the job, so Wood Green would be perfect. However, I now started to think differently, maybe working in Islington might not be such a bad thing.

Islington Families, that's what this new floating support service would be called. Well, I wanted to work at the other branch which was closer to my home. However, it felt right being here, it was freshly decorated, and new, just waiting for the lucky applicants, and I felt that I was one of them, I left the building that day with my job, as a support coordinator in my hand. Well, that's what I felt.

Two weeks later, I received a telephone call telling me congratulations you have the job, I went silent again, but this time was not because I didn't believe it, this was because my life was about to change, and I could not wait.

I felt on top of the world, and proud of myself for getting this job just because I was myself, and didn't pretend to be anything more. I was a professional now and most of all, supporting families and helping them to make a difference in their lives.

I felt that I had all the tools needed for this job, everything that I had been through during my life now made sense to me, the struggles I had endured, I now believed that I was the best person for this job, and they saw that.

I felt that this was my purpose, and that because of my life experiences, both positive and negative, I could use them in a way to reach people. I remember someone saying to me "Jackie you have so much to say, but you listen too, that's a skill, I've never met someone who could talk for England and listen at the same time, it's either one or the other, but you have both, that's a rare quality.

Getting prepared for work mentally, and physically, shopping for work clothes, was an experience, I had never done this before, it felt special, just standing in the shop looking, picking up clothes, telling myself that these clothes were for work.

Waiting for my CRB to come through was a long wait, I was ready to start work, but there were still references, to come through before I could start. It was summer, and even though I had been waiting for a few months, I took it in my stride, and was happy just doing whatever it was, because I knew that once I started working, my life would never be the same again.

Here I was with a job, just waiting to start. This was a far cry away from January, when I had started the year, feeling that my life was passing me by, no job, no money, and faded dreams.

I was depressed because I was at home all day, just watching television and sleeping my life away. My life had stood still, and I had become addicted to Maury Povich, Jerry Springer, Jeremy Kyle, and loose woman, then it was time to do the school runs, which I had literally stopped doing. I couldn't face my daily life. I couldn't face going to the school. I couldn't face even going outside. Sometimes weeks would pass, and I would not go out, and if I did it was in the car. I couldn't face outside. No sooner had I gone out there than I wanted to get back inside, where I felt safe with my boredom.

I prayed and I pleaded with God, "Please help me to find a job in 2008." There was no way I could go on like this, I told myself. I remember saying to Benji that by the end of the year I had to have a job, and a good one at that.

Financially we were struggling, drowning, that's what it felt like; and now what I had asked and prayed for I got. When I look back over the past two years and see the steps that it took to reach were I am now, I find it unbelievable.

I believe in destiny. I have faith and hope. I have courage and strength to get through, and most of all I have my beliefs. Oh yes, my beliefs. Without them, I probably would still be at home, watching my television, which I believe added to depression. Watching Jerry, Jeremy, and Maury contributed to how low I felt at that time; watching people's problems unfold on these shows just made my problem worse.

People who have something going on in their lives do not entertain themselves by watching theses programmes. It's only people like myself and others who have nothing going on in their lives at the time who are entertained by this kind of TV. Well, I was out of this trap now and, to be honest with you, have never watched any of those programmes again. I now have too much going on in my life to even take a minute to view.

Wednesday, September 10, 2008, and I had received my contract. I was very happy because this was my confirmation in writing; this was what I had waited for all this time. This was a day for celebrating, putting my past behind me, and moving on.

I read the letter with pride beaming from my face. Well, that was until I opened another letter which was still lying on the floor waiting patiently to be read. I opened the letter carefully because it looked important. Letters which didn't look important, I would just tear them open. Brown envelopes always looked important. As I slowly opened the envelope, I noticed the letters CRB, Criminal Bureau Check. I pulled it out of the envelope and started to read what it said. Written down in black and white was my past, twenty-three years ago. My past had come back to haunt me, buried in a grave it had laid, for twenty-three years; and now it had risen.

Twenty-two years ago, when it felt like I had been forsaken by the people I loved, my father, mother, sisters, brother, babies' fathers, and God, alone, with no one to turn to, no mother to help support me with my children, no father to look up to, no sister, no brother to cling to, no baby's father to turn to, not even for a penny to rub together, I had to steal to survive. Forget about support services, there were no Harts for Families to support me, no Heart stone to run to, no Family Action to ease my depression, just me.

I stood staring at the word *shoplifting* there in black and white. For a while I stood there mind blank, but waves full of shame and embarrassment flooded my mind. I felt so weak. I had to go and sit down. It was even worse when I came to my senses and realised that the company that I would be working for must have seen this, because that is what they were waiting for, I felt even worse when I thought about it. I almost sunk to the floor. I literally crawled up the stairs to my room with the letter in my hand, into my bed and under the duvet, with my shame in my hand. I rang my sister to tell her what that I had received my CRB, and it had shown my past offence of shoplifting. She then said to me, "Jackie, when you were filling out the application forms, did you fill out the part about convictions?" That's when it clicked in my head that I had not done that part. I remember the night when I was filling the forms, I had rang my sister to ask her the year when the incident had taken place, because it was such a long time ago that I had forgotten the year, and I had also moved on, leaving that part of my past behind me. I was no longer that desperate person that felt the need to have to go out there and commit a crime.

That night after ringing my sister, I had put the application down and fallen asleep. Well, the next day I put the forms in an envelope, had them checked, then hurried to the post office to post them recorded quick delivery, because the deadline was the following day. It was not until that moment that I had realised that I had mistakenly left that part.

Well, that night I was in such a panic, as I read the parts of the application form that were not needed to be sent back. Well, there in black and white it read that if I did not declare any past convictions, my job would be taken away. Well, could you imagine how I freaked out. I hadn't even had the chance to start my job, and I was already sacked. I sat down on my bed with my both hands on my head. I felt so ashamed. Would they understand that it was a mistake, or would they think that I had deliberately not disclosed that information? I must have rung every one of my friends that night, for reassurance, and I got it from all of them. "Jackie, this was a genuine mistake, and you know what, if they don't give you this job because of your mistake, then that's their loss, because they will have lost a great support coordinator." Well, I heard that from all of them, and I believed what they had said, and I started to think that way myself.

I woke up in the morning and very anxious to get in contact with them, to let them know about my mistake, was just about to make the call, when I heard the a bunch of letters come through the letterbox. Well, amongst all the letters was one that ready the company's name, when I opened it up, and read it, I realised that they had acknowledged my offence, my heart sank. Well, I couldn't ring the company any faster than I did.

I spoke to a lady, which I found out on the day when I went for my induction was my line manager Catharina. Well, I told her how ashamed I felt, and that I didn't think that I could face coming in on that Monday for the induction knowing that they knew of my past life. Catharina assured me that she believed it was a genuine mistake, and that we could talk about it on Monday, or we could put it behind us. Well, I chose not to talk about it on that Monday.

Lost so much weight in three months stress of the job, didn't know anything Carol said why worrying you been doing this for so long supporting people Jackie all you need to learn is paper work.

Chapter Twenty-Eight

Supporting with a Difference

2009

My role as a family support coordinator, helping vulnerable families, to empower and support, without passing judgement listening, being their voice when words are few, sometimes in life there are times when we lose our voices, we know what we want to say, but we don't know how to say it to make people listen, sometimes we may even feel like we are the only ones who are going through whatever it is that, we are going through at the time, we even believe that no one will understand how we feel, but were wrong, because someone does.

No matter how little, or big our problems are they still affect us all in the same way, problems have a way of staying in our heads, the only way that we can get them out is to talk about them, we can't forget them because problems don't let you forget, keeping them in your head causes depression. Well, that's what I believe. As a writer, I have always been able to write down my thoughts and feelings, on a piece of paper, good and bad thoughts, good and bad feelings, and that's how I managed to get through some of the toughest times of my life, with no support on the outside. Well, not everyone would be able to do what I have done, because it is hard to write these things down in black and white, because it seems more real, just like when we see a bill, in black and white, bills never have a tendency to make us feel good, the more you get, and the less you deal with them, then in creeps depression.

Well, being able to do the job that I do, has given me an insight into how people's lives are affected by everyday problems.

Supporting families and helping them to make a difference in their lives, as helped me to make a difference in my life too, It has made me look at my life differently today, it's made me realise how far I have come, in terms of wisdom, knowledge and understanding, given to me to do this job, and be the person that I am today.

Going back to when I was a child, I always had a caring nature about me, I was inquisitive too, I wanted to know everything, my mum would say "Jackie your to nosey, you're always listening, through walls, through doors.

Yes I used to eavesdrop; some may call it that including me, others may call it being nosey. but I learnt, from being nosey.

I remember there was one time when I had my head pressed against the door, and my mother opened it. Well, I fell flat on the floor. I remember another time when I got caught for listening to people's business, as they would say. I ran up the stairs so fast before the door could open, I nearly broke my neck. Since that day I never did it again.

I cared about some of the things that I heard, I even began to take it on, worrying how I could help, "maybe get a job as a newspaper girl, I used to think. Well, that would stop them cutting off the electric or gas I didn't want my parents to worry.

Reflection 1974

The first time that I discovered empathy was when I was ten years old. I was coming home from swimming with my brother Robin. We walked through the park, without a care in the world, as children do, then we came to a bench, and there sat this old tramp. Everyone knew who the tramp of Seven Sisters was. They even said that he used to have a home, family, and money; but he went mad, crazy.

People used to cross the road when they saw him coming. No one wanted to go near him. The children used to get close enough to him, to make fun and throw things at him.

Well, the Seven Sisters tramp sat on the bench, with his head hung down. We even thought he was sleeping, but he wasn't. Well, as Robin and I stood in front of him all I could see was a destitute old man, neglected, isolated, and hungry.

My little heart went out to this old man. I remember thinking to myself, where are children and his home? I felt sad for this old man, and I wanted to help him. Well, I figured, I could not give him a roof over his head. Can you imagine me bringing a tramp home? My parents would murder me or ground me for life.

His clothes were tattered and torn and looked like he hadn't washed them since he lost his home, family, and money. I thought about giving him one of my father's suits. There were so many of them, coordinated and hung neatly on expensive wooden hangers. Well, I could give the old man the one he used to wear to work, not a Sunday suit. Could you imagine me doing that? My father walking down Seven Sisters Road and seeing the Seven Sisters tramp in his work suit?

I even wished that we could have taken him home and put him in the bath. Well no, that was even worse than giving him the suit. My parents would sin if I did that. My parents have never sworn in their lives, but they would have on that day.

Well, we ran out of ideas. The one thing I could offer him was a meal, my parents' meal, which they would eat when they came home from work that evening.

I thought about the amount of food we had in our cupboards, and I thought about the amount in the pots, which was small compared to what we had in the cupboards.

We had to help him, and if it meant giving him our parents' meal, we would take that chance. If it meant getting a hiding from our parents, then so be it. This was another adventure for me and Robin, this was an emergency, this old man was starving, and we didn't want him on our conscience all night, We ran home as fast as we could. We then took out one of my mother's best Tupperware bowls, and we filled it to the brim, with every piece of food that was in the pot, then brought it to the old man. Well, the look on his face said it all. It was different to the face that we had always known. Gratitude shone on his face. "Thank you," he repeatedly told us, as he ate my parents' meal of salt mackerel, dumplings, green bananas, and yams. In no time the bowl was empty, like it had never been full.

We were happy at that moment because the Seven Sisters tramp was not hungry anymore. We felt that we had done something very special, and to feel proud about. Forget about the hiding, I told my brother to think about the look on the old man's face, and the feeling that we felt when we had helped someone, then the hiding wouldn't hurt so much.

When we got home our parents were there. They had come home from a hard day's work, hungry and ready for their meal. Well, when my mother opened the pot and looked inside, her eyes nearly popped out her head because the only thing left was the mackerel's head. "Where is the e dinner that I cooked? Who ate the dinner?" my mother shouted. My father was now sitting round the table with his knife and fork, waiting for his hard-earned meal. "We gave it to the tramp," I blurted out. "He was hungry, starving, and we wanted to help him." I couldn't believe when my parents agreed that it was the right thing to do. Even though they were hungry, they were still saying that it was okay to help someone in need.

From that day on, I never looked at the old man as the tramp of Seven Sisters; he was an old man who needed some support to get back on his feet again.

Chapter Twenty-Nine

Time for a Break

2009

I really needed a break away from work. It was four months since I had been working and felt that I had worked myself into the ground, I had managed to conquer the paper work. I remember when I had started working there for months ago, the paper work was my biggest fear, even the telephones, when they rang I would panic, I didn't know what to say. Well, one of my colleges, who I now see as a friend, supported me through that, and before long I was answering phones, and people were asking me to be their support coordinator, because I had been so helpful to them, I always said, if I could I would, but we don't work like that, I sometimes wished that I could choose my cases, because some of them, I felt that I could genuinely support that person, because I had experienced the same thing.

My first family cases were a mirrored image of my life, I couldn't believe it when I first got them. I really enjoyed my job, because practically, I felt that I was good at it, and I believed that I had the right tools to support these families.

I loved doing my job, at first, I had lost so much weight, because of the stress that I felt, my skirts were swinging around my hips, and my trousers were literally falling off, I couldn't control my weight loss. I felt so nervous each day, especially when I would approach the building, I now know that I felt under pressure, caused by Jacqueline La-Touché.

As I learnt to use the system, send e-mails, write supporting statements, fill charity, benefits, housing and medical assessment applications, I became confident. I learnt to fill risk assessments, support families to create a support plan in terms of goals. I became confident in my role as a support coordinator. Gone were the doubts and fears.

The last four months took a lot out of me, and I needed a much deserved break, so I decided to book a holiday, back to Jamaica, to visit my mother. It had been almost three years since I had last seen here. My sister Patsy, was now living in Jamaica with my mother, so it would be nice to see both of them again, and to go and relax, ready to come back to work refreshed.

Well, cheap offers for flights were floating around at the travel agents, so I felt that I had no choice but to book a holiday to Jamaica, before the deadline was up, which was in three days time, all weekend I pondered about going to Jamaica, could I afford it even though it was cheap, what month would I go, what date would I choose, I had three days to decide. Well, I chose to go in May, around my mother's birthday.

The months seemed to pass very quickly as I prepared for my journey. I was also taking Marley and Lourdes, the two of my youngest children. It was difficult for me to even focus on this holiday because of my job, which had become so demanding. Even preparing was hard, because I only had the weekend to do this. However, I only had my weekends to relax and didn't want to spend it on the streets hunting for holiday bargains, but I had no choice.

The months had flown by, and it was now May, and the time had come for us to go on our holiday. I was tired from working so hard, working full time and being a mother. I saw that as two separate jobs when I would come home from work. When I left work I would take off my professional cap, and when I got home I would put on my apron, and my mother's ears. I saw my job at home much harder than my professional role job.

Well, Lourdes and Marley were excited about going. I just couldn't share their excitement. I just acted like it was just a normal thing that we did all the time. Even when the day for us to depart came, it felt just like another day. No one would have guessed that I was going to Jamaica, because I never really spoke about it, and when I did, you would have thought that I was going to Blackpool for the day, not abroad.

Well, I must say that the journey was a nightmare, delayed by five hours, tired, fed up, and I just wanted to reach our destination. However, we had nine hours more ahead of us.

It's not that hard to get lost in time when you're on an aeroplane and you have a long journey a head of you. The first few hours are the hardest, but after that you just lose track of time and just make the most of the time you have, solving puzzles, reading the news paper, watching TV, sleeping, listening to your iPod, using your laptop, and having a drink of wine.

Well, for me it was different. I spent most of my time watching the kids and making sure that they were okay, helping them take their colouring books out, watching them watch TV, watching them sleep, watching the other passengers on their laptops, and watching them as they nodded their heads to music coming from their headphones, even watching some of them sleeping. Well, after what seemed like forever, countdown came. As we were told to fasten our seat belts and prepare for landing, I was too tired to feel excited. I just wanted to get off and reach my mother's house. However, we still had a long journey in front of us, a long journey before I could actually rest my head on a pillow and fall asleep.

Finally I was able to do so and woke up two hours later, at six in the morning, after reaching home, that's what I called it, at two in the morning, and going to bed at 4:00 a.m. after all the excitement and welcomes were over in Jamaica.

Even though I had only slept for two hours, I felt that I had slept for ages. Just the thought of being in Jamaica made me feel awake. Just the thought of not waking up to work and my other commitments and not having to watch the clock made me feel so relaxed and happy. Just walking outside onto the veranda and seeing the sunshine feeling it on my skin felt awesome. I felt like I had died and gone to heaven. What were our plans for the day? Well, I soon decided that this was a day for us to adjust, take things easy, and unpack our suitcases and just chill out with friends on the veranda.

The one thing that I loved about Jamaica was that the days seemed longer, because we woke up early and had more time to do the things that we loved like going to the beach and in the evenings going out, listening to music, which Jamaica is also about, and having a drink. That was enough for me. As my mother reminded me, "Jackie, remember you come to relax and rest yourself." I agreed with her, that's what my holiday was about. I had done the tourist thing so many times, Dunn's River Falls, Blue Lagoon, Green Grotto Caves, Portosico Beach, San San Beach, and Devon House, where they sell the best ice cream that I had ever tasted. Over the years that I had been to Jamaica, which was quite a few times, I had visited all those places. I decided that I would take the children to the local beaches. I didn't want to be a tourist this time, not this time. It was about relaxing and spending time with my mother at home. Well, that's what I thought, until I got there.

We arrived in Jamaica Thursday evening and reached my parents' home Friday morning, and Friday night I was ready to enjoy myself.

I called my friend Damian and asked him to come round. He knew that we were in Jamaica, but he waited for me to call him to come over. Well, the last time that I was in Jamaica was three years ago, which was a long time for me not to come back to see my mother. This was due to circumstances which were going on in my life at the time, depression, money problems, and debt which engulfed my life. I had lost confidence in myself, and I guess that time just slipped away.

My sister Mary was the one that encouraged me to take a holiday and helped me to focus on going. She also helped me to save for my holiday.

I had just not that long ago started my new job. Well, I thought that I would be more financially able, but it seemed like the more money I earned, the more and bigger the bills became. Outstanding debts had to be cleared. I didn't really want any debts hanging around, apart from the ones that I could not really avoid. However, with the help of my sister, my holiday was made possible.

Well, I never got the chance to see my friend Damian the last that I was here, so I could not make this time pass and not see him.

In 2006, I had gone to Jamaica with my sister, and we had taken the children, also our friend, Winston.

Winston was my best friend, a tall, funny man, with a big heart, and a sense of humour to match, he was the joker of all jokers, you wouldn't believe that he was a black man, he spoke like he had lived in the East End of London all his life, however he was true when it came to his roots of west Indian cultural food.

Winston was like family. We met as teenagers with responsibilities as young parents, Winston had stood by me through the bad times with, and long after Patrick had gone, initially he was Patrick's friend, however he became mine, Winston never supported the way that Patrick treated me, he would always curse behind his back, and say "Jackie if I had a Woman like you I would never treat her like he treats you, you deserve much more"

He was more of a father to my children, in terms of being there for them, parents meetings, meal times, shopping trips, when the boys were expelled, when they were at the police station, waiting to be bailed, when Patrick was nowhere to be found, he was there for everything, I relied on him heavily, and I guess it made him feel like he belonged in a family, even though he had two daughters, which he loved, there was something missing, because he was no longer living with them, however they always came first to him "my two girls", that's what he called them. The life he vraved he found with us, and that was stability and routine for him, We were never hungry when Winston was around, he became my hero. People always believed that we were a couple, we would recoil in horror 'errr', "no way you must be joking", he would even pretend that he didn't know me as I talked to him, he would even stop people and say "excuse me this woman's crazy, I don't know who she is, she's bothering me," we argued, we laughed, we cried together, he was my rock when I needed one to lean on.

He had always wanted to come with us to Jamaica, my mother and father had a soft spot for him, because they knew that we all loved him, the children too. So we planned a family holiday, all of us going to Jamaica, this was his first holiday abroad.

This was his first away and we wanted to make sure that he lived his first Jamaican experience. Well, every day we were so busy planning our day and going out with the children and showing our friend the sites that time slipped away. It was only at the end of our two weeks that I had realised that we did not get a chance to see Damian.

Well, he later found out that we were in Jamaica and came to visit us. "Why didn't you guys let me know you were here?" Well, we didn't really have an answer for that, because we should have let him know. I should have let him know, because he was my friend.

Damian had changed from when I had last seen him. He was a Rastafarian, and he now had dreadlocks which lay on his shoulders. He looked different to how I last remembered him. He even looked older because of his hair; he looked wiser too.

We all sat on the veranda with and spoke about our time in Jamaica. Damian also told us that he was into his music and spoke about songs that he had written, surrounding his life in Jamaica, and also his childhood. We wanted Damian to perform for us, so in true Jackie style, I put him on the spot and asked him to sing for us.

Well, he did, and we were amazed at what we heard, the lyrics, the talent. Well, the gift that he had was unspeakable at the time. We couldn't believe that we had met someone in person who was so talented with music. I couldn't believe that he was my friend.

I had never known that side to him. As far as I was concerned, he was this quiet person who listened, more than anything. Thinking back to when my father died, that's all he ever did with me, just listen.

Such a big voice coming from this young man, something that I had learnt about my friend Damian Cousins.

I felt a little sad, because I had never met anyone in person who had that talent. It was just flawless, and as we watched and listened in amazement on the veranda, lights turned off and just the moonlight, and the stars, glowing in the dark, it was perfect, and a night that we never forgot.

Well, here I was in Jamaica three years later, and calling Damian to come over and see me again. Well, that evening he came round, bringing along his two little daughters with him. My sister was sitting on the veranda when she saw someone coming up into the yard. The dogs were barking as they always did when someone came up into the yard. No matter where we were inside or outside, we knew that someone was coming through the gate. As the person got closer she realised that it was Damian. "Jackie," she called, "Damian has come to see you." "Okay, I'm coming soon." I quickly got myself together and went out onto the veranda, where he was now sitting.

Damian looked even more different than when I last saw him three years ago. His hair was on its way down to his waist. I could not believe it had left his shoulders three years ago and was now striving to reach the ground. Damian had a dark complexion, with very striking beautiful white teeth, I had never met anyone with teeth as white as snow until now, a lot had changed about my friend Damian, he had matured with time, and seemed a lot different to how I last remembered him. In three years so much had changed, I couldn't help but notice.

In three years so much had changed about him. "Hi, Damian," I said, "how are you?" He seemed very pleased to see me and then introduced me to his two little girls and their cousin who had come along. That evening was nice and relaxed. The children played with each other. His two little girls entertained us with their dancing. We had a laugh and a drink, and we all made plans for that night to go out have more drink and listen to more music, which we did.

Before we left for our music and drink, I gave him a present which I had brought from England. It was nothing much, only a T-shirt, just to let him know that I had remembered his friendship. He seemed really grateful that I had remembered him. However, later on he would tell me that I had just given him a present and walked away, and that's when he realised that the only feelings that I had for him was that of a friend and nothing more. He also told me that he felt a little rejected, because he always hoped from the very first time we met, maybe one day I would look at him as more than that.

Damian hoped for much more than I had to offer. He had always kept his feelings for me buried deep inside, and respected the fact that I was married, and would not think about approaching me in any way, that could have caused our friendship to die, so he just settled for being friends, nothing more.

Well, all that was about to change, without any of us really knowing that it would. That night was great, I hadn't enjoyed myself like that for ages, the music was fantastic, and soon as I got to the wine bar, there was no holding back, you see, I love dancing, I always had, you could never stop me from shaking a leg, as I used to say, for me music was the ultimate gift created, every chance I could get to dance, I would, even at home cooking on a Sunday, dancing was on the menu as well as our Sunday roast, I was so engrossed in music, and owned at least 500 CDs, which I had collected over the past years, and still collecting today. You see music had helped me throughout the years get through some of the darkest moments, heartaches, and happiness in my life, and I was dedicated, and so in love with my music.

So dancing was in sync with the music I loved. I never cared what people thought especially when I was on the dance floor, in the middle, I hated standing in corners, or around the side of the walls, I always expressed myself in the middle of the floor, why hide, I was proud to show that I loved music, and dancing, so tonight was no different than any other night it didn't matter that I was in Jamaica, where everyone was supposed to be able to dance, I was doing my thing, and lost in music, Damian soon joined us, and we all started to rave, even though we were the only ones, apart from a few other people who were now starting to dance, now that it had turned into a party moon. Come to think of it, no one was dancing until I arrived, now they were.

I was having such a great time, no work in the morning, no watching the clock, just dancing and having a drink with my mate Damian, judging by the way that I was enjoying myself, I knew that my holiday was going to end that way, I had started how I meant to go on, I thought to myself sorry mummy, I thought that I did come here to relax, and have a rest as you put it, but going out, enjoying myself for me is having a rest, and relaxing my mind, body and soul, with music.

Every day for the next two weeks were filled with fun, the children had a great time going to the beach, and so did I, the beach had always been about the children having fun, I would go to the beach, but I spent most of my time lying on the sand, shouting at them not to go too far into the sea, most people relax at the beach. Well, I never did, I was always looking out for the children and spoiling their fun as they would tell me.

Well, this time was different; I was out to have fun with them this time.

We were all off to the beach, Damian too, and we were going to have a great time, a picnic included, cooking on the beach is something that people do a lot in Jamaica, it's a beautiful scene, sunshine, blue sky, the sound of the sea, and a Rasta man cooking, yes that was Damian, we were both happy to cook for everyone, while they had fun in the water.

The sun was blazing hot as the flames from the fire, which he had put together from coconut shires and pieces of wood, crackled and popped. As we fanned the fire, and the pan sizzled I watched as he masterfully took over from me, something felt special about us cooking together, as we cooked, we laughed together and had fun, it felt good. I found myself staring at him, as he leant over the fire, cooking, For the first time since I had known him, I had never really noticed his good looks until now, I told myself why did it matter now, why was I noticing that he was a beautiful looking black man, with such an aura about him, which I found myself being drawn to.

After we all ate we relaxed on the beach, the children looking for shells, building sand castles, and laughing, at that moment the child in me surfaced, as it sometimes did, I was always told by my family that I was still a child at heart, all my childlike qualities never left they were never that far away, and would often come out. Well, that day they were out.

Lying down on the sand, looking up at the blue sky, with the kids playing in the sand, I sat up and started to play with them, picking up the sand and letting it slip through my fingers, then I said, "Why don't you all cover me up with sand, I had always seen people on TV covered from their neck to their feet in sand, head poking out, and I always wondered, to myself what must that feel like.

Well, no sooner had I said that than the children started piling sand all over my body. Damian helped them, as they laughed, I was laughing too, and loving every minute of it, the sand felt very warm as it covered my body, my legs were slowly disappearing, so were my arms, and before I knew it my whole body was covered with sand, and my head poking out, I was buried in a sand grave, I couldn't move, and just lay there laughing at myself, along with Damian and the kids, I felt happy. Well, I freed myself from the sand after I had received my memory.

Damian asked me if I wasn't going to go into the sea, I never really went into the water when I was on holiday, the furthest I got, was just wetting my feet.

I couldn't really swim anymore, after having a traumatic experience when I was a child, I was afraid of swimming pools, rivers, and the sea. "Come on Jackie, you can't come all the way to Jamaica and not go in the sea, I heard Damian say, "No I said I don't really want to, and besides that it must be cold, he replied no it's not. Well, by this time everyone who was in the water had come out, children were drying off, to put their clothes on, it was time for us to go, Come on Jack" Damian said, just a few minutes in the water hold your hand. Well, okay I thought, might as well, and he did say that he would hold my hand, so he held my hand as I followed him into the sea.

I was laughing as we walked out a little further "Come on Jack, don't be scared he said, I could see a wave heading towards us, like it was ready to knock us over, and I didn't really want to get fully wet, so I started to pull away from him, to get back to shore, but he sensed that I was about to do that and held on to my hand even tighter, as he guided me slowly back towards him.

We reached as far as I would let him go, and we just stood there, as the waves rushed towards us again, but this time I didn't run, I just stood there, I felt safe standing there, I felt secure knowing that I would not fall down whilst he was there holding my hand, suddenly a huge wave crashed against us, suddenly I felt his arm around my waist, this kept me on my feet as the water covered my body, and face, I could taste the salty sea, in my mouth.

Even though this had happened I still remained calm. His hand was still wrapped around my waist standing in the sea. He had made me feel safe. I felt protected by him, a million miles away from everything. At that very moment I felt that there were feelings for me, which had lain dormant for seven years. Standing there in the sea, I realised that not only did I feel that he had feelings for me, but I was enjoying the feelings that I was now feeling for him.

I didn't want it to end. If I could have stayed standing in the sea forever, holding that moment and feeling free, and feeling the power of someone else's feelings coming to the surface, I would have, so I took that memory and put it along with the other memories which I had now begun to accumulate.

As the days passed, more and more memories accumulated, and so did my thoughts and feelings for Damian. However, I just kept them to myself.

I started to question my feelings when I woke up one morning, with Damian on my mind. The first thing that morning was to ring him and tell him about plans for the day. My feelings were growing for him. However, I tried to ignore them, because we were just friends. I thought a lot about his age and the fact that he lived in Jamaica, but most of all because I was married, and I never wanted no more complications in my life.

One evening after coming from the beach, and having another intense moment, where I felt that he felt that, my feelings were also growing. Even though we never spoke about it, we both knew that there was something going on between us.

With our feelings for each other, it was weird because I had never ever thought of him as nothing more in my life than just as a friend, someone that I would see only when I went to Jamaica. I never really kept in contact with him after I had returned back home to England. There was only ever one time that I had spoken to him when I was back home, and that was three years ago, when he had given me his number. Well, I contacted him once. We only ever spoke for a few minutes, just to say hello, and how you doing, nothing more than friends. I soon lost his number and never asked for it again.

So here I am with my feelings on the verge of getting out of control, for someone eighteen years my junior, and I his senior. I was now forty-four years old, with a husband, seven children, three grandchildren, two dogs, and a cat, and a whole lot of baggage, and falling slowly for my friend Damian, the Rasta man, who was twenty-seven years old, and not nineteen years young. Well, even though he was older, he was still younger than me.

That even we sat down under the mango tree just talking about life in general, I also wanted to know more about his life. Damian had grown up with his grandmother. What sort of life did he have as a young child? Where were his parents? Where did he live? I wanted to know about my friend, but I didn't want it to be in a way which made me sound like I was being nosey. However, I do have a skill getting information out of people in a nice way, which is an asset to my job.

Well, it wasn't that hard for him to tell me about his life, in the short space of time, under the mango tree. He spoke about his grandmother with great respect, and I thank her for the upbringing of this soul. He is the positive side to the three Cs that I knew, conscious, caring, and charming, the opposite to the three negative Cs which I had in my life, when I was fifteen years old, charged, convicted, and condemned, between us good and bad. However, the good always overrides the bad. Good lives on, and bad must eventually come to an end.

Over the remaining days I began to admire his honesty and respect his consciousness. He had so much knowledge for someone of that age, and it was hard to believe that he was the age that he was. I found myself speaking to my friend about my marriage. I found it easy to talk to him. He listened to every last word. He never once judged what I had told him. Well, that was the first time in my married life that I had ever opened up to anyone. I had never gone into depths of my marriage with anyone before. I had always kept my thoughts and feelings inside. It was easier to just carry on from day to day. I had accepted this was my life, and I just had to get on with it, the best that I could, but I wasn't getting on with it. I was unhappy. I couldn't have spoken to Benji more than I had, so I guess I just gave up, so here I am sitting under the mango tree, with my marriage being questioned, by me.

Damian asked me how long had I felt like this. He even asked me, did I feel like this when we first met seven years ago? Well, I replied yes, that's how I felt when I came to Jamaica for my father's funeral.

The next day Damian took me to meet his grandmother, who seemed like she was very familiar with my name. She even spoke to me like she had known me for a long time. I later found out that he had spoken to her about me for the past years. She even knew my age, and she knew that he had always felt more than just being friends.

Damian's grandmother and I had a bond, with England; she had visited England a few times, so she was familiar with the weather, and that was one of things that we spoke about, amongst other things.

She had her posh English accent which was probably for me. My parents were like that too. They had accents for special people, so I guess that in Damian's grandmother's eyes I was special too.

Damian grew up with his grandmother living in a fine house, probably the best house on the block. Well, that's what I thought. It looked grand from the outside, and on the inside it was just as nice. For some reason I thought that Damian still lived there, but he didn't anymore. He lived by himself, after his relationship ended with his children's mother.

I was curious to know where he lived, because it could not be better than this. Why did he not come back to live at his grandmother's home after his relationship ended, because his room was still there.

He also explained to me the reasons why he did not go back home to live with her. I respected his reasons.

Well, I now wanted to see where he lived, and I wanted him to take me there, so I asked him to show me where he lives. He hesitated, and then he said sure. Walking through bushes, we came to a little house hidden by hedges and trees. "This is where I live," he said. "Okay," I said.

We walked up to the door, me following behind. He opened the door, and we walked in. That evening he taught me the true meaning of never judging a book by its cover.

He taught me how to be humble, to be true to myself and be happy. I was on my way to falling in love from that night on with my friend. He had such sincerity in his voice, in his eyes, my feelings were confirmed.

My sister had always spoken about going to Bob Marley's museum. Well, I wasn't really keen on going. The journey was far, and the kids would probably be sick, so I wasn't really bothered about going even though I had heard that it was something to see. Well, I sat there smiling then saying aloud, "Boy, I feel like I'm in Damian's museum. One day when you are famous, I can say that I have sat on Damian Cousins, the great music artist's bed. I don't need to go to Bob Marley's museum to sit on his bed. I would rather sit on Damian Cousins, who is alive, bed." We laughed about it; however, I believed it. I believed that one day I would.

As I sat on his bed and looked around, there wasn't a lot in that little house, but it felt like a home, and even if there was not a lot of material things, there was a lot of peace and tranquility in that little house, covered by the surrounding trees.

The countdown to days were left time to go home. Two weeks had passed, and it was now time to go home and leave this all behind. It was difficult, because my feelings for Damian had grown to another level. I was slowly falling in love with him and him with me.

Time to say goodbye came back to haunt me, for this was exactly what I had already been through when I met my Benji. I was now an expert at this procedure and could explain to Damian what it felt like before he experienced it for the very first time, and I the second time around, thinking that it would be easier, but it was just as hard as the first time around.

That evening, we stood in the airport with tears streaming down our faces, embraced to say goodbye, feeling like we were torn apart. There was definitely a connection between me and Damian.

Well, it was difficult coming back on the aeroplane. I couldn't get him out of my mind. All I wanted to do was hear his sweet voice. To be honest he has the sweetest voice ever. I kept on hearing his voice inside my head, and I just couldn't wait to hear his voice again. This time I had his number, and it wasn't on a piece of paper for me to lose. It was etched in my memory.

I missed him so much, and I was still in the airport to get back home safely. I had to put my holiday to the back of my mind, but each time I tried it didn't last.

The children were happy to get back home; that's all they ever spoke about. They were excited, and I felt that they were rubbing their excitement in my face. They couldn't hide it. *How selfish of them*, I thought, *here I am feeling that I could never be happy again, after experiencing such bliss for the past two weeks.* I didn't want that to end, but it had.

All my family were happy for our return. I was happy to see them too. We spoke about our holiday. We gave gifts, which we had brought from Jamaica for them. This took my mind away from how I was really feeling, then slowly my mind started to drift away, back to Jamaica, and I was thinking about him again. I wanted to ring him, to hear his sweet voice again. Well, I couldn't hold out any longer so I slipped away to call him, and when I heard his voice, a great big smile lit up my face. We spoke for a while, he spoke about how he felt, and how much he missed me, I missed him so much, more than I cared to realise at the time, which I would soon find out as time went on.

Chapter Thirty

Falling Deeper

2009

Things got back to normal very quickly. I returned back to work and was greeted with eight new cases, families to support eight of them one time. Imagine if this had happened before I went on holiday, before I felt like I had someone who loved me. Well, I would have freaked out, but I didn't. I just took them out of my pigeonhole and carried them to my desk, like presents, putting them down and going through them one by one, then ringing the families to tell them the good news. "My name is Jacqueline La-Touché, and I have been allocated to be your support coordinator." I quite enjoyed doing this; it felt easy doing this, when it once felt hard. Knowing that a person feels loved makes them feel like they can take on anything and conquer it too. Well, that's how it was.

Nothing really seemed to get me down anymore.

I kept in contact with Damian, speaking to him every day. It had become the norm. Our telephone calls had become precious. They were full of magic, laughter, fun, and learning everything about each other, singing, listening to music together on the phone.

Damian began to love all the music that I loved. We had very deep spiritual conversations on the phone. We spoke about what we did during the days. He respected my job and was interested in the line of work that I did. He began to know me, and I began to know him inside out too.

Damian and I developed a strong connection between us. We even discovered that we both had telepathic communication skills. We would think alike. He could even finish my sentence, if I hesitated to carry on. I even did the same with him; it was spooky. We even played guessing games, as to what the other was thinking. We always got it right. We would laugh about it like we were a couple of kids. Things got more crazy when he would call me with music in the background, and I would also have music playing in my background. He would ask me what song I was listening to, then I would tell him, and then he would tell me that's what he was listening to now. No, I couldn't believe it. Well, that's until he turned up the volume, and it would be a word behind or in front of mine. It was amazing.

My creative side became more apparent; it came flooding from my head, through my body, to my hands, through my fingers, through a pen onto paper as poetry. My feelings became poetry, my life became poetry, and I was able to express my feelings to Damian, through a pen. I would write poems and send them by text. They just could not stop coming.

I had always loved writing, and so did Damian. He was passionate about writing his songs. We started to write together. He once started writing a song, and I ended up writing one of the verses, which had just sprung to my mind, as we were having fun being creative on the phone.

Damian was a songwriter. Both of us inspired to write the way we do, and the things that we write about. Inspiration comes from anywhere and grabs you anyplace anytime. We both know as writers, we cannot think about what to write. It is given to us just like that. I once tried so hard to write a joke for Ms. Meryl. Well, could I get one, I sat there all evening, and not one inspirational funny thought came to my head. My head was blank.

I wanted to write some new jokes for Ms. Meryl, so I thought that it was easy to do. This was at the beginning of my journey with Ms. Meryl. That was when I did not understand my gift, and how it worked.

Now jokes for Ms. Meryl they come to me, just like a letter in the post.

Sometimes I get them one after the other, coming so fast, and so fast to write down in, so you see, Damian and I had a connection, with thinking, we had the gift of being able to express ourselves through writing, music poetry, and writing jokes for Ms. Meryl, Damian even wrote, and recorded a song for Ms. Meryl, then sent it to me, it was hilarious. Each time I listened to it, I smiled. I guess that was intended, to make me smile.

We understood our gift, and that's what helped to bring us closer together, and it was easier to fall in love. Soul Mate, that's what people say. Well, I've never really used that term before now, maybe I'd never felt so connected to any man, to give them the title of a soul mate.

All those years ago, I had fallen in love with Benji, I loved him enough to want to marry him, but this was completely different, I felt so connected to Damian, we fell in love completely over the telephone, I even joked, to him, that Graham Alexander Bell, was the man who invented the telephone, the next greatest man to God, because with his invention he made it possible, I said to Damian that we had to thank him, for giving us this opportunity to communicate with each other, because we felt that this was the next best thing to being together.

I always said that we were still together, we were always in each other's heart, his voice was always in my room and mine his, I would always start off our conversation with "What are you doing, or ask him where he was, funny enough, I always pictured him lying down on his bed talking to me, when he sometimes would say, that he wasn't at home.

I used to tell him what I would be doing, even if it was looking outside my window, I would even say to him follow me downstairs to get a snack; he was now in my kitchen.

We would tell each other everything, talk about our day, sometimes I used to think I was boring his ears off, I would say it at the end of a conversation, his reply would be Jackie you could never bore me because you have so much to say, there's so much I want to know about you, because I love you, I he would reply, "Damian you're the sweetest man I've ever known, and I meant every word of it, because

He truly was.

September, and my birthday fast approaching forty-five years old, I would say, he would say no you mean forty-five years young. I Started to think about the number 45, I didn't really know how I felt about that number, I remember my mother at that age, and I thought she was old, imagine, it took me until I reached the age forty-five years old to realise that she was still young.

Well, I started questioning the happiness, I had in my life before Damian came along, looking back to May, was I happy before then, I tell myself no, I was comfortable, like an old pair of slippers, I was tired, I felt tired like an old sheep dog, I felt miserable, as a child does on a rainy day when they cannot go outside to play. Well, that's fine for others. I started to do a self analysis, looking at the kind of personality that I had. I was vivacious, very energetic, and intelligent to know what I wanted out of life.

I was articulate in the things which I did, very creative, imaginative, so why should I settle for any less than being happy, but I had. Finding peace in heart, that's all I had ever wanted, I wanted to feel loved and needed in return, and I had found that, in Damian. Until now I had not realised how much I had needed to be happy. Well, I could not go on feeling the way that I had for so long, it wasn't fear to all three of us, me, Benji, and Damian.

During the past three years, I felt that my relationship with Benji, had hit rock bottom, we were going through a very difficult time in our marriage, even then I felt that there was no hope for us. However, we managed to get through that time, but even though we did, things still remained the same, we chose to stay in our relationship, but there were never any changes between either of us, I guess it was easier to stay together than to leave the relationship.

Now three years on, the inevitable was here, and my relationship was at its near end, In a million years I could never believe that it would.

I had become more distant from Benji, I don't even know what he thought, did he notice. Well, if he did he didn't say anything me, I thought that it could not get any worse but it had.

Benji was oblivious to the distance that had grown between us, and was happy to plod along. Well, that's the impression that he gave. I felt so alone now, more than ever in this relationship, it was far from being right.

Well, I continued to live a single life in my mind, in this relationship I made decisions on my own, I slept many nights on my own, for the past nine years, I had spent Valentine's on my own, for the past eleven years since we had been married. I have been out for the past eleven years on my own, and I have been crying inside on my own, for the past eleven years.

Well, forty-five years old, and its Saturday morning, and was going to ring the travel agents and book me a flight to Jamaica, I wanted to see Damian again, that's all I could think about night and day, I had to see him, I never thought twice about going like I did last time, and this time I was going alone, I had never been anywhere by myself since I started a family.

The more I thought about the idea of being on my own fascinated me, I thought about the whole experience of feeling that It was just me, and no one else to think about but myself, I wanted to experiencing saying that I only ever thought about myself for once instead of always thinking about everyone, my husband, my children, my dog, my cat, my job.

I told Benji that I was going to Jamaica, it had got to that stage, where I never asked, I just did whatever suited me at the time well, flight booked for November 16, I was off to sunny Jamaica, it felt a little weird but it was real, I was going to Jamaica, tickets' in my hand reading my flight details to Damian over the phone, we counted the days that I had left to come, it seemed like forever, with the way that I was feeling, my love grew to another level, we would fantasize about the things that we were going to do together, the fun we were going to have, meeting at the airport that was a big one, the airport scene, we called it, we would even act it out on the phone, I even told him something that I wanted him to ask me when we first met and you know he did.

16 November, packed and ready for Jamaica, it was raining outside, but I didn't care because I knew that tomorrow, I was going to be in the sunshine. The weather had just started to get bad, it was winter now, what a time to be going to Jamaica so close to Christmas, I was happy about going, but when I thought about the little time I had when I came back from holiday to get Christmas together for my family, I felt scared thinking that it would be impossible, if

I felt the way that I had imagined when I came back from Jamaica, broken hearted.

Going to Jamaica I did have mixed feelings, some of the time, I would think about my departure, and my arrival in Jamaica, the thought about leaving Damian made me feel sick, the thought of seeing him again made me feel happy.

My journey to Jamaica started in a minicab, to the train station and sitting on the Gatwick Express.

I made sure that I had fully charged my iPod which I had especially purchased just for my holiday. As I connected the earphones to both my ears, I relaxed back into the seat and closed my eyes. This was awesome, and I hadn't even moved from the station.

Locked in my world of music, I didn't realise that we had now reached Gatwick. I struggled off the train with three suitcases and hand luggage. A good Samaritan carried them all the way into the airport and straight to the check-in desk. *What an angel,* I thought. *Thank you, God, everything is going smooth. So far so good.* Well, I sailed through check-in, through immigration, no liquids for them to throw away. Angel and Hypnotic Poison sweet-smelling fragrances lay buried in the bottom of my suitcase, on the way to the aeroplane before me.

That was easy, I thought, not like the last time, when they confiscated my hair products. I felt angry and even felt like I wanted to cry, when I remembered that I wasn't going to bring them in the first place. I had forgotten them, so I turned back to get them.

Well, everything continued on a role. Sitting in the departure lounge, still listening to my iPod, walking through the shops, through duty free, smelling all the different fragrances, spraying them on me, sitting down having a quick meal, and no one to interrupt me, to take them to the toilet. It was pure bliss.

I even gave Damian a call to find out how he was and to let him know that I couldn't wait to see him again; he felt the same way too.

Well, I was just sitting down thinking about how lucky I was to be able to have quality time with myself.

I took my time to walk down that long pathway to board the plane. Flight VA 1 to Kingston was now boarding, the big screen tells us. All the passengers start getting up from their sits, one by one, and picking up their bags, newspapers, and children, following me down the long pathway to the boarding lounge, where we all wait patiently to start the second half of our journey.

Finally I am on my journey, walking onto the aeroplane, leaving all my cares behind me, my family too. I was about to take off into the sky, above the clouds. God must have been smiling down at me, because I got the perfect seat, right next to the window, and the first as you walk in. I felt no different to a passenger sitting in first class.

I fastened my seat belt and pushed my seat way back. I placed my pillow behind my head and covered myself with the red blanket, still with music flowing through my head. I closed my eyes as the plane pointed its nose to the sky and started to make its journey up above the clouds, which now begun to look like balls of cotton wool, I smiled. It was amazing, and even more especially after I had drunk one, two, or maybe three glasses of wine. I felt like I was actually floating amongst the clouds, and all I could hear playing in my head at that moment was Mariah Carey's song, "Fly Like a Bird." It was such a beautiful memory that I must always treasure.

All the thoughts of being alone on this journey that I had previously thought about were coming true. This was better than imagining it. This was actually feeling it. I had so many things to occupy my mind, my puzzles, my newspaper, my laptop, and my music, and Damian on my mind. I felt like I was in heaven.

Lost in everything I would fall asleep and only woke when I smelt the aroma of food being passed round. Even the food I enjoyed, which I never really did. I always said that aeroplane and hospital food tasted like the packaging it came in, but this time for some reason it tasted different. I was eating like I was in a restaurant.

In front of me sandwiched between the middle of the back of the seat was a little TV screen, with a map of my destination, and a little aeroplane pointing towards Jamaica. Occasionally I would look at it, to see where we were, Barbados, Guyana, Trinidad, St. Lucia, Antigua, I told myself that we were probably passing there.

Cuba and America, I knew that we had definitely flown past those two, because the seat belt sign has come on. When you see flight attendants walking around gathering earphones and blankets and handing out immigration forms, then you know that it's almost time to land and get off this long ride.

I'm in Jamaica, as the plane starts to turn its nose down.

My stomach starts to feel pangs of excitement, the little dots which I noticed from above, were now turning into houses, the little spots of light began to get brighter as we get closer to the ground, and before I know it, I am walking through the airport fanning myself from the heat, a far cry from where I had just come from. I started to undo my jacket, taking it off and placing it over my hand luggage. People standing patiently, some impatient little children holding on to their parents still not fully awake from staying awake most of the journey, then falling asleep in the last hour.

After waiting anxiously in the immigration queue with almost 300 people, I couldn't believe it when I walked into the baggage lounge, and found that someone had taken all my luggage off the conveyer belt, and placed them within my reach, for me to check out straightaway. *Thank you, God,* I thought.

With more immigration procedures, and suitcases to search, I take my time, making sure that I have everything. Well, before I took another step, I made sure that I looked good, checking my clothes, and applying my lipstick, walking outside was always another memory, people waiting for their loved ones, mothers and fathers waiting for their sons, and daughters, brothers and sisters waiting for their brothers or sisters. Lovers waiting for their lover, and Friends waiting for their friend, everybody waiting for someone, and everybody feeling the same way.

Rows of faces lined the airport grounds, cars, taxi cabs, and vans parked waiting for their passenger to come. it's a wonderful feeling waiting for someone to come out, and it's an awesome feeling coming out, I can tell you.

Looking for Damian, and my sister Patsy, who was there to meet me, I scouted my eyes around, and then I heard someone say "there she is" then I looked over, and saw my Patsy, and Damian, I could not believe here I was again, with Damian, I now loved him even more than I did yesterday. We greeted each other, with a little caution, we loved each other. However, no one really knew how much, apart from us, so it was hard trying to hold back how we really felt, but we had to.

Sitting with Damian in the van going home to my mother's house was another memory, which I still smile at when, remembered.

Music blaring, and drinks flowing, he whispered in my ear, what I told him to ask me, after five months he had still remembered, and laughed after he had whispered in my ear.

My third, and final part of the journey was a happy one, with Damian sitting next to me. We all sung away, as the van hugged the corners of the road, I slumped from side to side to side, that was funny, especially when Damian was trying to stop me from falling, I remember him still holding onto his drink, and trying to save me from ending up on the floor, I remember thinking that I wish that I could hold this moment, I didn't mind this journey being long. However, this time it went quickly, because you know what they say, time goes quickly, when you're having fun. Well, I was and it was a shame that it had to end. However, I knew this was not the end of my fun, and not the beginning, the beginning had started five months ago, and there was lots more to come.

He always made me laugh, I don't think that there has ever been a day since I met him that he hasn't put a smile on my face, we make each other laugh, all we have to do is look at each other, then we both would smiles.

Everything that we had spoken about on the phone, the fun that we wanted to have with each other, the place we said that we would go back to, the beautiful things that we said we would do for each other, we now had the chance to do, we were not dreaming anymore, we weren't imagining this day anymore we were together, living the dream, it felt real, it felt natural as Damian would say.

That was one of Damian's, favourite words, when something was said which he agreed, and we both did. Well, it was real.

My time in Jamaica was magical, the first week, I savoured every moment, because they were so special, I felt like crying because I'd never felt so happy, in such a long time. Come to think of it, I never really felt complete happiness the way I did, at this time, everything we did together was so special, it felt like we belonged together, everything was so romantic, from the very start.

Our first day together was a day that I can never forget, we were so happy just being together not doing much, we walked down to my father's grave, and I just stood there resting on the grave just like I always did, and taking in the sun, feeling so happy.

I always felt at peace when I vested my father's grave. My father was buried on the Land, right in front of the church that he built, which was the reason for coming back home to Jamaica when they did, I was glad that my father had fulfilled his dream, and was now resting here, in front of it.

Damian knew how much my father meant to me, in life, and in death, because I always came down here to his grave, and I always spoke about my father to him, like he knew him before, he passed away, but he didn't, Damian knew how important it was for me to come here, each time that I came to Jamaica, I remember the last time that I was here, it was Damian and me, who sat down, and painted my father's grave, back to snow white. He would say to me Jackie the grave could do with washing down, we'll do it later, or another day, so you see, he knew how much coming down here to my father's grave, meant to me, because when I first met him, it was almost nine years ago.

My father had just passed away, and I was attending his funeral in Jamaica, it was a very difficult time for me, and I was full of grief. I was there to help with funeral arrangements, and to support my mother through this terrible time.

Being strong for everyone was hard, because I was breaking up inside, the only person who really understood how I felt inside was Damian.

Overwhelmed with grief, I stood on the grounds of my parents land, just staring into nowhere, I was completely lost, just standing there, staring down to where my father would be buried, on this land, which was his final request, his resting place. As I stood there I noticed a young man standing in the distance just staring at me I didn't know who he was. Well, I stared to walk towards him, when I noticed an uncanny resemblance to someone I knew, I remember saying to him, that he looked like someone I knew, he smiled, this was not a chat up line, I then asked him his name, and was shocked at his answer "Damian" he said. Well, that was spooky, because not only did he look like someone I knew, he now had the same name.

From that day, we became friends, I spent one week in Jamaica, which felt like forever, the days just dragged by, there was nothing to smile about.

The next few days were just a blur, it felt like they had been erased from my memory. Well, that's until Damian retrieved them, and filled in the gaps of my time spent, in Jamaica, which was the saddest time that I had ever gone through in my life.

He became my rock. I have since realised, reflecting back to when my father passed away, that Damian Cousins had held a torch for me from that time. I must say that he held it well.

I now ask him, if he had liked me all those years ago. His reply was "Sure, I have always liked you and hoped that one day it would be possible for us to get together." I couldn't believe that my friend had thought more about me. He even said to me, "Jack, when I first saw you standing there in the yard, you looked so lost and helpless, and I didn't want to take advantage of that. You came here for your father's funeral, nothing more." I even asked him why was he looking at a big woman, when he was only nineteen years old.

Damian had told me that he was twenty-five years old, not that it mattered because I never thought of him in that way. Damian thought I was twenty-five years old, even though I did tell him that I was thirty-six years old at the time. He told me that age didn't matter. Well, it did at the time, because I was thirty-six, and he was nineteen.

Well, during my week spent in Jamaica, attending my father's funeral, he became my support system. He stayed with me throughout the days.

He would now tell me that I would mostly talk about my father during those days. Damian would follow me down to my father's grave, where I would often sit, sometimes twice a day. He told me that he would light my cigarettes for me and that each morning I would greet him with a glass of rum, which had become my daily medicine, my antidepressant. Rum numbed the pain, rum made me smile, rum became my best friend during those days, so did Damian. He even told me about the funeral service. He also told me how he stood beside me at the graveside, while I cried. He told me how he had comforted me, with his arms around me. Well, I was in disbelief, asking him a barrage of questions, which he thoughtfully answered. He was able to fill me in, on those missing parts of my memory which I now remember so vividly in my mind, and here I was back to where I had first met him. Here in sunny Jamaica.

That day the sun was blazing as we walked around looking at the trees, in the churchyard. We sat under the mango tree just chatting away in disbelief that we were here together. We sat for a while, then we got up, ready to go back up to the house. Well, as we stood there Damian put his arms around me, face to face, my back turned towards the sun.

I could feel the heat of the sun on my back, as we stood embracing each other. Well, something very special happened between us, something we could not explain to anyone, only ourselves. For a while as we stood there, I could feel some kind of energy flowing through our bodies. We could not move. It was unbelievable. We actually felt like our hearts were connecting together. When we came to ourselves, I remember saying to him, "What just happened there? Did you feel it?" "Yes," he said. I asked him, "What did you feel?" You know what, he explained it to me exactly the same way as I had felt; something happened that day, something very special between us.

I will never forget that day, and the memory of it, I hold in my heart along with all the other memories. So here I was with Damian, who actually came into my life almost eight years ago.

Spending time alone together was incredible. We were both so in love with music. There was not a moment, a day, a place, or a time we never had music with us. We did so much sharing with music, singing, dancing, we would put the iPod earphone in our ears, one in the left and other in the right, and we would dance to the sound of our favourite songs, which seemed to be most of them. We would be on the beach just looking up into the blue skies lying down next to each other locked in music. We would be sitting down having a drink in a bar, listening to our music; it was amazing.

Our imagination took control of whatever setting we were in. On the beach staring into the sea, we saw a ship out in the far distance. We imagined being stranded here, on an island, our island Jackie and Damian, no one to rescue us, but ourselves.

Waving to the ship, even though it was just a dot, in the distance, no one could see us, and we'd be here forever. The thought of that was amazing. We would even imagine pirates taking us away. We even made vows to love each other forever. I was so happy, us two alone on a beach, walking along the seafront, me picking up shells and shouting out, "Damian Cousins, I love you always." He laughed and told me that I was different. He must have told me that a thousand times, or more. He never failed to surprise me. One of the greatest moments I remember was having a drink and dancing away enjoying myself, while Damian was busy doing something else. I was even talking to him whilst I was dancing, not really focusing on what he was doing, then all of a sudden he turned the lights out, and to my surprise the room was lit so brightly, with little candles, that looked like stars, shining in the night. They were everywhere, right around the room. I looked around.

I couldn't believe that someone had taken the time to do this for me. It was so beautiful. I really wanted to cry, but instead I told him that he was the sweetest man I had ever known. It was so funny though, because I did not even realise what he was doing. I did see him stretching up, bending down, and walking around the room. Funny thing is that I was even talking to him while he was lighting the candles. However, I was blind to what he was doing. We laughed about it, when he asked me, "Jack, didn't you see me doing it?" I said no, I really didn't.

Well, there were so many times he would surprise me with little things that were so big to me, dancing together outside in the night, with just the stars above us, and music from a party which we were supposed to go to. I didn't really want to go. I became very selfish with him. I never wanted to spend my time with Damian and other people. I needed to have him to myself. That's how we both felt. I asked him if he was upset that we didn't go to the party, and he replied, "Jackie, that party happens every year, and I have always gone alone. This would have been the first time I ever went with someone I loved."

He didn't let it bother him that I didn't want to go, because we were here on the veranda dancing under the moonlight and stars. This was actually better than going to the party.

We would point to the stars, and I would tell him that the brightest one that was shining over his house was me and that every time he missed me, just go outside and look over the house, and there I would be.

Waking up in the middle of the morning and taking me by my hand to look at the sunrise in the morning was awesome. I'd never seen that happen before. It was an orange glow and looked so near yet so far. We felt so in love; it was crazy. He made me feel like I had never felt before, a woman, a lady, even a girl again, he brought out the child in me, I felt special, he made me feel like I was the most important person in his life especially when he said my name, "Jacqueline La-Touche", Damian was the only one who ever managed to make my name sound beautiful, I felt special each time he called my name, I guess it was the way he said it, He said my name with such a difference. I never really loved my name, until now.

I loved cooking for him, breakfast, lunch, and dinner, when I had the chance. It felt so natural. Damian thought I was a fantastic cook, and he always commented on how lovely my food tasted.

I was a great cook, I must say. I had been doing it for many years, and I enjoyed cooking for someone who I felt appreciated what I had taken the time to prepare for them. It felt so good to be doing something for someone whom I truly loved, to be sharing something, that I wished that I still had with Benji. Everything was divided between me and him. The last time that I can remember really feeling in love and sharing washing up the plates was when Benji first came to England and broke my heart with his confessions of infidelity.

Sunday afternoon, a week into enjoying my holiday in Jamaica, when I received a telephone call from my daughters, blissfully happy and unaware that my secret had been exposed. Between the two of them they had put two and two together and come up with four. They knew about Damian, and no one had told them. They had guessed. One thing I must say is that between them they make great detectives.

I had been rumbled, and the bubble of happiness that I was in burst. "Mum, is it true?"

"What?" I said.

"Is it true that you're with Damian?" I just stood there with the phone in my hand speechless, thinking what to say. I was always a quick thinker, but this time I was lost for words. "No," I replied, "where did you hear that from?"

"Is it true, Mum?"

"No, it's not," I said.

"Don't lie, Mum, swear on your life, swear on Marley's life, and Lourdes's life, it's not true." Well, they had backed me into a corner. "Yes, it is," she said, "because if it wasn't you would have sworn on their lives already. How could you, Mum? He's just a bush boy. He has nothing to offer you, and he's young." Straightaway when she called him a bush boy, my defences went up. "Yes," I said, "I am with him, and you know what, how dare you ring me up and ask me this. Why not wait until I come home to confront me."

What did they have to achieve by doing this now? What is going on over there? I thought. Did Benji know that this was circulating? Would they tell him? I felt my world falling apart. He didn't deserve to hear this from them. No matter what had happened between me and Benji I still loved him, maybe not in the way that I had loved him once. However, I respected him for being there for me, throughout some of the tough times, especially with the children. I couldn't let him find out like this. I owed it to him to tell him to his face. I hadn't been entirely honest with him. If I had then I wouldn't be here, because there would be no way that he would have allowed this. I felt desperate enough to deceive my family, to be here. Benji knew that things were not right between us, but I don't think he realised how bad they really were. He didn't have a clue about how I felt, even though I had told him so many times. Well, here I am on the telephone, being interrogated by my daughter.

I remember saying to them that Benji already knew that there was someone else in my life, and that was true because he did, whether he knew I was serious or not. One thing that he didn't know was that this person was in Jamaica. He did know that it was a younger man. However, we did not speak about it. We just carried on as normal, our normal, just ignoring things as usual.

I always spoke about the way I felt to him. I had been doing it for years, so he always knew how I felt, and I had always been open with him about everything.

I remember telling my daughter that she would never understand how I felt in my life and that I hoped she never had to experience how I felt, with any man. She was engaged and going to be married, just like I was eleven years ago, and now here I was telling her that I hoped she never ended up sitting on the right side of the chair while her husband sat on the left, with distance between them, and the sound of silence when communication has died. I even told her that I would walk out on them all if they ruined my happiness.

I felt threatened by them, and that's probably why I said that. However, I loved my children, and I would never forsake them, like my parents did with me, to go back home to Jamaica. My children had always been my world; everything was always centered on them. As long as they were happy, I was too. And now I had made them unhappy, enough for them to ring me on a Sunday morning, with this interrogation. I loved them, but I loved Damian too, and there was nothing, or no one, not even my children that I was going to let come between us, and the love that we felt for each other.

After I had defended myself, I pressed the red button on the phone and walked out of the room. I was still in disbelief. All I could think about was what was going on over there in England. What if Benji already knew? What was going to happen when I returned home? Would they all be waiting to attack me? That's how I felt. My sister Patsy told me not to dwell on it. "Jackie, don't let them ruin your holiday. I know it's difficult not to worry, but you can't spend the rest of your two weeks dwelling on this. What are they going to do to you when you get back? What can they really say? If you love Damian, you can't change how you feel."

Well, I rang Damian straightaway and told him what had just happened. He couldn't answer me straightaway. I remember saying to him say something then. "Jack, what do you want me to say? I feel really bad for you, and they were wrong to do that to you, but we have to deal with it." I got the feeling that Damian probably felt free to know that he was no longer hidden from everyone. When you love someone you want everyone to know, even though it wasn't the ideal situation, at least he was not a secret anymore. Come to think of it, I always used to get scared when I thought about this day, the day when they would find out about him, and you know what, I didn't care who knew about him, because I loved him. I didn't care who didn't approve either.

Well, Benji rang that day, and he was oblivious to what was going on. I felt really bad, because he missed me very much, but I felt more relieved that they had not told him.

It was coming to evening, and Damian had not arrived yet. He was always here around this time. I decided to ring him, to ask why he had not come yet. Well, he was at home and felt really down because he knew how much I loved my children and how much I felt hurt from the call, and he thought that he had now come between me and them and probably thought that I would agree with them that he was a bush boy and to stop all arguments in my family end our relationship.

"Are you coming?" I said. He told me that he didn't feel happy about what had happened. "Well, neither do I, but what do you want me to do, sit down for the next two weeks fretting about when I get home? Damian, if you want to lie down and take it on then that's up to you, so are you coming or not?" Well, as soon as I said that the tone in his voice changed, and before long we were sitting on the veranda together. He later told me that he realised how much I loved him that day, and he loved me even more than he did before, for standing up for our love.

Countdown to my happiness was fast approaching. My sister would joke about us, how we would cope when the time came for us to say goodbye.

My mother could not understand what was going on between me and Damian.

Damian was slowly becoming a part of our family. He got on very well with my mother. Even when I was not in Jamaica he would always go and visit her. Sometimes I'd call him, and he would tell me that he was with my mother. I guess that he was happy being around her. He even told me that he felt closer to me when I was not there, when he was around my mother, because she reminded him of me. She was funny, and that's why he loved being around her. She was also fearful of unwanted visits from creatures, lizards, mice, cockroaches, you name it she would scream if she saw them, just like I did, so there were many similarities he admired about her, and being in her presence he enjoyed.

My mother comes from the old school where marriage is for life. She was married to my father for fifty-six years, until death stole him away from her, so you see it was difficult for her to understand how I felt about Damian, even though she liked him a lot.

"Jackie," she would say, "Benny is a good man, you have a family with him, and he is a peaceful man, you have to try and make your marriage work. Look, me and daddy was married for all those years, and things was hard at times, but we still manage to stay together." I remembered replying that I didn't want to manage to stay together. I tried to explain to her how I felt. My mother had always known how I felt in my marriage and knew that I was not happy. However, she would tell me to stick it out. Well, I didn't want to stick it out anymore. I was here and the happiest I'd ever been for years, and that was all because of one person, Damian.

Even though she spoke like that, deep down she did understand, because she later told me that she wanted me to be happy, and whatever decision that I made to be happy, as long as I was, then she was too.

As my sister joked about the countdown, Damian and I looked at each other. Why was she reminding us of the time we had left? First there were seventeen days, and now you both have less than seventeen hours left. Well, we knew that because we had started counting from the first night, since the first week started. Sometimes it was hard for us to talk about it, because we felt that we would note cope with saying goodbye. Even though we felt like this, we made a vow to enjoy our last days and live each day as if it were our last.

My energy began to leave my body as the hours slipped away. I felt so weak; we both did, as I sat down watching him fold up my clothes, neatly packing them away in my suitcase, remembering the day that I wore some of the clothes which he had in his hands. I had asked him the night before if he could help me pack, because I didn't feel that I could do this alone. At first he said no, because it would feel that he was helping me to leave. I didn't want to leave him; however, I had no choice, because my ticket said departure December 3.

I started to think back to earlier in the day, when we went back to the beach for the last time, both of us standing in the sea just holding hands looking around, looking up at the skies, reminiscing about the last time when we were here, remembering seeing a aeroplane flying between the clouds, until it was out of our sight, Damian standing there saying, "I can't imagine the day when you leave me to go back. When you're back on the plain again, I will watch it just like this one, until you are out of sight." I thought to myself, *Not out of your mind though.*

Well, here we were suitcase packed, and our last night together, I just could not think straight, it's like Damian became my rock, I knew that he felt as weak as I did. However, one of us had to be strong, I could see that he was struggling to be strong, our faces were etched with sadness, it was hard not to notice.

I had started to cry about leaving from the first week I arrived, Damian too, he would just stare at me, while I slept, and he would cry, he could not imagine me not being with him always, and he wasn't ashamed to tell me that's what he did. I always thought that it took a real man to cry, and crying did show that we had feelings for each other.

I was torn between where I would spend my last night, would I spend it with my mother, or Damian, my love for him was so strong, I couldn't spend my last night in Jamaica, in my mother's bed, don't get me wrong, I always loved sleeping with my mother, from a child right up till now. However, the way that I was feeling that night, so sad, I don't think that she could have helped me, the only person who could help me was Damian, at least we could be sad together, and comfort each other, because we both were going through the same thing.

Feelings of loss, followed us that night, we could either be sad or happy. Well, that's what I told him, "Damian do we really want to spend our last night, just sitting down looking miserable, not really talking to each other, because we didn't really know what to say anymore, counting down the hours, "No Damian said, "well let's make the most of our last night, lets live it like it were the first night when I arrived, we both agreed. Well, that was the night when he surprised me with all the little tea lights, flickering and glowing in the dark, at a time like this he still had the strength to surprise me and never ceased to amaze, even on our last night together.

I lay there throughout the rest of the night, I didn't really want to sleep because, if I did, morning would steal the night away, and then it would be time for me to leave, lying there with tears falling down my face, I turned around and watched as Damian slept, he looked so beautiful, as I stared at his face, I felt a wave of deep hurt just come over me, how was I going to manage without him, I was so use to seeing him every day, how was I going to get through the day, knowing that I wouldn't even see him at the end of it.

For the past seventeen days we were like Siamese twins, always together, and now we were going to be apart, how could I bear that, as tears rolled down my face, I just couldn't bear crying alone in the dark anymore, "Damian, wake up," I said. "I'm so sad I can't stop crying I miss you already and I haven't gone yet, we held each other in silence.

Morning was here, and time for me to leave, I didn't want to get up, I didn't want this moment, or any of the past seventeen days to end, but I knew that it had to.

I gathered all my belongings together, ready now I said, we both stood looking at each other, as I gazed around the room for the last time, I noticed the two wine glasses that sat on the centre table, always clean and ready for us to use, Damian would always dust them off before he poured out the drink. Well, leftover Rum and Pepsi still in the bottom of the glasses which we had left, from last night.

I was going to miss this little sanctuary, where I had found so much peace, where I had fell more in love, where we had sung, and danced, and laughed like we'd never done before, I didn't want to leave, and he never wanted me to leave either, but my time here in this little place was up for now.

Walking up the road, going home, this was the last time I was walking up this road, everything was the last time right now, we even said it last night when we were walking down, last kiss last hug, last everything we said.

We arrived at my mother's house, the long sullen walk from Damian's house to my mothers had left me feeling hot and exhausted, I had to get myself, and my luggage together, I had less than five hours to sort myself out.

I felt like a robot, just walking around going from room to room looking to see if I had gathered everything together, time just slipped away as I walked around, with tears in my eyes just thinking about leaving.

I sat down outside on a bench, just looking around and just lost in my thoughts, I could see Damian in front of the fire that he had made, to roast breadfruits for me to take home. Well, he could see that I was crying, but he never came over, because he knew that he would probably end up doing the same as me, I just sat there saying to myself that I had to find a way to make him understand, I had to find a way to make Benji understand. I could not go on like this, I could not go back home and carry on as normal, everything had changed, how could I ignore everything, like it never happened because it did, and was very much real.

Time had passed and it was countdown through the last hour, as I stood in the garden with a pair of scissors in my hand, looking through the full head of hair on Damian's head looking for a part of him to take back with me.

I had asked him for a lock of his locks to keep as a memory. I loved his hair, to me it was so beautiful, not only was it long it was well groomed, and he would sometimes put it in different styles, which I loved, sometimes I'd see him just sitting there playing around with his hair making it into a creation, I'd often play around with it to, running my fingers through his hair until I reached the end, his hair was so long, you couldn't help yourself but touch it.

He also had a little plait, in his beard, which I would always fiddle with, he told me that he always plaited it, every week, he even made creations with it.

As I looked for a lock to cut, I was spoilt for choice, brown ones, black ones, brown and black, single ones, double ones long ones, shorter ones, chubby ones, slim ones well I held on to one, and carefully put the scissors through it, until it was freely in my hand, as I looked at it, I noticed that there were five fine locks, joined to one. I was amazed by this because I had only cut one.

I felt happy, because I had only planed to take one, and here I was with five joined to one lock, in my hand, I showed Damian, I even told him sorry for taking so many, he said, "Jack it was only meant to be one that you cut, but it's all good, in Damian's term, "natural," anyway I don't think, he would miss them, because he had so many, hundreds, I thought.

I told him that I would find a good home for them, and a good place to keep them, and that having them with me would keep him closer to me.

On our Journey to the airport, I didn't talk once, I just silently cried, my heart felt so heavy, my legs felt like felt like jelly, and I wanted to be physically sick. My head hurt so much from all the silent crying that I did on the way to the airport, the silence in the car between me and Damian was not golden, it was blue. I couldn't even look him in his face, let alone his eyes, I didn't want us to break down, because we were both on the verge of doing that, so we tried to avoid any facial contact, for now.

I just sat there deep in thought, thinking about the night I arrived in Jamaica, driving up the airport road, loving all the landmarks which I now hated.

As we approached the airport road, as we called it, our hearts sunk further to the bottom of its pit, we could see the floor mill in the distance, we could see the Port, this was the landmark for the airport, I always hated this road, the road that led to our departure.

The closer we got to the airport, the more landmarks became visible. The palm trees that decorated the airport gardens meant that we had arrived at the dreaded destination. We both looked at each other, as if to say, "Oh well."

Checked in cases and found out that the flight would be delayed; this made us feel happy for a while.

We felt like they were telling us we had another day together. We had at least two hours together. With time to spare, we walked around the airport yard. People were saying their goodbyes. We even looked over to arrivals. Oh, how I wished that I was over there, walking through like the happy people over that side. We were the sad people on this side. I watched them with envy as they hugged and loaded their cars and vans with luggage, ready to start their holidays, and my one was now ending.

Damian and I felt a lot more relaxed with each other than we did on the journey here. We even forgot that we were sad, laughing away, taking pictures. We even had a meal. I hadn't really eaten much over the past few days. My appetite was asleep. Well, now it seemed to be awake. We stood outside savouring our last moments. It felt like we were clinging on to each other. My sister Patsy came to the airport with us. Well, she started teasing us again, "You two start saying your goodbyes. I told you that your time was up. Come on give her a kiss. She has to go through now." Go through now, no, I had thirty minutes left. It wasn't time yet. she followed her joke with a lecture on why I needed to go through now.

As we walked behind her, we muttered to ourselves, "She wouldn't understand how we feel."

"Yeah," Damian said, "does she think it's a joke? Half an hour is a long time, and she wants you to go through now. No, man, she can't do that to us."

Time to say goodbye. I felt like I couldn't breathe. I had been here before time and time again. I stood there with my sister hugging and saying goodbye, putting aside all the jokes. She whispered in my ear then said aloud, "Jackie, follow your heart. Don't let anyone tell you how to live your life. Be happy." She repeated this more than once and then walked away, leaving me and Damian alone to say our goodbyes.

As we walked through the airport, my heart felt a bit stronger. I thought, *Thank you, God, for giving us those two hours, because it has helped me to be stronger in myself, and me feeling stronger has helped Damian to be stronger.* When we thought and felt like there was no way we could cope, we seemed to be doing okay, for now.

He followed me as far as he was allowed to go. When we reached our final port of embankment, we held on to each other as if we were still on that beach, on our island, waiting for the pirates to take us away, as we embraced to say goodbye for the second time around.

Damian held me just as he had held me seventeen days ago, down in the churchyard, as we kissed goodbye.

I let him go slowly, as I walked towards the entrance leaving him behind, not knowing what our future held.

As he walked away never looking back, I stood there just staring at his back. I loved him so much. Words could never say how much. As he got to the door he turned around, we waved, and I blew him a kiss, then walked through, with tears in my eyes. Only God knows how we never fell apart, because all the times we thought about this day. It always felt inevitable.

Alone again, I always thought about this part. On my way here I was happy to be alone, enjoying my own company, and now on my way going back home, I was sad to be alone, and I was no longer enjoying my own company.

I put my iPod earphones in my ears, but the music didn't sound so sweet anymore, and I could not find one song that didn't remind me of him; they all did.

I sat down with all the other passengers, just staring into space, listening to them, but couldn't understand a word they were saying. My mind was not here. I had left it with Damian Cousins.

I had to try and retrieve my mind and concentrate on making this journey back home alone.

As I walked down the long and winding walkway in Kingston airport, bound for England, I scouted for upbeat songs on my iPod and walked as fast as I could with tears streaming down my face. Not even an upbeat song could help me. They sounded sad. Everything was sad around me at that moment.

Back on the aeroplane again, I didn't care what seat I had. I didn't care about my laptop. I didn't want to read. I didn't want to listen to music. I didn't want to drink any wine, not even see the TV screen which was sandwiched between the seats, with the little pointer aeroplane heading back in the direction it came from, England.

I just wanted to curl up and sleep, not waking up until I reached England. I wanted to go home and get into my bed, with my head under the duvet, and cry.

Chapter Thirty-One

Declaration of Love

2009

Arrived back in England, as the plane landed there were no lights, that shone, just grey dismal looking buildings a far cry from the place I just left, behind. As the passengers gathered their hand luggage, jumpers, coats and scarves, and kids, we all waited for the doors to open, flight attendants telling us goodbye.

I walked down the airport isle, it seemed endless I was back where I started; I just wanted to get out of the airport and get home.

After going through immigration I was now free to get my suitcases and go home I didn't really know what to expect, I stood there watching the conveyer belt rammed with suitcases, of all shapes, sizes and colours, go by, people fighting with their cases as they went round and round on this merry-go-round.

I saw people leave one by one, until I was the last person standing there still waiting, wondering where my cases were, I even began to think that they were probably left behind in Jamaica, when I noticed one, then all.

I walked out with nothing to declare but a broken heart. My husband, Benji, was there to greet me, probably waiting anxiously with anticipation, I knew that he would be happy to see me, it had been seventeen days since we last saw each other, when he left me at Victoria station, boarding the Gatwick Express, I remember that day very clearly, making sure that I got on the train with all my luggage, Benji knew that I always had a tendency to forget, or even lose things, and always said that it was because I had too much to think about, too much on my head, so he made sure that I had everything, and that I was comfortably seated before he kissed me goodbye, and told me that he loved me.

I always knew he loved me, in his own way, but things were far from fine, between us, we both knew this.

Well, he would be here now, just as he always was for me despite everything. As I walked through arrivals, I gazed at the crowd of anxious anticipating people, waiting to hug their loved ones. Well, there was Benji, I slipped away, before he could see me, I needed to go and change into some warm clothing. he didn't notice that I had come out.

I had changed my clothes, taking my time, I thought what was the hurry, it's not like I had anything exciting to look forward to, I picked up my belongings and walked back out into arrivals to meet Benji.

I walked up to him and called his name, and the first thing that I did was have a moan, not even greet him, as a wife would do. My heartfelt heavy, because it was not him that I wanted to see, I wanted to see Damian, I had grown so use to him that it felt really hard for me to go back to how I was, before my holiday, I had changed in more ways than one.

The next few days after I had arrived back home were terrible. I had created an atmosphere which a knife could cut. I never spoke about my holiday. When asked, I never really wanted to speak at all. I just wasn't the same person anymore.

Benji even told me that I brought sadness back into the house. They were all looking forward to seeing me come back, but this was not what he had imagined. It was true, what he said, and I felt really bad about that, but I really couldn't help the way that I felt, because I missed Damian so much. It was really hard for me to hide my feelings. I felt cheated. One day I was happy in Jamaica and the next day I had been transported into unhappiness.

I was happy to see my children and pleased that everything had been taken care of. Benji had done his best while I was away. The home was well taken care of, so were the children. They were all happy while I was away.

Benji had always been a great father. He spent so much time and gave them so much attention. I always used to wish that he gave me a little of this attention and time. However, it was great seeing him with his children and watching him while he took care of them. In my past relationships most of the responsibility was always on me, and then when those relationships ended, so did their relationship with their children, so this was different because I had one hundred percent support from Benji.

I became more distant during my return. Benji continued to act as if everything was fine, even though he knew that something had changed. I just could not listen to his questions anymore. "Where did you go in Jamaica? Did you eat any jerk chicken? Did you go to the beach?" I just couldn't listen to anymore. I just had no answers for him. Well, he finally said to me no one would believe that I had just come back from holiday and that all the other times that I had gone away I always had so much to talk about on my return, but this time I had nothing to say.

Even though I had told myself while I was in Jamaica that I had to find a way to tell him, I never knew that it would be at that moment, same place in the kitchen where he had broken his news to me, eleven years ago, where he had confessed about his infidelity, and here I was eleven years later just about to confess mine and declare that I had fallen in love with another man.

As I made my big confession, the silence echoed around the kitchen as he took it all in. I didn't really know what to expect, when I broke the news to him. However, I felt free, probably just as how he had felt eleven years ago, but this time was different, because I was now telling him that our marriage was over, because I had fallen in love with this person, who felt the same way about me.

I told him that I could not go on feeling the way that I had done for the past eleven years, and I was now happy and that I couldn't go on as I had done for the past years.

Benji's world fell apart because he still loved me, and this was a total shock to him. He had never really seen this coming. I tried to explain to him that this was coming for quite some time now. I even told him that I still loved him. However, it was not the same way as I used to. He just could not understand and didn't want to accept what I had just told him. How could I expect him to accept that I was leaving him for someone else?

I had just dropped a big bombshell; my life had now changed again, for the fourth time in my life.

For the next few days everything was a mix of emotions. It was like someone had just died, the grief was unbearable. Seeing Benji in that state was more than I ever imagined, if our relationship should come to an end, I watched his sorrow turn to anger. I watched him plead and cry, begging me to change my mind. He told me that he had never realised that I had felt like I had done for all those years and that he should have taken care of my heart and not all the things that he had taken care of around the home, putting the children first all the time, when I should have come first, all the things that he should have done for me, that he never did, he should have, but he never got the chance because of everything else that had happened over the years.

I felt really sad. I felt like I had done something terrible, but how could falling in love be so terrible? Benji had given me so much, done so much. However, it never felt enough, because all I ever wanted was to feel loved and happy in my relationship. I never wanted to feel alone, but truth is, I did.

Benji spoke about his plans, which he had for me, when I came back from Jamaica. After he had walked away and left me on the Gatwick Express, he realised that something had to change and that he had always loved me but never really showed me or told me as much as he would have wanted to. Benji wanted a second chance to prove his love to me, but I felt that it was too late.

Questions after questions, right through the day and night, there were times when we would sit down and reminisce, over the years. We spoke about the problems which we had over the years. We spoke about all the factors which impacted on our marriage, him working during the nights and having no time for our relationship, also his infidelity. I even questioned why he had married me without being honest about the child which he had in Jamaica. We spoke about when we first met. We spoke about everything, good and bad.

Benji wanted to know things about Damian, and I wanted to tell him how much of a good person Damian was and how much he loved me and that it was not a joke, even though he probably thought it was one.

Well, as the days slipped into Christmas he still thought that he would wake up and find out that it was all just a bad dream or that I was joking, but it was no joke.

I wished that I could turn back the hands of time, to a time where we were both happy. I wished that he had never spoilt our happiness with his confession, because that was the start of why we were now standing here, with our marriage in tatters. I wished that we had taken the time to try and mend what had been broken, but we didn't, and now here Benji stood with his heart broken, and mine breaking because his was.

Benji asked me to change my mind, but it felt too late to go back, because I didn't really have anything to hold on to, no good times together, no precious memories, during the past eleven years. I had always held on to the precious memories that we shared before he came to England. Those memories had always stopped me from leaving in the past. However, now, they were not enough for me to hold on to, like the ones that I had now with Damian. I could not hold on to past memories and stay with Benji because of them, because I had held on to past memories for so long.

In my heart I felt that it was time for me to move on with my life. My relationship with Benji had become stuck.

"What about the children?" Benji asked me. He even told me that I didn't care about them because if I had, then I would change my mind. I loved my children, and they have always come first in my life, and I have always put myself last.

I realised that I had to come first, because if I was not happy, how could they be? I knew how much Benji loved them, and they adored him, but was that enough for me to stay, because if I did, I would never be happy. That's how I felt, and I would only be staying in this relationship because that is what he wanted. How could I stay to please everyone, but myself?

Benji pleaded with me to give Damian up. "Ring him and tell him that you're staying with your husband. Tell him that you will settle for being friends instead."

I wished he could listen to himself, because this never made sense to me. How could I ring Damian and tell him that I didn't love him anymore, because that's what I would be doing? How could I tell him that I wanted to be his friend instead of his lover? How could I tell him that I was staying with my husband because it was the right thing for me to do because of my children? How could I break our hearts, when we really loved each other?

How could I forget about the past five months, and all the memories that I had accumulated, and my time spent with Damian, this was a win and lose situation, and I started to feel like I was in the middle between the two men in my life, my husband and my lover.

I was taunted by Benji telling me that my children would never accept my new relationship, and my mother would, not either, he even said that he could not believe that I would ever dream of looking at someone like Damian, a Rasta man, he thought that I would have gone for someone who had wealth, someone who could take care of me, financially "what are people going to say about you" well I never thought, or cared about what people would say, I had spent my life worrying about what people thought about me, but not now, that had passed. I knew that my close friends would not judge me; they would support me because they had always known how I felt.

Returning to work was like a godsend, I could escape my torment, and focus on my work, instead of the past few days since coming back to England.

My home had become a psychological prison, I could not get away from the questions, the pleading the crying, the anger, work was my only escape, a place where I felt at peace, no confrontations, just peace to get on with what I was doing.

At work I would say to myself, Jackie "imagine you're here, helping people to sort out their lives, and right now you can't even sort out your own.

At the end of my working day, leaving work to go back home became difficult, I began to dread, going home, because I knew what I was facing.

Well, each day my return home was different, some days, I would go home to find Benji crying it broke me down, I don't think he knew how much, but then why should he, when he said that I didn't care, and it was his feelings that were now hurting, it was all about Benji, right now, my feelings didn't seem to matter, he even told me that my heart was hard, and that I had no feelings, because I had not cried, I don't think he really understood how I felt, because I had cried for so long inside about the death of our relationship, that I had nothing left to cry about, that's how I felt.

I had become immune to everything but it didn't mean that I had no heart, because I would sit down and put my arms around him as he cried, holding onto his hand as if he were a child, I knew he was in so much pain, and couldn't handle the fact that our relationship could possibly be over.

The affects of the following days leading up to Christmas began to take its toll on me, in such a short space of time I had lost so much weight, I couldn't eat, sleep, or even think straight whilst I was at home with Benji, there were times that I would just sit down and listen to him, pleading and crying, and just get angry, because it now started to feel like he was using psychology on me, even if he never knew it, he was.

I would sit down and take it in for hours, then get up, and it's like I would come round to what he was doing unintentionally, and without a moment's thought, shout at him, "Can't you understand I love him, you were not interested, you took me for granted until another man came into my life, I always told you that this would happen, and now it has, deal with it.

In some ways I resented Benji, for neglecting my heart, and giving me the opportunity to make someone else come into my life.

Well, Christmas Day came. Only God knows how I managed to get it all together, but I had to, whether I had the strength or not, and for Marley and Lourdes. I even surprised myself with buying presents for everyone, which was something that I thought that I would not get around to doing because my mind was not here this Christmas.

Benji and I tried to put our differences behind us, just to concentrate on Christmas, because we could see where the day was going to come and go, and no preparations made or presents bought. We had always made sure that everything was always sorted out for Christmas, food, drink, and presents. I had always done my Christmas shopping with my daughter Chantal. She always helped me, but this year it was different. I was on my own, without her help. I was still upset at the way they had treated me over the phone.

The relationship between Chantal and me was now distant. I had not made the effort to approach her or speak about the telephone call which she had made to me, whilst I was in Jamaica.

I had heard that my other daughter Sacha was also spending Christmas at Chantal's house. They were all going to gather around there for this big Christmas feast, just as they had always gathered around here on Christmas Day for every Christmas that they ever had.

Well, Christmas Day, they came around to deliver their presents. This was the first Christmas that we had not exchanged presents together. I gave Chantal's present to my grandson to give to her, and she did the same to me, then left.

As I watched them walk through the door, I couldn't help but feel sad. I knew that they felt the same way too, but there was so much left unsaid that needed to be said.

Well, I wasn't going to let this get me down. They gave Benji an opportunity to rub this in my face. "Look how you are tearing your family apart. You are letting them down when they look up to you for everything." Well, I knew that Benji was right when he said that they looked up to me. However, they were now adults and had their lives in front of them. They never really knew how I felt about being in this relationship, because I never really spoke about it with them. I didn't see a reason to, so I just carried on as normal.

They always came round to visit regularly, and they were used to seeing me and Benji in the kitchen cooking and hardly ever saying a word to each other, but I guess they were comfortable with seeing that.

Benji did not ill treat me, like Patrick did, so how could they understand what was now going on between me and Benji, and how I felt?

This Christmas was the first year that there was no music playing in the house. For the past years, music was one of the biggest features around Christmas. From November you would hear me playing my Christmas songs, but not this year. There was nothing to sing about. The house stayed silent, with just the sound of me and Benji's voices.

Chapter Thirty-Two

Acceptance Must Come

January 2010

What a way to start the New Year, waking up this morning to another year, and taking parts of the past year into the new, unresolved issues that needed to be spoken about, left unsaid, however better to be spoken about.

January 1, 2010, thank God the New Year had finally come to an end, and the new one was here, I knew that this year was going to be like a roller coaster ride, with feelings and all.

The relationship between me and Chantal, had come to a standstill, past issues and now present circumstances embedded between us, without a moment's thought I reached for my phone like I always did when I was about to ring her before conflict took its place in our lives surrounding the new man in my life, which I had given my heart to as well as accepting his.

Our love for each other was unacceptable to my family, what did they think? Was I having a mid life crisis going crazy, fooling myself, or did they think that I was trying to recapture my youth with a younger man, No.

I wasn't losing myself, I had found myself again surrounded my reciprocated love, in the arms of a man eighteen years my junior, eighteen years his senior, but very much head over heels in love we were, and to everyone did not account for nothing, but heartache I was made to feel that it was wrong, forbidden love, which had no happy ending, but tears and tissue at the end.

The only thing that I felt was wrong was that I was still married to my Benji, who I had known for nineteen years, and married to him for almost twelve of those nineteen years, I had broken one of the Ten Commandments, "Thou shalt not commit adultery."

I had committed a sin according to the book of matrimony, which said, to love honour, cherish and obey, but the thought of how anything so wrong could feel so right, came in between everything I once believed in.

For richer or poorer, in sickness and in health, till death us do part, that's what we had promised to do. However, the love that I now felt for Damian took president over everything else, my relationship with Benji had stood still for so many years, it had lost its voice and had become silent, a relationship that had lost Its sparkle with time, and circumstances that helped to drive a wedge between us steeling our power to communicate with each other.

Here I was standing in the middle of a sea of happiness, but drowning in a river of tears, which ceased to fall because my heart had cried so many times in my life, for past relationships that had ended in tears. Well, my heart was now telling me that it was time to stop crying, and start to live again.

As I stood by the window looking out, I felt that I was made to feel as if I had committed a crime, which I was now paying time for. I felt as if I was standing in the dock at the court of love, charged and now sentenced to a life of unhappiness in my heart.

For the past eleven years, our relationship had become stuck, we were moving forward with family life and everyday commitments. However, our commitment to each other had began to become fragmented.

Over the past years, the distance had grown between us like a malignant tumor, and silence didn't feel so golden, and dwelled in the midst of this relationship.

Arguments were petty, and caused mostly by me, I sometimes felt resentment, trapped that's what I used to say, I would always blame Benji for making me unhappy I always told him that he should have given me a choice to stay or go, I felt deceived and feelings of hurt and anger haunted me for so long, letting go was slow, I managed to let room in for forgiveness, but not forgetfulness.

I managed to learn to move on quite a bit from how I felt when it first happened, it was difficult at first, but I had to, especially if I chose to stay.

Benji tried his best to please me, doing whatever he could around the home, he became a great father, and even more as the children got older. My life was comfortable, I had all the makings of a nice home, food on the table, clothes on my back, and a man who still loved me, but there was something missing.

Each day I look in his face I see how sorry he is, for the life that I should have had but didn't because of deceit.

What more could I want, that's what everyone thought, "Jackie is lucky, and I was, but something was missing. Everybody who came round to our house always had something good to say about Benji.

"I wish that I had a husband like that, who cooks, washes cleans, and helps me with the children, even take them to school sometimes. "You're lucky" that's what I was told.

Well, I knew that I was lucky to have a husband, who supported me like he did, and I should have been on top of the world but I wasn't.

Even though our relationship was not as we would have loved it to be, we were okay, that's what most people around us thought, I even told myself "Jackie this is it, this is your life, just get on with it.

No two relationships are the same, some people expect more than others, some are quite happy with the basics of life, and having a house husband. Well, I was not, I wanted someone for me, to give me that undivided attention, that I believe that every woman is deserving of, well, all that became lost along the way.

Night work came back to haunt me, letting me know that it had stolen my relationship, and taking the main ingredients which keeps it together 'communication'. Baby mother always lived in the background of my mind; arguments hurled their fists around the room hitting out at every chance it could get.

Feeling ashamed that my husband had never taken me out haunts me until this day.

I began to live a single life, I might as well have been, that's what I told myself. Well, he is never here, and when he is all he does is sleep, family parties became our date. Weddings they were the best, sitting in the church listening to two people take their vows, has a way of making every relationship, good, and bad sound, special as it use to be. You would sit and hold their hand, squeezing it gently, and then remember when you stood at the altar and said I do.

Years of pleading with my Benji for change had passed. I had become accustomed to the way our life had become. I even started to feel sorry for him because he knew no other way. It just was not in him to be romantic again. It felt like he had given up on me. Come to think of it, we both gave up trying. We had become victims of our own circumstances. I knew that Benji had taken up a lot of responsibility when he came to England; he lived a single life before now.

Remembering back to when we were at the height of our relationship, when nothing stood between us, no night work, no children, no financial pressures, no baby mother, when we were blissfully in love, lying down in each other's arms wrapped up with love, thousands of miles from where we are now, in Jamaica.

I remember saying to Benji if it ever got to the stage where we both ended up sitting on the opposite side of the sofa, then it was time to call it a day. I remember truly believing this. We both agreed at the time that neither of us wanted to sit at either end of the sofa, him reading the papers and me reading a book. I had told myself that I never wanted to feel alone again in any relationship. Now, we lived together, but we were miles apart. I thought back to when I first met Benji, and what I loved about him, I still loved those things, but a lot was missing, from our relationship. If I could turn the clock back I would, but I couldn't. I wish that I could say what Benji wanted to hear, but my heart would not let me. Benji blamed himself, he blamed the children, the one person that he did not blame was me. He said that if he had taken care of my heart then it would not have been open for someone else to walk in and take.

Living with regrets, that's what Benji was doing now, I felt so sorry for him, but I knew that I could not stay for that reason. We reminisced about the past, the good times, we laughed, and spoke openly about how we felt, we listened to each other for the first time in years, but it was too late, even though Benji had reminded me of when we first met, and I said to him that I was going back home to England and it was too late to get to know him now, his reply at that time was that it was never too late, and he was right at that time, however this was a memories that were good, I could not stay in this relationship, living in the past. Circumstances had stolen everything from us.

Chapter Thirty-Three

Soldiering On

2010

I managed to get through 2009, and made it into 2010, even though I had started a new year, every day for me since then has been a physical and mental struggle, with my emotions, everything that had once felt easy and that I loved seemed hard.

Waking up in the morning and going to work felt really hard. Getting ready for work was always easy, my colleagues would ask me, how did I manage to put myself together, coordination of creating colours together, which you wouldn't think of putting together. Well, I now stood in front of my wardrobe, packed with everything a girl could ever want, and as I looked inside my wardrobe all I could see was the four corners, not the clothe, my wardrobe seemed empty, I felt like I had nothing.

Laughing was my youth; it was my medicine for being who I am, no matter what I have been through in my life, I have always been able to look on the bright side of life. Well, at that moment, there was no bright side of life, everything was slowly creeping up on me.

Day after day the talking between me and Benji would start again, the confessions, of love, the blames, the sorry, the chances, the anger and frustration, the pleading the pain, and tears.

I began falling apart at the seams, and I began walking around in a world of my own, carrying my burdens, my worries, my fears my pain, and my confusion on my head and shoulders, my heart ached, and the pain was written all over my face. Benji began to pay me all this attention, that I was not use to, it felt really strange coming from him, it felt like the attention was coming from a stranger and not my husband, all this attention was new, and unwanted, at this stage of the relationship. I became distant, to my family, friends, and my job, and Benji.

I found it difficult to function on a daily basis, I would go to work, and as long as the day lasted, I would sit there feeling suppressed, unable to take in any kind of information. However, I still managed to find the strength.

For the next few weeks, I left work exactly at four o'clock, I couldn't bear to be there a minute longer, I couldn't get out of the door any faster than I was now doing.

In the office, I had always been happy; I got on very well with all my colleagues, and was the joker, always smiling, I always appeared to be happy, always being positive, and being myself, so here I was now sitting secluded, and isolating myself from everyone, how long was this going to go on. The dynamics changed when my emotions, took me over, and my tears began to make their way down my cheeks every day. Questions, after questions, I began questioning my questions, I started from the day that I got married, right up until now.

I questioned Damian too. I became confused about everything. However, the one thing that I was clear about was how I felt about him. Knowing that he loved me gave me the strength to move forward.

The breaking point came for me when I collapsed at my friend's house after enjoying myself all evening. Our night ended with us all questioning my health. My friends were worried about me. I had given everyone a fright. All I can remember was opening the double glass doors to walk through. The next second I was flat out on the floor. I woke to find people crouching and leaning over me, calling my name. As I lay on my side for a short while, stretched out as if I were in my bed, I started to wonder what I was doing down here. It felt like I was sleeping and I had just woken up, but confused. I couldn't make out the faces of the people crouched down beside. As I began to focus, I realised that it was my friends who were gently shaking me and helping me to get up. I couldn't believe what had happened. They sat me up. As I leaned against the table, they asked me questions. I was very detached from what had happened. As they were helping me up from the floor, I asked them, "What just happened to me? How did I end up waking up on the floor?"

"Jackie, you fell, you collapsed." I just looked at them, still detached from what had just happened. I had given everyone such a fright.

As I sat down in my friend's kitchen, she made me a glass of water, adding sugar to it, to take away the shock; that's what they say, sugar and water is good for shock.

As I sat sipping away, my friends still looked worried. "I'm okay," I said. "I'm fine. I had never felt better." Well, for some strange reason that's exactly how I felt, "better."

My friends stood over me, watching and waiting while I drank the potion of sugar and water. "Drink it," she said. I had drunk enough and didn't want to drink anymore. Well, all of a sudden my friend shouted at me, "Drink the sugar and water now. You come to my house and collapse, drink it now." Wow, that was the first time, since my mother and father, that anyone had spoken to me like a child. Well, I tried to tell her that I was full, but I didn't even get to say it, because she shouted again, even louder, "Drink it!" I never had another thought. I just did as I was told.

When I reached home, I felt great; I felt that something big had changed in my life that night.

I wanted to ring Damian, because I noticed that I had a missed call on my phone. He always spoke to me before I fell asleep; even if it was just to hear my voice or tell me that he loved me, he would phone. I had to call him back, just to let him know that I had got home. Well, he answered the phone. He sounded like he was waiting to hear that something had happened. He told me that as soon as the phone rang he had said to his friend who was with him, "What's happened, why Jackie's ringing?" Damian had never questioned why I rang, until now. It's like he sensed that something had happened to me.

Sunday morning I opened my eyes and just lay in my bed thinking deep thoughts, with my eyes wide open. It's funny how when I think sweet thoughts, I always close my eyes.

I started to question last night, what had happened to me. As I turned to lie on my side, I noticed that my ribs were aching, and I could just about lift my arm. I had no recollection of anything. I didn't feel scared. I just ached. This was the first time I had ever fallen down and not felt it.

Well, late that day I spoke to my friend. I thanked her for the evening and felt that I had ruined it for all of us. Well, as I asked my friend what happened, she told me that she had been right behind me. I had fallen heavily and lay there with my eyes wide open and shaking. I started to think about how lucky I was to be here, in one piece. I then realised that's where my aches were coming from. I even asked my friend what side did I fall on. She told me right, but that didn't explain why I was aching on the left.

I started to think about the double glass doors and that huge solid dining table and how I ended up on the floor near the table leg, like someone had put me down to sleep. I thanked God.

My friend asked me to keep in contact with her more. She was worried and felt that I was not taking care of my health. I wasn't eating properly, drinking, smoking, and abusing my health, so on the outside, I was immaculate, and on the inside, I was slowly deteriorating. I agreed to keep in contact and said goodbye, feeling lucky to be here, alive and with my family; things could have ended much differently.

My health had deteriorated. I could not manage to go to work for a full week, at the start or end of the week. It became one problem after the other, all different kind of aches, tummy, head, chest, back, but the worse pain of all was the emotional, not the physical pain.

My heart felt tortured and hurt, and my mind felt like it was on a merry-go-round. My head felt jumbled, but now everything began to make sense. All the anxiety of everything that was coming down on me at one time had gone. My stress levels had dropped, and everything that made me feel stressed no longer had the effect to do so again.

I felt like I was given another chance. From that day on, I was like the old Jackie again; I started to smile and genuinely felt more at peace on the inside. I felt emotionally stable, no anxiety, tears, and overwhelming feelings written on my face anymore.

I became disciplined, focused, and driven to reach that positive state of mind that I had been in before my life got on this rollercoaster of emotions, with my husband.

The only way was up, that's how I started to think, "There's nothing that is going to stand in my way." I know what I want, and I'm going to make sure I get it. If it's the last thing that I do, I want to set myself goals, and I'm going to reach them.

I promised myself to do all the things that I've wanted to do, or be, "I wanted to be a DJ. I had dreamt of that for so long. I know my music, and I would like to touch people with my music, because I knew that I could."

I wanted to make people dance around their living rooms, just like I did, on a Sunday, when I felt the groove.

Music to me is like medicine to the sick. Yeah, I want to do Ms. Meryl. There were so many things that I wanted to do, but the one that I wanted to do the most was to finish my book. I had a story to tell, and I wanted to share it with everyone, because I thank God for bringing me this far, and with everything that I have encountered in my life, I am able to now share my hopes and dreams with everyone.

I have realised that if you believe in yourself, all things are possible, and it's up to us to look inside ourselves and find our gift, because we all have one. Some of us have multi, others a gift, but they're all gifts that have been given to us, and we need to find them, realise what they are, and use them, and they will change our lives, in some way.

For the past few weeks I haven't been able to write a single word in this book. As a writer I have always felt that my mind has to be free to write. However, this was not the case, because clouded judgments were in my jumbled mind. It was difficult to make sense of anything, at home and at work. Now my mind feels free to continue with my writing.

I know that every word I write from here on will bring me closer to the end of this chapter of my life.

Writing my autobiography, well, I call it my life story; I didn't expect to be reliving it through every chapter of this book, right from my life at the age of fifteen years old to the age of forty-five years old.

I remember once, thinking that people spent years writing about their lives in a book. Well, it took me almost four months to complete this book. Some of you may find this hard to believe, but my friends and family will know that I would be determined to reach the end, the fighter, the survivor. I have noticed that it took a big change in my life to start writing this book, and an even bigger change to finish writing it.

Chapter Thirty-Four

My Lifelong Achievement

Entry written on 27 February 2010 my thoughts,

February 27, 2010 is one of the most proud days of my life, the day my beautiful daughter Chantal graduated as a Teacher. My daughter teaches Theatrical and Media make up, and I am very proud of what she does, she is one of the best in my eyes, especially when she makes me look like a celebrity, Women, imagine having a daughter and she is able to make her mother look beautiful, how great that is.

I remember going to a concert with my daughter Chantal, to see the great R&B soul singer Baby face. Well, that night we were mistaken for celebrities, that was so funny.

I couldn't believe it when two people came up to us and asked us if we were special guests, and wanted to show us to the VIP lounge, I didn't know what to say, I did say no but thought maybe we should have said yes and see what happened. Today we still smile, and laugh about it, that night I remember saying to Chantal did she really think that we looked like celebrity guests, and she laughed and said, yes mum.

Chantal has worked so hard to reach were she is today, and I am very proud of her for more reasons than one.

I can remember my fortieth birthday, and for one of my birthday gift, Chantal took me to London fashion week, I was so proud of her for her achievements, and for giving me the experience of going to a place that I never

ever really would have gone too, I can never forget that birthday, I felt special, mingling amongst some of the most beautiful looking people that I had ever seen in one place.

Well, today my daughter is here to collect a certificate for a lifelong achievement in teaching.

As I sit feeling like the proud mother I can't help but wish that I had stood in front of a crowd of people to collect a lifelong achievement, but then I remember standing in front of a crowd of people collecting my certificate of lifelong achievement for being a parent, when I was attending the parenting course.

For me, being a parent is a lifelong achievement, for the many nights my sleep was disturbed, sitting up in the bed, baby in one hand, bottle in the next with my eyes closing down, and mistaking eyes and nose for mouth, years of teaching, bleaching,(No sleep), laughing crying, going to and from the school, gates, I know that they still need me to be there for them, not just when they were children, but adults too, and this is the reason why I am her today sitting in the Chapel in the front row waiting for my daughter to walk through the door, my lifelong achievement.

Sitting quietly waiting for the ceremony to take place, I can hear people all around chatting away, and waiting for that prouder moment, not just when the graduates walk in, but when they are recognised for their achievement, and accepting their certificate.

I feel a little emotional, as a write this final chapter of my book, a very proud moment and precious memory, that I will treasure in my heart forever.

Locked in my thoughts I think back to when Chantal was born almost thirty years ago it still feels like yesterday, watching her go through each milestone, the first time she reached for her bottle, her toys, her shoes, it's funny how we feel, when we revisit old memories, they have a tendency to make us sad, even the happy ones too.

A fifteen-year-old teenager today, and tomorrow a sixteen-year-old mother, that was me, what a big jump. This has proved to me that I must have done something right as a teenage mother, young mother, and an older mother like I am now.

Three stages of motherhood, some people have been through one or two, stages, but me, I've been through all three and every one of those stages have been a struggle right up until now, but I'm here today and my struggles have not been in vain, I'm not saying that I am the perfect mother, because I am not, some may think that there is no room for mistakes when it comes to being a mother, but there has to be.

In order for us to become better mothers we have to learn by our mistakes, big and small, so no one can ever be the perfect mother, as we would desire to be.

Mothers don't just stop learning when they have children, we learn from them and them from us. There are times when I wished that I could have done more for my children, I guess we all feel that way, but love is all they really need.

I can't help but think how my daughter must be feeling, waiting outside with all the other graduates, excited and nervous.

The silence in the Chapel came, as the sound of the recessional music played, beautifully mastered by the gifted and talented, musical students of Canterbury Christ Church University.

Slowly walking into the chapel were these very important looking people, dressed in gowns fit for a professor, judge, or a doctor, one man walked slowly into the chapel, with a big sector on his shoulder, I could not help but think it weighed a ton, because the man's face looked red as a beetroot, he managed to steadily put the sector in its rightful place.

As they all took their seats, the graduates made an entrance, a long trail of them, including my daughter.

I become overwhelmed as I see my daughter walking into the Chapel, in her blue graduates

Gown to take her seat, and wait for the ceremony to start; I have to take a deep breath to stop myself from crying. Chantal looked so beautiful, her faced looked immaculate, she always managed to do her makeup beautifully flawless, to enhance her natural beauty, I guess that she had many years of practice, and that's what brought her hair today. I was proud that she was my daughter, not just because she was pretty, but because she had managed to achieve her dreams, a very ambitious young woman, with the world at her feet, who would go far in life.

As the awards were presented, I watched as people after people follow suit, as their names were called out one by one, as I sat there I couldn't help but wonder what type of teachers they all were.

Well, I could see Chantal looking over in my direction as she walked along, I can't explain the feeling that came over me, true pride that's what it was, and even though Chantal had stepped into my shoes, she had managed to step out of them, and she has never stopped walking to where she is today.

For me, my daughter is a role model for all the teenage mothers, she was also sixteen years old, when she became a mother, since that day she has worked hard towards being here today.

Names after names were called as each graduate graduated the moment when they received their lifelong certificate in teaching diploma.

"Chantal Amara, Smith," I heard them say. I clapped the loudest clap ever, and I made sure it lasted the longest. I even felt like getting up and shouting out, "That's my daughter," Julia Roberts Style, but I had to respect the fact that we were in a chapel, and not at a concert. I laughed and lost the thought.

I didn't want them to say, "Silence in the court," or throw me out and miss the ceremony.

The only ceremonies that I have ever been to in a chapel were weddings, funerals, and christenings, never to a graduation, until today. I hoped that it would not be my last.

I loved the sincerity about this place, my grandson, Chantal's son, two generations, my daughter, and now her son. We were both teenage mothers, both at sixteen years old. I am here for my daughter, and he is here for his mother. I asked him if we would all come back to Canterbury Christ Church University one day, and he said yes, and who knows, there may be three generations of us there on that day.

Chapter Thirty-Five

The Three Gs, Accepted

2010

Someone once asked me, did I cry when I was writing my book, reliving my life, going back in time, to the days when I fought my way through each day. Well, you would think that it was inevitable, that I would shed a tear or two but I didn't.

I now realise that it has been very therapeutic, because it has helped me to look at my life for what it is today, and be thankful for what I have, and not to look at the things that I don't have. Well. it may not be much, what I have, but when I look back over my yesterdays its more than I had back then.

I have my faith, I'm thankful, that I was able to hold onto that for dear life, when I needed confirmation from my prayers that I was not alone. I know that as long as there is life there has to be hope, because faith and hope walks hand in hand, you see even a leper is still hoping for a cure, and a man on his deathbed is still hoping that his heart won't stop beating.

Believing that God had a purpose for me, to use me in this way, I believe that I could not have come through life without, scars, bitterness, hurt anger and pain, resentfulness, blaming society, I have learnt to forgive, everything, and everyone that has hurts me in some way or other.

I have told myself that there is no need for me to hold on to the negative things in my past, because they can stop the positive things from coming into my life and besides, I can't carry them around with me forever, so I let them go.

Today Patrick and I are friends, just like we were before we got together, it seems like we are better friends than we were partners. Patrick is still there for me, and I know that I can now call on him.

To be able to forgive is a wonderful thing; I figured that God forgave me, so I just follow in his footsteps.

I had a purpose to fulfill. Well, that's what I was told as a child, "Jackie, God has a purpose for you." Well, it's taken me until now to believe this.

I never ever imagined writing about my life, but I believe that everyone has story to tell, and I thank God for giving me the gift of writing. Being able to tell my story through a book has been a great experience. I hope that whoever reads this book will be able to take whatever it is they receive from this book and find hope, faith, belief, and peace in their lives.

I also know that no matter how happy I feel at this moment, life has its ups and downs, trouble comes, and it goes, problems come and problems are solved, but it's how we deal with them, overcome them, that are what counts.

Today I stand firm, I stand strong, whilst writing this final chapter, it suddenly dawns on me that I no longer question my questions, and my faith and my belief has grown. At this moment I feel that I have arrived at my destination, and there is nothing stopping me from reaching my goals.

Everything that I have wished or dreamt about is within my reach, and all I have to do is reach out and grab it. I thank God for walking beside me, and carrying me this far when I felt that I could not go any further, now I can finally stand on my feet, and tell myself that I am here and I have finally found solid ground in my mind, heart body and soul.

Sometimes it's easier to go back than forward, that is because a lot of us don't like changes, we become too complacent in the way we think, see and live, we get comfortable, even when things are not right in our lives, sometimes we feel that it's easier not to change the things that we don't like about ourselves, and our lives.

Changes can be good, bad, happy or sad, and were afraid of feeling those emotions, good or bad. Some of us say" I'm afraid to fall in love because it can hurt, some of us say "I am afraid of moving, because I might not like where I am going to, some of us say "I can't change my job because the company might go bust, life is about changes, and embracing them. Well, a change had to come in my life, I had patiently prayed each day, for a change to come.

Well, here I am moving on to another chapter in my life, and for the first time, I don't feel afraid.

There are some things that can be fixed, and there's something's that cannot be fixed.

If there is anything I will take from all of this is that I had to go through this to be the person that I am today, a strong independent woman, who does not carry a chip on her shoulder. Life is the most precious gift there is, and it's how we live our lives, which makes us the person that we are at this very moment in time I thank God for helping me to recognise my gifts and to start using them in ways which God intended me to do. I never would have considered myself as a comedian, to bring a character like Ms. Meryl to life, with her own identity, not even a poet writing such deep poetry which makes me look at my life, in so many different ways, and most of all being an author. The first time that I really acknowledged the title next to my name I laughed and said proudly with my head held up high, "Me Jacqueline La-Touché an author." I repeated it several times for it to sink in, but I don't think it ever will, because to me I am still Jacqueline La-Touché, the fighter, the survivor.

As I write these last few lines, I sit in my bed. My fingers suddenly feel light. It's like they are floating along the keyboard. As I bite my lip, to try and control the overwhelming emotions from coming out, I tremble with elation. I feel so thankful. I radiate gratitude to God. I am amazed.

I would never have imagined ever feeling these feelings at the end of writing my book, so this is a total surprise to me. Unexplainable feelings, that I have never felt, all I can say is that it's above all happiness that I have ever felt at some stages in my life, this is an awesome feeling, and a wonderful experience, which I am grateful for.

I acknowledge my gifts, the three Gs, that's what I call them, my God-given gifts. During this journey I have been able to remember, some of my gifts and talents, which I had forgotten about. My musical gift of being able to play the guitar, and the piano, which I inherited from my father, who was also talented when it came to music, especially when it came to playing the mouth organ and his much loved guitar, my father's guitar still sits in its case today, with no one to pluck its strings.

I come from a family of musicians and singers, even recording artists, and I discovered my musical abilities when I was just a young child.

Reflections 1972

Playing around with my father's guitar and just watching him strumming away, I would wait until he left the house and then sneak into the place where he kept it, then I would sit down strumming away, until I had managed to accomplish some kind of tune from this instrument.

I remember one day asking my father if I could have a go of his beloved guitar. His guitar even had a name, and my father even spoke to it. Well, to my surprise he said yes. My father could not believe his ears when I started to play and sing. He was in awe as I played "Amazing Grace." My father started to sing along. We had many sessions of strumming and singing after that day.

My father encouraged me to play music when he discovered that I had the ability and was willing to learn.

Well, my teacher Mrs. Henry was giving away her old piano and asked my father if I could have it. I couldn't believe it, a piano. Well, I couldn't play, not even a key. However, that didn't stop my father from going all the way to Wembley for this old piano. Well, by time we got the piano back home to Tottenham, every key was out of place and out of tune, but that was soon fixed.

My father had got me a piano, and I couldn't play it, but I soon learnt to play the piano by trial and error.

I taught myself to play the piano beautifully. My father eventually sent me to piano lessons, after church on a Sunday, and I hated it. I didn't understand a word of music, only how to play it. My father soon realised that he was wasting his money and stopped me from going. However, I continued to play each Sunday at church without fail. I must say that there was times that I hated it, because I felt like I had no choice but to play for the congregation. I even encouraged and helped my brother Robin to learn to play. Well, he couldn't really play that well, like I could, but it was better than nothing. Sometimes he would give me a break by playing with his one finger at church, banging away. I don't think my father really minded as long as someone played. At fifteen years old all that stopped when I became a mother.

So here I am today, remembering my God-given gifts, and never in a million years would I have thought that would I be writing a book or feeling these emotions at the end of this chapter. Well, you know what, it's like I am saying goodbye to the end of my past life.

I know that I will always revisit only memories, but that's life. I will cross that bridge when I come to it. Crossing rivers, climbing mountains, building bridges, I've done it.

This Is Me

I am me, can't you see, this is who I am,
This is me faults, mistake and all I have embraced them,
Memories won't let me erase them,

I am me there's only one created, Troubles and Trials
sometimes I felt hated.
My spirit is strong, and I have the strength to go on, that's me.
I love being me, I give thanks each day, for this gift that'
Lifts my heart in such a way
My dues I have paid so many nights I have laid, asking god to be
my guide, as I take this earthly ride.
I am me can't you see, this is who I am.
This is me, giving thanks, to the almighty creator
Peace in my heart has come sooner than later

By Jacqueline La-Touché

Lightning Source UK Ltd.
Milton Keynes UK
21 June 2010

155918UK00002B/5/P